To Succeed or Perish

TO SUCCEED OR PERISH

The Diaries of Sergeant Edmund Trent Eggleston,
1st Mississippi Light Artillery Regiment, CSA

EDITED BY LAWRENCE LEE HEWITT,
THOMAS E. SCHOTT, AND MARC KUNIS

WITH A FOREWORD BY ANDREW STEVENS

Voices of the Civil War
Michael P. Gray, Series Editor

The University of Tennessee Press / Knoxville

The Voices of the Civil War series makes available a variety of primary source materials that illuminate issues on the battlefield, the home front, and the western front, as well as other aspects of this historic era. The series contextualizes the personal accounts within the framework of the latest scholarship and expands established knowledge by offering new perspectives, new materials, and new voices.

LIBRARY OF CONGRESS CATALOGING-IN-PUBLICATION DATA

Eggleston, Edmund Trent, 1833-1896.
 To succeed or perish : the diaries of Sergeant Edmund Trent Eggleston, Company G, 1st Mississippi Light Artillery Regiment, CSA / edited by Lawrence Lee Hewitt, Thomas E. Schott, and Marc Kunis ; with a foreword by Andrew Stevens. — First edition.
    pages cm
 Includes bibliographical references and index.
 ISBN 978-1-62190-122-8 (hardcover)
  ISBN 979-8-89527-085-1 (paperback)
1. Eggleston, Edmund Trent, 1833-1896—Diaries. 2. Confederate States of America. Army. Mississippi Light Artillery Regiment, 1st (1862-1865) 3. Soldiers—Mississippi—Diaries. 4. Mississippi—History—Civil War, 1861-1865—Personal narratives. 5. United States—History—Civil War, 1861-1865—Personal narratives, Confederate. 6. Mississippi—History—Civil War, 1861-1865—Regimental histories. 7. United States—History—Civil War, 1861-1865—Regimental histories. 8. Georgia—History—Civil War, 1861-1865—Campaigns. 9. Tennessee—History—Civil War, 1861-1865—Campaigns. 10. United States—History—Civil War, 1861-1865—Campaigns. I. Hewitt, Lawrence L. II. Schott, Thomas Edwin, 1943- III. Kunis, Marc. IV. Title.
E568.81st .E44 2015
973.7'462—dc23
        2015004306

CONTENTS

Illustrations

Figures

Maps

FOREWORD

I was born in Memphis, Tennessee, and raised in the South. I was the only child of parents who in their youth migrated with their respective parents, my grandparents, from various parts of Mississippi in search of better jobs in the city of Memphis. My entire family and extended family was from Mississippi. My father was born in Indianola, his father in a town called Kosciusko in the Mississippi Delta, and his mother was from Duck Hill. My mother's mother was born in Marks, Mississippi, and both my mother and her father, Thomas Ellet Eggleston, were born in Yazoo City.

Much like regional dialects in England, they all spoke with distinctly different southern accents with different inflections and colloquialisms, based on the regions their mostly English, Irish, and Scottish ancestors had hailed from when they settled in Mississippi. The Egglestons proudly declared that they were "Englishmen," even my bombastic maternal grandfather constantly said, "I'm a Englishman! A Beefeater."

I remember visiting the family home in Yazoo City where my grandfather's mother, nick-named "Dandy," then still lived in the family home where her father, Edmund Trent Eggleston, had resided. The house was white wood, with a modest colonnade in front. It had survived the Civil War, but cannon shot had either been embedded and/ or chipped away parts of the colonnade that had later been repaired. I remember eating wild duck at a family Thanksgiving gathering and decidedly not liking the gamy flavor. Years later when I moved to Hollywood and began my respective careers in the entertainment business, I met the prolific producer brothers Larry and Chuck Gordon, who informed me that their grandfather was the first Jewish mayor of Yazoo City, Mississippi.

In my early childhood in Memphis, I was raised by both sets of my grandparents, sharing time alternately between my mother's parents and father's parents. My grandparents had little formal education beyond high school, and my paternal grandfather only attended through the sixth grade before going to work to help support his family. He spent his career climbing poles and hanging transformers for the Mississippi Power and Light Company, and later as a foreman with a small bucket truck and crew for the Memphis Light, Gas and Water Company. My mother's mother did go to nursing school and ended up working at Veterans Hospital in Memphis. Before that she traveled all over the rural areas around Marks, Mississippi, with a doctor in a Model A Ford making house calls on the sharecroppers and birthing lots of babies. My father's mother attended one year of college and actually taught school briefly in Mississippi, then, after moving to Memphis, worked in a department store called Goldsmith's. My mother's father, whose grandfather is the subject of this book, worked in Yazoo City, delivering Coca-Colas and, after migrating to Memphis, worked the rest of his life as a foreman on the graveyard shift at International Harvester.

My mother's mother was a self-proclaimed pack-rat and always had any number of things crammed into closets, drawers, and into cubbyholes in a freestanding antique secretary desk in a corner of the living room. One day during my middle school years, I was nosing through my grandmother's desk and I happened across an old, tattered, small, thin, black leather book, with a leather strap that slipped into leather loop to hold it closed. After questioning my grandmother about it, I learned that it was the diary of my grandfather's grandfather, Sergeant Edmund Trent Eggleston, who had fought in the Civil War with a light artillery regiment on the side of the Confederacy.

I remember looking in amazement at the diary, its aged and faded pencil writing (some pages of which my grandmother, much to my chagrin in later years, had traced over in ink, so that the fading pencil lead would be more legible). I remember the musty smell and imagined as I read the sights and sounds and smells and horrors depicted in the pages of my ancestor's diary. I was also fascinated by a few papers that were tucked into a small collapsible accordion sleeve in the inside back cover of the volume. There was a parole document: my great-great-grandfather had been captured as a prisoner of war and later paroled back to his home in Vicksburg with "one shotgun, one rifle, one revolver and ammunition" for hunting in order to provide food for him and his family, so long as he performed no military duty whatsoever and paid proper respect to the authorities in his locality.

As I grew older, from time to time I would ask my grandmother to see the diary, and I remember questioning her about how the penmanship of my grandfather's grandfather was so elegant and beautiful, and his words and language so gentile, educated, and erudite. None of that elegance and grace existed with any family of ours that I had come in contact with on either side of my family. Her answer was a simple one, but it resonated with me. "Well, sugar," she said, "We lost all our money in the war and nobody could afford to go to school much. We all had to work." This was clearly an epiphany for me, and I think I understood for the first time that financial wherewithal equated to the ability to pursue an education.

I have come to embrace my heritage and am fortunate and proud that the legacy of my ancestor has been commemorated in print, which may endure for my children and their children to come.

Andrew Stevens

PREFACE

A few years ago my good friend Marc Kunis came to my home for dinner. He began the evening by dropping a photocopy of a hand-written diary on my desk. A few weeks later when I looked through it, I discovered it had been written from November 1, 1863, to December 31, 1864, by a Confederate artillery sergeant who served in the Western Theater. Aware of the rarity of such a source, particularly for that period of the war, I researched the author and discovered that his service record ended in April 1864 with his being listed a deserter. The diary indicated otherwise, which made the manuscript more intriguing to me.

During fifty years of researching the Civil War, I have discovered thousands of soldiers on both sides, often killed in action, who have been falsely labeled deserters. I also discovered hundreds of individuals who had served in the Confederate army for whom no service record exists. Checking the individuals mentioned in the diary against the existing company records—*which end in April 1864*—I found examples of men who died while on active duty even though their service records ended with their being "Present." I turned up at least one soldier who joined the outfit during the final year of the war for whom no service record exists. After having traveled the country speaking on "Slandered Heroes: Deserters Who Didn't," I found myself with a manuscript that not only documented what I had been espousing but also appeared to merit publication in its own right.

Wondering how rare such a diary was, I consulted Larry Daniel's *Cannoneers in Gray: The Field Artillery of the Army of Tennessee, 1861–1865.* As Daniel's "Bibliographical Essay" notes: "The diaries of one officer and three enlisted men are known to survive and, though none spans the entire war, they provide valuable insight into life in the western artillery."[1] Eggleston's diary was not one of the four.

Andrew Stevens, of Dallas, Texas, is the current owner of Eggleston's 1863–64 diary. He inherited it from his maternal grandfather, the late Thomas Ellet Eggleston of Memphis, Tennessee, who was a grandson of the diary's author. After Andrew graciously allowed us permission to publish the manuscript, Marc and I began transcribing the volume. Before we finished, however, we encountered two unexpected and potentially terminal roadblocks.

First, I learned that the diary had already been published, or rather, partially published. Fortunately, what appeared in the *Tennessee Historical Quarterly* in 1958 was a highly abridged, lightly edited version, under "Notes and Documents."[2] The second obstacle appeared more formidable: the project we originally envisioned could not merit publication as a stand-alone hardbound volume because of brevity. So I decided, first, to include a history of Eggleston's unit covering its service beyond the period Eggleston wrote about, and second, to compile a roster of his comrades that would include information about them similar to what Joseph T. Glatthaar presented on the sample group in his *Soldiering in the Army of Northern Virginia: A Statistical Portrait of the Troops Who Served under Robert E. Lee.*[3]

At this point, with obstacles overcome and the end in sight, Terry Winschel notified me that the Vicksburg National Military Park had a copy of Eggleston's diary. But this one ran from April 26, 1862–May 9, 1863. The discovery of this additional diary, along with several manuscript collections relating to Eggleston's relatives and other members of the battery, forced a reassessment of the project and eventually a decision to produce two smaller volumes that would do justice to Eggleston's diaries and his unit in a way that a single volume could not. This is the first of those two books.

Unfortunately, the current location of the first volume of Eggleston's diary, if it still exists, is unknown. The following cover letter accompanied the typescript copy of that volume at the Vicksburg National Military Park:

> This Diary of E. T. Eggleston was presented to me a number of years ago by my friend Jasper T. Brinton, 1425 Spruce St., Philadelphia and now Resident Judge of the Eru Mixte, Alexandria, Egypt. Judge Briton [*sic*] is a son of the late John H. Brinton, M.D. of Philadelphia , Pa. who was a surgeon of the staff of General U. S. Grant

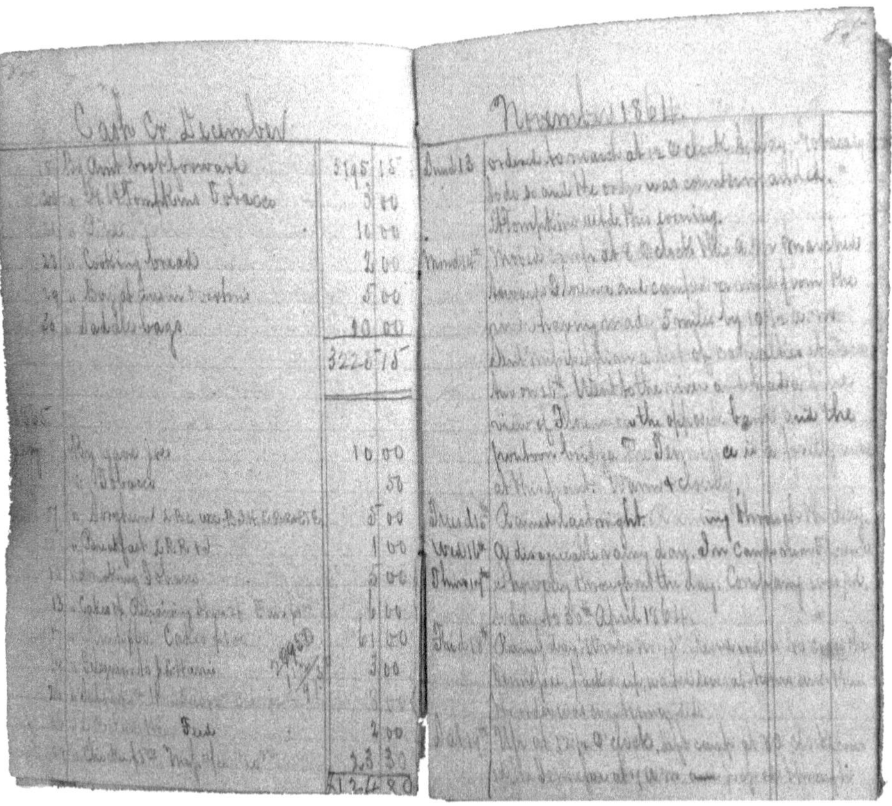

1863–64 Diary of Edmund Trent Eggleston. Courtesy of Andrew Stevens. Page 84 (left) is typical of his ledger entries, while page 85 is representative of the diary entries.

at Cairo and in the campaigns of Fort Henry and Fort Donelson and latter [*sic*] transferred to Washington D. C. to adi [*sic*] the founding the Army Medical Museum.

The diary was among the effects of Dr. Brinton after his death in Pheladelphia [*sic*] March 18th, 1907 and is presented by me to the Vicksburg National Military Park, Vicksburg, Mississippi this 27th day of September 1940.

Edward T. Stuart
Church Road
St. Davids, Pa.

No connection could be found between Eggleston and Dr. John H. Brinton, and it is possible that Brinton never possessed the original diary. There is no reason to doubt the diary's authenticity, however, because of the people and events mentioned. And the writing style found in the typescript matches that of the original second volume, including Eggleston's habitual spelling of "to day."

A few passages in the typescript are missing. At some point after the invention of both photocopying and the automatic feeder, a copy was made of the manuscript and the copy, rather than the original, was returned to the file. Unfortunately, as was common with automatic feeders, the bottom of some pages were cut off. Those passages are indicated with "[text missing]".

Eggleston divided the pages of the second volume of his diary—and probably his first, too—into two columns. Material written in the narrower left-hand column appears at the beginning of each entry followed by a colon. The text following is from the wider column on the right. All places are in Mississippi unless otherwise stated. The names of members of Eggleston's company appear in bold text. More information about them can be found in Appendix D. Unless otherwise indicated, all unidentified first names refer to Eggleston's immediate family: wife "Molly," and children Annie, Bob, Johnny, and Matty/Mattie. All references to "sister" refer to Mahala Perkins Harding Eggleston Roach. Her 1862 diary survives. Entries from it pertinent to her brother are interspersed among his.

Obvious typographical errors in the first volume have been corrected, but otherwise the text of both volumes has been reproduced as written by Eggleston. Where Eggleston occasionally divided a word at the end of a line without inserting a hyphen, these words appear undivided.

ACKNOWLEDGMENTS

Maybe a child does need a village to rear them. This book wouldn't exist without the assistance of the following individuals. In addition to their actions described in the preface, I wish to thank Marc Kunis for transcribing the 1863–1864 diary and Andrew Stevens for providing various family items, as well as the foreword. A valued friend for nearly four decades and a collaborator on several volumes in the past, Tom Schott's insight proved as invaluable as his editorial skill, as always. Therese Winschel opened her home to me during my stay in Vicksburg, all the while providing the hospitality for which the South is famous, including waving to us with a smile as I stole her husband Terry away from his chores to show me various sites around the city and to assist me with the records now housed in Lieutenant General John C. Pemberton's former headquarters.

All of the following went out of their way to render assistance above and beyond: Gordon Cotton, George C. "Bubba" Bolm, and Jordon Rushing of the Old Court House Museum, Vicksburg; Grady Howell of the Mississippi State Library and Archives, Jackson; Lauren Stealey of the McCain Library and Archives, University of Southern Mississippi, Hattiesburg; and, especially, Therese Odlevak of the Chicago Public Library. Several individuals assisted in locating, copying, or allowing the reproduction of the illustrations. In addition to Andrew Stevens and Terry Winschel, they are Stuart Salling, Michael K. Roach, Tiffany Coyle, Warren E. Grabau, Timothy B. Smith, Ted Savas, David Friedrichs, Brian S. Wills, Michael Shafer, Leon McElveen, Virginia DuBowy, and the late William R. Scaife. I also wish to thank the Kennesaw Mountain Historical Association and Savas-Beatie, LLC. As he has numerous times in the past, Bruce S. Allardice proved a valuable resource for genealogical queries. I am especially grateful to my wife Donni Case, who brought a keen reader's eye to the "finished" manuscript. Her diligence enabled us to enhance the clarity of the manuscript in several places.

Without the aid of these individuals and organizations, as well as the entire staff of the University of Tennessee Press, this book would not have been possible. Emily Huckabay probably surpassed Scot Danforth in patience, and Stephanie Thompson designed a cover that aptly depicts the volume's contents. My thanks to you all. I alone am responsible for any errors it contains, even ones of omission. With an accompanying volume on Cowan's Battery being planned, I gladly welcome suggestions and comments from the readers of this one.

Lawrence Lee Hewitt

INTRODUCTION

Possibly the best insight into any previous time, at least the most "close to the ground" knowledge, is contained in the letters and diaries of its contemporaries. They, unlike any other source, enable the reader to relate personally with past events. And among the most valuable of these manuscripts are those from authors of certifiable veracity who provide the sole eyewitness account of historical events. The diary of Edmund Trent Eggleston is such a source. Like all such sources, it reflects a personal, singular point of view, sometimes, as in all times, based on erroneous information and colored by the *Weltanschauung* of the surrounding society.

Even though thousands of diaries written by Civil War soldiers have been published, Eggleston's stands out as unique. Simply the fact that he served as a Confederate artilleryman throughout the war in the Western Theater makes his account one of only a handful. That he never rose above the rank of sergeant cuts that number in half. Lastly, as a near-neighboring Mississippian, he was well-acquainted with President Jefferson Davis. Eggleston's life before enlisting in the Confederate army also differentiated him from the average Civil War soldier. Though literally to the manor born, financial reverses suffered by his father resulted in his being able to live in reasonable comfort only through employment by an aunt. At twenty-eight, not only was he older than average, but he also had a wife and children. And the amount of time his family spent with him in camp and him away from camp visiting relatives would seem impossible in time of war.

Eggleston enlisted in Company G, 1st Mississippi Light Artillery Regiment, in April 1862. Captain **James J. Cowan** commanded the battery throughout the war. For the next year, the unit did garrison duty near Vicksburg, which was hometown for many of its members. There wasn't a better morale-boosting assignment in the army. "Molly and the children came to camp and spent the day with me," Eggleston wrote about one of his wife's visits, "and I went home with them. Her visits to camp are sources of much pleasure to me and have a happy influence serving to break the monotony of camp life."

The battery's first engagement with the enemy came at Champion Hill on May 16, 1863, where Eggleston spoke with Brigadier General Lloyd Tilghman just before the general was mortally wounded. "It was some little time after the General fell before his son, a youth, could be found," he later recalled, "and I shall never forget the touching scene when with grief and lamentations he cast himself on his dying and unconscious father. Those of us who witnessed this distressing scene shed tears of sympathy for the bereaved son and of sorrow for our fallen hero, the chivalrous and beloved Tilghman."

During the retreat from Champion Hill, the company divided: a portion of the battery served at Vicksburg during the siege, while the remainder, including Eggleston, were posted in central Mississippi under General Joseph E. Johnston. Reunited that fall, the battery retreated into Alabama with Lieutenant General Leonidas Polk's Army of Mississippi, following Major General William T. Sherman's successful Meridian Campaign early in 1864.

In May, the battery accompanied the Army of Mississippi to northern Georgia, where it was absorbed into the Army of Tennessee. During the Atlanta Campaign, Eggleston's unit was engaged at Resaca, Cassville, New Hope Church, Kennesaw Mountain, at the Chattahoochee River, as well as during the siege of Atlanta. "I pity the true citizens who have fallen under the Yankee yokes," Eggleston lamented the night the Confederates evacuated the city. In late September, the battery marched north with the Army of Tennessee and saw action at Allatoona on October 5. The army marched west into Alabama, where the "battery suffered severely" during an attack on Decatur on October 26.

The battery crossed the Tennessee River on November 19 as part of General John Bell Hood's advance into Middle Tennessee. Left behind at Columbia, Tennessee, Company G missed the Battle of Franklin. During the Battle of Nashville on December 15, the battery was removed from its position on the siege line and ordered to the left, to stem the Federal assault, but it arrived only in time to be overrun. "The infantry ran like cowards and the miserable wretches who were to have supported us refused to fight and ran like a herd of stampeded cattle," wrote Eggleston, "I blush for my countrymen and despair of the independence of the Confederacy if her reliance is placed in the army of Tennessee to accomplish it." Two cannon were assigned to Company G that night, for it had lost all its guns, but they were not engaged the following day when the "army was flanked and badly whipped."

Those Confederates who managed to reach safety south of the Tennessee River had every reason to believe their cause was lost. But Eggleston thought otherwise:

> The last of the eventful and disastrous year 1864! May a merciful Father vouchsafe that the coming year may be more propitious to our cause and may he grant us peace and independence ere were are again called upon to record the departure of another year. We have met many reverses and have lost many brave and gallant souls but our Cause is not hopeless, we can yet achieve our nationality with the aid of the All powerful God of battle—we must bear our reverses with the fortitude of heroes, buckle on our armor and calling on the God of Truth to be our ally resolve to succeed or perish.

In January 1865, the remnants of Hood's command were broken up. Most of the artillery units, including Cowan's Battery, were ordered to Mobile, Alabama. While participating in the siege of that city, Company G was captured, along with most of the Confederates defending Fort Blakely, on April 9, 1865. Eggleston, however, was in Mississippi at the time and missed the fall of Fort Blakely as he had the siege of Vicksburg. Because of his absence, those two events are not covered as fully in this volume as some readers might wish.

Eggleston found himself with few options at the end of the war. His family moved in with his mother in Vicksburg, where he found a job clerking. After a decade of hard work, he owned his own business and was a prominent member of the community. Luck turned against him in the late 1870s, however, and he was forced to relocate to Yazoo City in 1881 to find employment as a clerk. He continued to reside there until his death in 1896, when his body was taken to Vicksburg to be buried next to his wife.

PROLOGUE

Edmund[1] Trent Eggleston was born on September 12, 1833, at Learmont, the family plantation in Wilkinson County, Mississippi, the fifth of six children of Dr. Dick Hardaway Eggleston and Elizabeth Stark Gildart Eggleston. Though he started life in a well-to-do household of one of the state's first families, his future would prove to be more turbulent than those of his ancestors.[2]

In the summer of 1635, Richard Eggleston arrived in Jamestown, Virginia, seeking his fortune. Either sixteen or twenty-four at the time, his life in the New World began as an indentured servant. He apparently lived in the Eastern Shore before patenting land in James City County in 1653, 1655, and 1662. His son Benjamin, born in 1652, patented land there also in 1690 and 1698. He and his wife, Elizabeth Hartwell, had Joseph in 1678. Joseph settled near Hampton and married Anne Pettus of Hanover County on January 20, 1719. He represented James City County in the House of Burgesses from 1727 until his death on November 24, 1730. The couple had five sons and two daughters, including Richard in 1720 or 1727. Richard married Rebecca Clough on August 21, 1749, and Richard Jr. was born on March 19, 1752. Richard, Jr. married Judith Moulson on November 21, 1783/5, and their youngest child, Dick Hardaway, was born on November 20, 1796. Though several collateral ancestors had fought Indians and the British, it appears that among his direct antecedents only his grandfather Richard had any military service. He had served as a member of the Cumberland County Committee of Safety (1775–76).[3]

Elizabeth Stark Gildart's father, Captain Francis Gildart, was born in Liverpool, England, on December 2, 1758. In October of 1780, he came to North America to fight the rebellious colonists as a lieutenant in the British Legion. The infantrymen of the Legion that survived the Battle of Cowpens were converted to cavalry in February of 1781, and Gildart was promoted to captain to command what became Gildart's Troop of Light Dragoons under Lieutenant Colonel Banastre Tarleton. Gildart and his command became prisoners of war when Major General Lord Charles Cornwallis surrendered Yorktown, Virginia, on October 19, 1781. He went on half pay in 1784 and resided in Shelburne, Nova Scotia. He married Sophia Stark on January 8, 1792, at Winchester, Virginia, and the couple eventually settled in Wilkinson County, Mississippi. Sophia had been born in South Carolina in January 1775, the daughter of Colonel Robert Stark and Mary Hall. Colonel Stark had been born in Prince William County, Virginia, in 1740. Having moved to South Carolina, during the Revolution he commanded a regiment of militia in the Cherokee Expedition and during the siege of Savannah, Georgia. After being captured at Charleston, South Carolina, he was shackled and confined in the cellar of the Royal Exchange and Custom House. He moved to the vicinity of Natchez, Mississippi, upon a Spanish land grant after the war, but when the grant was later revoked, he moved to Winchester, Virginia, where he died on May 28, 1806.[4]

A native of Amelia County, Virginia, Dick H. Eggleston earned his medical degree from the University of Pennsylvania in 1819. The following year he moved to Wilkinson County, Mississippi, and purchased a plantation five miles south of Woodville, taking up the professions of both physician and planter. In 1825, he owned twenty-eight slaves; by 1830, he owned forty. He married Elizabeth Stark Gildart, nine years his junior, on June 5, 1823. Their first child, Horatio, was born in September 1824 and died that same month, and their first daughter, Mahala Perkins Harding, was born on the following September 6. An unnamed son died at birth in May 1827. Dick Henry was born on December 12, 1828, followed by Edmund Trent five years later. Though less than a year old, Edmund made the news on June 28, 1834, when his mother advertised the theft of a silver cup with the name "Edmond Trent Eggleston" inscribed on the inside and offered a five dollar reward for its return. Elizabeth Sophia Gildart was born on July 21, 1837. Her father, who had been chronically ill for nearly a decade, died on October 24, 1837.[5]

When the family faced a financial crisis in the aftermath of the panic of 1837, Edmund watched the silver spoon he was born with go the way of his engraved cup. The plantation had to be liquidated. Five slaves were sold by sheriff's sale on October 1, 1840, and eleven more on December 1. On February 23, 1842, administrator Field Davis auctioned off an additional fifty "acclimated" slaves at the Woodville Court House. They included "a first rate blacksmith; his services being worth the last season $600," as well as hands "considered very likely and superior cotton pickers." Davis also sold two yoke of oxen, seven mules, six horses, one horse wagon and gear, and one ox wagon, and the following day at the plantation, ten cattle, "some of them being good milch cows," one set of blacksmith's tools, ploughs, hoes, axes, plough gear, and other items.[6] Privileged planter life, at least for the time being, was over for Elizabeth and her children.

The family moved to Vicksburg, where Mahala married James P. Roach on November 26, 1844. While serving as a private in the 1st Mississippi Infantry Regiment during the Mexican War, Dick Henry was killed at the Battle of Buena Vista, Mexico, February 23, 1847. The widow Eggleston continued to reside in Vicksburg in 1850, with Edmund and Elizabeth, he working as a clerk and she attending school.[7] She still owned fifteen slaves.[8]

Tragedy still stalked the family. On August 30, 1854, the younger Elizabeth died, and Mahala's husband died on July 1, 1860. But the family also gained some new additions: Edmund married Mary Susan "Molly" Read[9] on December 21, 1854, who gave birth to Robert Read on October 11, 1855, Elizabeth Sophia Gildart on January 6, 1857, and John Fox on August 6, 1858, though the latter's older twin was stillborn. Dick Henry Thomas died shortly after birth on September 30, 1859.[10]

In 1860, Edmund and his family resided with his aunt, Sophia A. Fox, on her plantation in Warren County.[11] In addition to working as her overseer, he owned $6,000 in personal property, including seven slaves.[12] His wife Mary gave birth to Anne Eliza on June 9. Edmund's mother continued to reside at Springfield, her house at the corner of Fayette and Farmer streets in Vicksburg.[13] She owned $2,000 in real and $4,000 in personal property, including five slaves. Edmund's four-year-old son Robert kept her company, possibly grandma's favorite, who unlike his siblings, owned personal property. His $1,500 included a twenty-five-year-old female and two young male slaves, one eight and the other five years old.[14] But he, along with thousands of others, was about to have his fortune washed away by a tide of blood that had already started to rise.

Edmund and Mary Eggleston. Courtesy of Andrew Stevens.

In 1860, Vicksburg was the second largest town in Mississippi behind Natchez, both bustling ports on the Mississippi River. The city's residents included 3,158 whites, 31 free blacks, and 1,402 slaves. It also had something of a cosmopolitan flair: Warren County had the second largest number of foreign-born white residents behind Adams County, which included Natchez. Most of the 1,041 foreigners were Irish, German, or British. The majority of the county's population lived in the rural countryside beyond the limits of Vicksburg: 3,738 whites, 6 free blacks, and 12,361 slaves. With a total population of 20,696, Warren County ranked twelfth in the state.[15]

The fighting did not reach Vicksburg during the first year of the Civil War, but the conflict impacted the region. Warren County had contributed at least thirteen companies, about 1,000 volunteers, to the Confederate army[16]—a number approximating that of every native-born white male in the county between the ages of 18 and 35 in 1862.[17] But still more soldiers were needed as the war entered its second year.

On April 16, 1862, the Confederate Congress passed the first conscription act which required all able-bodied white males aged 18–35 to register for military service. A thirty-day grace period allowed men to avoid "the odium of being forced into service." This enabled volunteers to join existing units or to organize new units in which they could elect their own officers, as long as they did so before being enrolled for conscription.[18]

Seizing this opportunity, 86 men gathered in Vicksburg on April 26 to organize a new company of artillery. Available records indicate that over 70 percent of the volunteers resided in Vicksburg or Warren County. Within two weeks they were off to Jackson to fight in the war. Within two months, they were back in Vicksburg and had brought the war home with them.

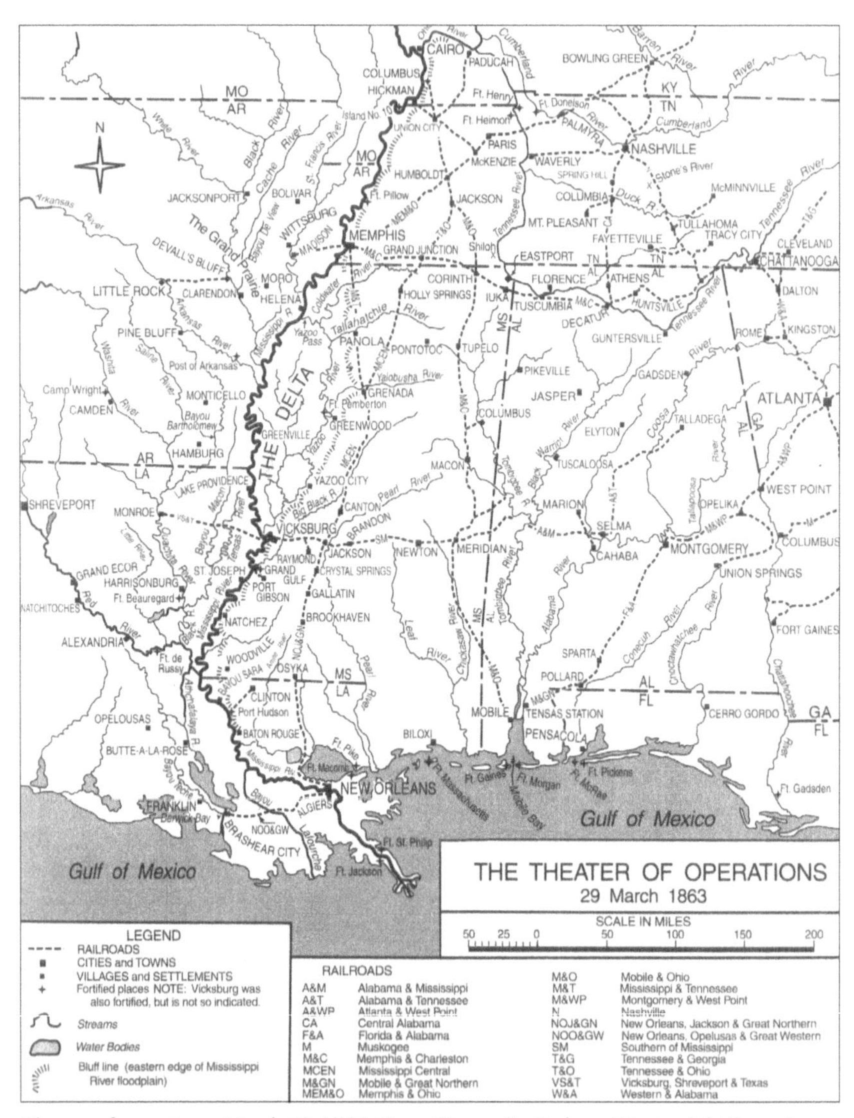

Theater of operations, March 29, 1863. From Warren E. Grabau, *Ninety-eight Days: A Geographer's View of the Vicksburg Campaign* (2000), 535. Used by permission.

Diary of E. T. Eggleston: Volume 1

1862

April 26th: I was mustered into the Confederate service this day as a member of Capt. **Jas. J. Cowan**'s Light Artillery Company; said Company belonging to Col. W. T. Withers[1] Light Artillery regiment.[2] Got a furlough to the 12th of May.

May 5th: Elected officers to day **Jas. J. Cowan** Capt., **Geo. H Tompkins** 1st Lt. Sr., **T. J. Hanes**, 1st. Lt., Jr., **Ben C. Edwards** 2d Lt. Sr., **L. B. Cowan**, 2d Lt. Jr.

12th: Joined the company at Jackson Enjoyed the novelty of the appearence very much.

[Mahala Roach's 1862 diary, May 12: "Trent went to Jackson today to join his Company—the house seems lonely without his cheerful voice and bright presence."

May 17: "Trent came home today on furlough for a few days."

May 20: "Called at Mother's and sat for half an hour, and then had a pleasant ride back to Woodfield, arriving at dusk. Trent was displeased that we left without letting him know, and I fear I answered him rather rudely when he spoke, but tried not to keep vexed—"[3]]

June 9th: Left Jackson for Vicksburg to day.

10th: Camped last night one mile from Raymond.

11th: Camped last night on the west bank of Big Black and got to V'Burg to day and camped in the pasture of T. J. Finney.[4]

20th: Four men were executed to day at the Heavy batteries by sentence of Court-Martial three for desertion and one for mutiny.

21st: Moved our camp to Rocky Springs the enemy fired some shells which pop[p]ed over our camp at Finney's.[5]

28th: Were on picket in V'Burg to day, got wet coming to camp all quiet.[6]

29th: Moved camp onto Fort Hill.[7] On picket again. The shells fell round us quite thick.[8]

30th: On picket still.

July 1st: Company still on picket.

2d: On picket still. Moved our camp to Willis[9] woods back of the grave yard.[10]

3d: Considerable firing last night.[11]

5th: Company still on picket.

6th: Company still on picket.

8th: Moved camp to Caphell's hill.[12]

12th: Commenced picketing to night in V'burg again.

[Mahala Roach's 1862 diary, July 12 (at Miss Bigelow's near Bovina): "We heard there of the death of our dear Cousin Harry Eggleston, he was instantly killed in the late battle . . . dear Harry, we regret his death very much."[13]]

15th: The C.S. gun-boat Arkansas was out of the Yazoo river to day and successfully passed through the Yankee fleet unhurt herself[14] but having damaged several of the Yankee vessels. Every one is elated and astonished at the daring achievement. The Arkansas was commanded by Capt. Brown.[15] Still on picket. A part of the Federal fleet passed by to day.[16]

16th: Last night of our picketing.

22d: One gun-boat passed down this morning, heavy firing.[17]

24th: Ordered to do picket duty again.

25th: On picket last night.

26th: On picket last night.

27th: On picket last night.

28th: On picket last night.

29th: Received marching orders to day and ordered to have three days provisions cooked Order countermanded in the evening.

Aug. 7th: Struck tents to day.[18]

9th: Moved to Mrs. Cowan's pasture.[19]

[Mahala Roach's 1862 diary, August 9: "Trent came home from Camp sick with chills and fever."

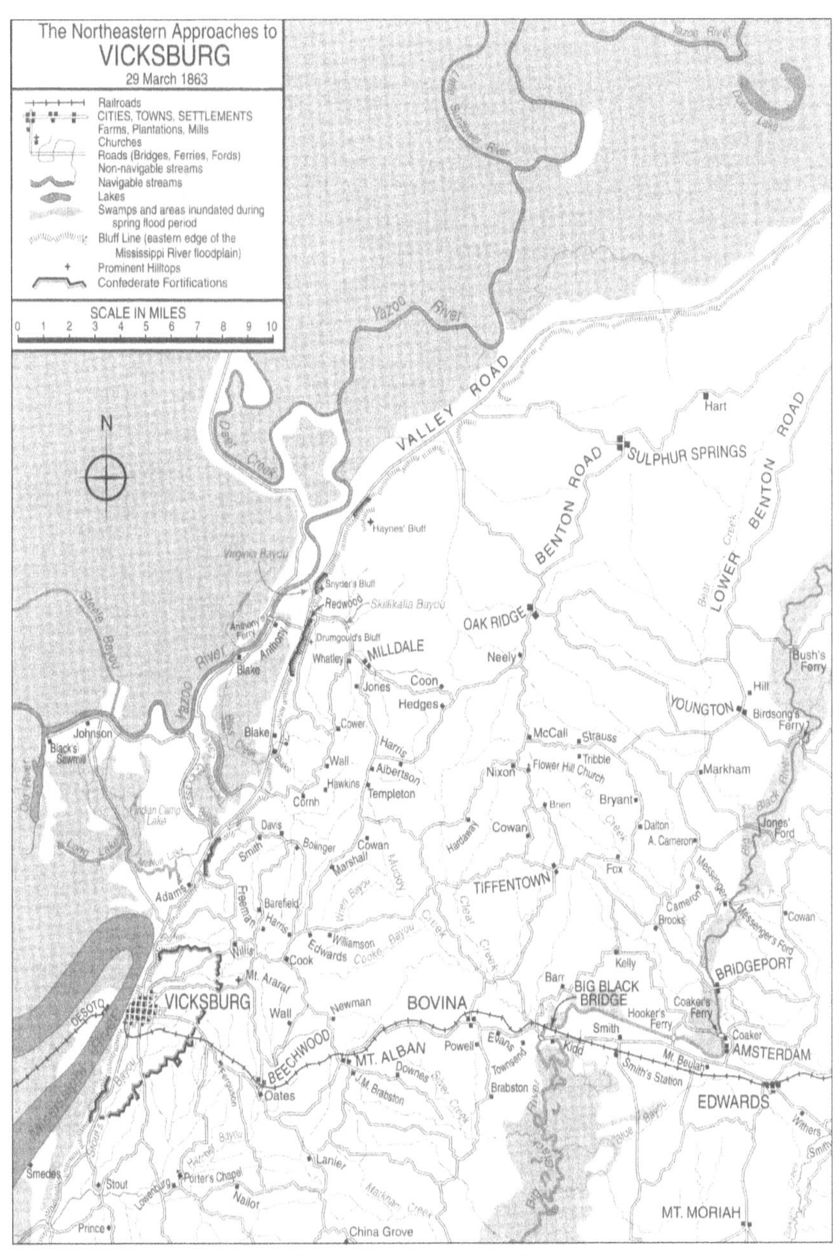

Northeastern approaches to Vicksburg, March 29, 1863. From Warren E. Grabau, *Ninety-eight Days: A Geographer's View of the Vicksburg Campaign* (2000), 551. Used by permission.

August 11: "Trent had a hard chill today."[20]]

16th: [text missing]

27th: I went home to day and returned.

28th: **Vaughn Noland** left to day.[21]

Sept. 5th: The Abolitine gun-boat Essex came in sight of one battery exchanged shots with us and went down the river again.[22]

6th: Received marching order to day which were countermanded. Heavy firing up the river this morning from 5 O'clock to 6½ O'clock; supposed to be a fight between our light artillery & the gun-boats.[23]

[Mahala Roach's 1862 diary, September 6 (Mahala's birthday): "Trent came out tonight to stay till tomorrow evening, his Company are under marching orders, perhaps for Kentucky—"[24]]

7th: Spent the day at home, had a chill and could not return to camp.

8th: Got back to camp feeling feeble, Horses being shod and battery being put in marching condition. The negro man *Jim* died to day.

9th: Molly came for me and carried me to Mother's[25] where I had a chill and a very hot fever.

18th: Returned to camp to day after nine days absence on account of sickness. Found nearly all the company had gone to V'burg to attend Thanksgiving services as requested by our Chief Executive for the glorious victories vouchsafed us by the Supreme Ruler of the Universe.

19th: Doing nothing, all quiet no picketing or drilling.

20th: Sent our gun-carriages to V. to have the lines cut.[26] Still putting the battery in marching order. Quite cold this morning. Regular fall weather.

21st: Got a letter from home to day. Bob quite sick with measles. **Charles W. Powell** died to day.[27]

22d: Very cloudy all day. Heard through Jackson's official report of the capture of Harper's Ferry [VA] with 11,000 prisoners and 6 ps artillery.[28]

23d: Rained throughout the night last night.

25th: **Luther Reid** returned to camp & duty.[29]

Octo. 1st: Clear and pleasant drilling daily.

4th: Molly and the children came to camp and spent the day with me; and I went home with them. Her visits to camp are sources of much pleasure to me and have a happy influence serving to break the monotony of camp life.

5th: Returned to Camp this morning.

6th: Went to V. voted[30] and dined with Mother.

16th: **Craig**[31] went to Bruces[32] to day. I stayed in V. with Molly at Mothers.

17th: Molly returned for me.

25th: Rode home this morning & returned this evening.

26th: Frost and ice this morning.

27th: Heavy frost this morning. I went to V. visiting.

Nov. 9th: Spent the day at home with my family and returned to camp at night.

12th: Had a good rain; the first we have had for several months. The dust was laid and the roads were much more pleasant to travel.

Sunday 16th: Still camped above V'Burg near the swamp. Expect to go into Winter quarters near Milldale. The weather quite warm for the season with appearence of rain.

Thursday 20th: Had a regimental review and inspection to day. A flag was to have been presented to the regiment by Gov. Pettus[33] but the Gov. failed to arrive and the presentation was postponed.

[Mahala Roach's 1862 diary, December 20: "Trent came from Camp this afternoon to make us a visit, he is looking very well."[34]]

21st: The flag presentation came off to day and such an affair! Gov. Pettus presented it and Col. Withers received it. The speeches were long to say the least of them.

[Mahala Roach's 1862 diary, December 21: "Trent left at 2 for Camp."[35]]

22d: Went home this evening.

23d: Returned to camp this evening.

Dec. Friday 19th: Moved into Valley Forge, our Winter Quarters at Milldale or Snyder's Mill as the "post" is called.

Friday 26th: The Yankee-gun-boats and transports with their hooks intended for the seduction of V. make a landing at Mrs. Lake's plantation on the Yazoo river and we had a skirmish with a portion of their forces.[36]

27th: Heavy skirmish near Chickasaw Bayou to day. I was appointed First Sergeant to day one month.

Sunday 28th: The Ab[olitionist]s. continued to attack our trenches. We repulsed them again.

29th: The battle of *Chickasaw Bayou* was fought to day. The Abolitine loss was heavy, ours light. We gained a signal victory, took 400 prisoners.[37] The prisoners state they expected a thrashing and *that they got it too.*

[Mahala Roach's 1862 diary, December 29: "Sister [Eggleston's wife] went to Camp at daylight."[38]]

1863

Jany. Sat. 3d: Everything has been quiet since the 29th and it is expected the enemy has gone up the Mississippi, an attack was expected at this point yesterday morning and we had gathered a considerable force to resist it. The 40th Ala, 3d Miss., 17th La., Hebert's Brigade[39] of veterans, and Adams cavalry regiment[40] were in readiness. The report was unfounded the enemy did not show themselves and the troops dispersed. I hope the rascals have found the taking of V'Burg impractable and have returned to their northern dens. Perhaps Braggs successes at Murfesburo [TN] and the raids of our dashing cavalry forces upon their railroads and ways of transportation have compelled them to return northward.[41]

Jany. 4th: We had a very hard rain last night—the only hard rain we have had since our company has been in service—say for eight months. The swamp is now rendered unfit for the military operations of the enemy until next spring.

Wednesday 7th: Went home to day on a visit.

8th: Returned to camp.

20th: Went home to day.

21st: Returned from home.

23rd: Molly and Aunt Mary Wilkinson[42] came to camp to day and returned home this evening. Left Bob with me. The little fellow is perfectly delighted and I am happy to have him with me.

Sun. 25th: A quiet Sabbath. The enemy has not again appeared in the Yazoo. He seems to have changed his base and is landing troops in La. on the peninsula opposite Vicksburg. What their purpose is no one seems to be able to fathom though the general supposition is that they intend planting a battery below V'Burg to prevent us from navigating the river to Port Hudson. Some think they are going to attempt to run barges through their famous canal and then run their iron clads by our batteries and make a landing at or near Warrenton. Time will reveal their schemes. Our commanders say they are ready for them whenever and where ever they may make an attack.[43]

Frid. 30th: Went home to see Johnny who is quite sick.

31st: Ret'd. to camp to day.

Feb. Sunday 1st: A Rainy day. Mr. Markham[44] came out to keep his appointment but the inclemency of the weather prevented his doing so. He, Sert. **Bentley, Duke Askew, H. N. Spencer** and **Ben Hicks**, had some sacred music in our cabin.

Sketch of Rebel fortifications at Haynes's Bluff. From *Official Records of the Union and Confederate Navies in the War of the Rebellion* (1894–1927), ser. 1, vol. 24:590B.

2nd: A gun-boat ran by V'Burg to day (the Queen of the West) apparently unharmed.[45]

Sat. 14th: Heavy firing at V'Burg about midnight last night. It is said another of the enemy's boats ran by our battery without damage. The night was very dark and cloudy and was quite favorable for the undertaking.[46] Vaughn Noland[47] came to camp to day. He and Hall[48] are both in the Militia.

15th: Molly sent me a cow to day and did not write I am *so disappointed* & greaved at her neglect of my claims upon her. If she only knew how her precious letters are prized she [text missing]

24th: Returned to camp to day feeling "blue" as usual after I have been with the dearness at home & have to leave them again.

March 1st Sunday: A most delightful, balmy spring day. The clouds which have been towering over us so long threatening a continuance of the rainy spell we had had so long, all disappeared last night and the heavens are perfectly clear this morning. What a calamity it is that "grim visage war" stalks through our beloved land carrying misery, desolation and anguish in his trains. Oh how I hope that he may soon "smooth his wrinkled front" and stay the dire calamities with which we are afflicted. I have just received a letter from my precious wife; all are well at home. Mr. Markham preached us an excellent sermon to day, and was listened to with marked attention by a majority of the camp. Spent the day in camp quietly as was proper. The Co. is now doing picket duty (a section at a time) on the grave yard hill fronting Blake's[49] quarters. Commenced last Wednesday night the 25th February. It appears to me a useless exposure of the men tho' I suppose Genl. Hebert[50] who is commanding this post deems it necessary to prevent a surprise. "Eternal vigilance is the price of Liberty".

Tuesday 3d: Went to V'Burg to day on company business. The first time I have been there since the 23rd of Dec. The appearence of the roads between here and the city and the city itself have been so changed by the felling of timber, removing of fences and construction of fortification that I almost felt as though I was on a strange road and visiting a strange city. Finished the Co. business and then went home got there about 9 O'clock and found a rough crowd of soldiers in the parlor playing cards, Aunt, Sister, Molly & Lt. Barnes[51] were playing Eucher.

Wed. 4th: Ret'd. to camp to day.

Friday 6th: I went to day to the *Chickasaw Bayou* to view a military execution. The condemned was *Sergt. W. H. Brown*[52] of the 1st La. Artillery who deserted from our army at Fort Jackson[53] and was subsequently taken prisoner in the Yankee army duped in the Yankees uniform. The prisoner was a young man of fine appearence between 20 and 25 years of age, Capt. Estelle[54] who was the officer appointed to superintend the execution told me he never saw more equanimish displayed by any one. The unfortunate man was perfectly calm and self propelled. When the [text missing] to day for the same crime, and another by the name of *Dennis Kean*[55] in the presence of Genl. Stevenson's command.[56] Thus ends their party in the tragedy of civil war, and thus have they paid for their crimes of treason & desertion.

Saturday: We had a tremendous rain last night. Pleasant to day some what cloudy. **Van**[57] went to V. to day on "detail" to carry in the Co. pay rolls and return tomorrow. I had the pleasure of getting him this privilege and am happy I did. The Conscience of having done a kind act always makes me feel better toward myself and the balance of mankind.

Sunday 8th: **Craig** paid us a visit last night. The first time he has been to see us since he was detailed in Nov. Cloudy & windy regular March weather. Got a letter from Molly to day all were well at home. Lt. Barnes still there and quite sick.

9th: Turned quite cold last night. Cloudy to day. Was dull in camp. Nothing exciting to be seen here and no army intelligence of any importance on hand.

Tuesday 10th: Very dark and cloudy last night. Heavy firing at V'burg. Learned this evening that another Yankee boat passed by our batteries.[58] I hope and expect she will fall into our hands as the Queen of the West and the Indianola did. Very windy and rainy to night and cold. Company still on picket by sections.

Wednesday 11th March: Cleared off in the night and bright and pleasant this morning. Relieved from picket duty to day.

Thursday 12th: I had a slight chill and fever to day. The Yankees are reported in Yazoo River with 5 gun-boats and 30 transports number thought to be exaggerated.[59]

Sunday 15th: Had a severe chill on yesterday. Molly came to camp to day and carried me home with her.

Sunday 22nd: Returned to camp to day after having been at home for a week. I was very sick on Monday, but missed my chill on Wednesday and have not had any since. Had a pleasant time the dear ones at home, and left my darling wife in tears and sorrow this morning. May God bless her for her love and devotion for me, and reward her for it by protecting me from all danger and return [text missing]

Tuesday 24th: A very hard rain this morning, cleared off beautifully in the evening, though rather cold. I saw two Yankee deserters and a captured negro this morning at Hebert's H'd. Qtrs. They were taken in the Yazoo swamp. I had some conversation with the Yankees and they told the same old tale of disaffections and desire for peace. The negro said he belongs to Mr. Watson, and was the bearer of Yankee dispatches to the fleet; the dispatches were in a plug of tobacco. Very cold to night for the season.

Wednesday 25th: Some frost last night though not enough to damage the fruit crop or to injure early vegetables. Our batteries at V'Burg effected a glorious achievement this morning. The Yankees attempted to run two boats by; one a large transport boarded up and the other an iron clad gun-boat. The former was badly damaged and the latter was sunk in full view of the city, and opposite the fair grounds.[60] She turned bottom upwards as she sank, and with only a small portion of her stern floated down the river until it got beyond the range of our guns where the Yankee boat Albatross lying below the city tred her in to bits. The Albatross had previously taken the other boat with her. A beautiful day. The Memphis Appeal Battery[61] and a portion of Hebert's Brigade have been ordered to Yazoo City,[62] and an order has been received from Pemberton's H'd. Qtrs.[63] ordering Genl. Stevenson[64] to reorganize the Lt. Art. in his command and bring the first corps of the 1st Miss. Regt. together under Col. Withers, so we will go to V'burg.[65]

Thursday 26th: Molly sent Emanuel to camp this morning with a ham and some butter. The 28th La. Regiment, Col. Thomas, went to Deer Creek to day.[66] Cool & cloudy; appearence of rain.

Friday 27th: Battery was ordered into the trenches this evening upon the supposition that the Yankee gun-boats were coming up the Yazoo. Staid out all night. **Capt. Cowan** went to V'Burg to day and didn't return to night. I was acting Lieutenant. Staid out all night and had a slight shower to fall on us.

Saturday 28th: Returned to camp to night. Battery remained on picket. Saw four Yankee prisoners to day, one of them a mere boy; some of our men who talked with them said he was the sauciest one among them, talked very defiantly, and was confident the North would subdue us. The **28th LA.** Regiment did not go to Deer Creek. they returned to V. to day. Genl. Lee having [missing text] [67]

Sunday 29th: We had a tremendous storm of wind, thunder and lightning last night. The large oak tree which stood in the rear of our kitchen was blown down and the kitchen was torn all to pieces by the roots of the tree which ran under it, and lifted it up, turning it almost completely over. **Mark[,] Granville, Silas** and **Chars.**[68] were in there at the time but luckily escaped without a scratch. The tornado was a fearful one and I hope to hear of the destruction of many of the enemys boats and vessels.—"An ill *wind* that blows no body any good." Heard at Headquarters this morning that Banks has evacuated Baton Rouge[69] [LA] that the Yankees have left Deer Creek, and that Genl. Featherston's expedition was returning.[70] The Yazoo river is said to be falling rapidly. The understanding is that Banks is going to cooperate in an attack upon Mobile [AL].[71]

Received a letter from my dear wife to day in which she tells me that all of our heaven given treasures are well. Mr. Markham dined with me to day. He says we are not going to V'burg but the Co. there will be brought here.[72]

Monday 30th: Featherston has gone to Greenwood.[73] Heard to day that we have had a fight at Fredricksburg [VA] in which the enemy was defeated and lost 30,000 killed and wounded, doubtful.[74] Very cold for the season. I fear a frost which would destroy the fruit.

Sunday 31st March: Very cold last night, had a frost enough to kill the fruit crop I fear. Saw a Yankee deserter, a captured citizen who says he was a Lt. in the 21st La. Regiment of Infantry and a negro belonging to Mrs. Col. Bankam at H'd. Qtrs. The deserter was a member of the 15th Iowa Regt., and [sic] intellectual man and told me there is more dissatisfaction in the Yankee army than we hear of.

April 1st: Three or four Yankee boats paid us a visit to day. They came up to Blake's quarters and threw a few shells at our works and then went off down the river.[75] Battery still in the trenches and likely to remain there. Fine weather indeed.

Thursday 2nd: Everything quiet on the Yazoo, received a letter from Molly all well at home. The Co. returned to camp leaving the guns in position with ground. Weather fine. There are 3156 troops at this point.

Friday 3rd: Nothing of importance to day. I had a slight chill to day.

Sunday 5th: Left Valley F. at 7½ O'clock A. M.: An order was received last night for us to go to Greenwood immediately to reinforce Gen. Loring;[76] we cooked three days rations and left Valley Forge at 7½ O'clock this morning and came to Haynes Bluff to embark. The order for us to get to Greenwood was suppressed this morning and we are ordered to remain at the bluff to await Genl. Pembertons decision.[77]

Monday 6th: Ordered to return to camp and got back at 11½ O'clock.

Tuesday 7th: Went home to day on a 24 hrs. furlough. Had a chill on road.

Wednesday 8th: Capt. Craig[78] came out this evening to pay off our Co. It is rumored that the Yankees had reached Snyders Mill and had ordered all the women and children out of Cowan's battery as they were going to shell this place.[79]

Saturday 11th: Craig paid off the Co. to day for two months and will pay us next week to the 1st of March. Quite Cloudy and I hope we may have a good rain.

Sunday 12th: Molly wrote me and sent my chains. Rain last night. Mr. Markham preached to us this evening.

Monday 13th: Molly came to camp from home to day. Rained all the morning.

Tuesday 14th: Rainy and windy last night, cloudy to day. Molly returned my cow. Cool for the season.

Wednesday 15th: Molly sent Emanuel up after Bob Wilkinson[80] to go down to see his Mother and sister who reached Woodfield[81] from New Orleans yesterday evening. Cleared off in the night and we have had a beautiful sunny day. No news afloat.

Thursday 16th: The raft at Snyder's bluff broke this morning.[82] Issued clothing to the company to day.

Friday 17th: I went to V'Burg to day, found Mother well. The Ab[olitionist]s. ran the gauntlet of our batteries last night & had two boats destroyed.—One was sunk and the other burned. The boats were Cotton and gun-boats.[83] A deserter from 81st Tenn. Regiment was shot to day at V'Burg. Company paid to 1st of March.

Saturday 18th: Nothing transpired to day of any importance. Lt. Col. Parker[84] arrived from Port Hudson [LA] on a visit. Warm and cloudy.

Sunday 19th: Quite a storm of wind last night accompanied with a shower. Cleared off beautifully to day. **Reid** ret'd to camp. Lt. Col. Parker paid us a visit this P.M.

Monday 20th: Went home this evening on 24 hours leave. Rode my horse (Selvin) which had been sent to camp with Bob Wilkinson.

Tuesday 21st: Ret'd to camp this evening. Stopped at Dr. Scotts[85] to avoid a rain, which detained me an hour and a half, and caused me to overstay my time about two hours. **Capt. Cowan** threatened to confine me to camp for forty days; but I hardly think he will be so unjust.

Wednesday 22nd: Cloudy and appearence of rain.

Thursday 23rd: Six boats ran by V'Burg last night one reported sunk and two disabled.[86]

Friday 24th: Nothing new or important to day.

Sat. 25th: Heard to day that 300 Feds. had penetrated the state of Miss. as far as Newton Station and had destroyed two trains of cars, burned the depot and paroled all the citizens. It was a bold and daring raid. Where were our authorities? "A sleep"?[87] Mrs. Reid[88] visited camp to day. I had a slight chill & fever after dinner.

Sunday 26th: One year to day since the organization of this company. Molly sent to camp this morning and wrote me. Cloudy this evening, appearence of rain. Mrs. Brin sent me some strawberries & lettuce.

Monday 27th: Rained last night. Firing at V'Burg at 3 O'clock this morning.[89]

Tuesday 28th: The enemy ran a tug-boat by V. last night.[90]

Wednesday 29th: Very heavy firing down the river to day; supposed to be below Warrenton.[91] Yankees have reached Hazelhurst on the N.O. & J. R. Road[92] our battery ordered to the trenches this evening. Yankees in considerable force have appeared in the Yazoo.[93]

Thursday 30th: A number of transports and several gun-boats are at Blake's lower quarters. A transport and two gun-boats engaged our [text missing][94]

Friday May 1st: The Yankees have been loitering to day on this side and the other side of the river. We shelled them and caused them to "get" back to the Quarters, where they have been seen through the day. The gun-boats have not renewed the attack.[95] A Yankee deserted to day and came riding into our lines huming for Dixie and Ky. He says we will have to fight here. He came directly across the field in front of our pieces and had to swim his horse through the back-water. He was very drunk.[96] The mortar's shelling us this evening.[97] One of Co. A's horses killed yesterday and three men wounded at Hy. Batteries.[98] Aunt Mary, Ross and Mollie[99] came to Penders to day and I went up to see them.

Saturday 2nd: The Yankees departed last night and battery ret'd. to camp.[100] Fighting at Grand Gulf and Port Hudson on 31st and 1st inst.[101]

Sunday 3rd: Rec'd. marching order yesterday. Harpes [?] came from home to day.

Tuesday 5th: Left Valley F. to day at 2½ O'clock under orders to report to Genl. Bowen,[102] arrived at Bovina at 9½ O'clock A. M. to report to Genl. Loring.[103] Temporarily assigned to Genl. Tilghman's[104] brigade and camped in Whittaker's pasture near Baldwins Ferry.

Friday 8th: Lt. Barnes and Tom[105] came for us this P.M. to take part in the expected fight.[106]

Saturday 9th: Barnes and Tom returned home this evening there being no prospect for a fight.[107]

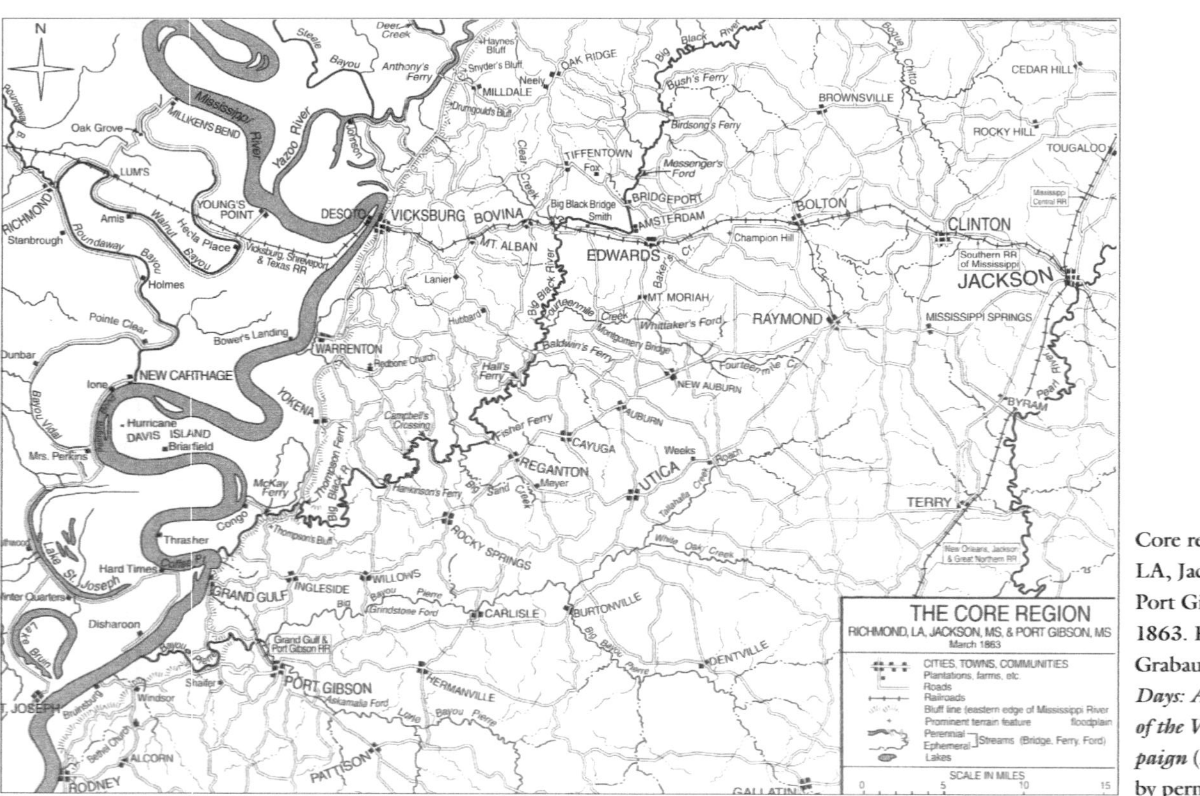

Core region: Richmond, LA, Jackson, MS, and Port Gibson, MS, March 1863. From Warren E. Grabau, *Ninety-eight Days: A Geographer's View of the Vicksburg Campaign* (2000), 539. Used by permission.

Though Sergeant Edmund T. Eggleston and his comrades had been in service for a year, their combat experience had been limited to enduring a few sporadic bombardments and, perhaps, exchanging fire with enemy warships while sheltered behind earthen fortifications. But that type of warfare was coming to a close for Company G. On May 5, 1863, they departed their camp near the Yazoo River and marched south to join the ad hoc army that Lieutenant General John C. Pemberton was throwing together along the Big Black Bridge-Warrenton line.[1] About midway along that line was Lanier's farm.

Early on May 5, Major General William W. Loring established his headquarters at Lanier's farm and had Brigadier General Lloyd Tilghman deploy his brigade in the vicinity to defend against a Union advance by way of Baldwin's Ferry. That evening, after covering about thirty miles, Company G joined its new brigade. The artillerymen remained there for a week, with nothing to do except construct earthworks while they awaited the enemy's advance. After it became clear that the Federals were moving on Jackson, Pemberton advanced eastward on May 13 to what Loring described as "a very strong position . . . about 1 mile south of Edwards Depot, our left resting on the railroad and the right not far from Baker's Creek."[2] On the fifteenth, the Confederates resumed their march eastward, crossing Baker's Creek. About dark, Loring's Division bivouacked at Mrs. Ellison's.[3]

At 6:30 the following morning, the battle opened on the Raymond Road east of Tilghman's camp. Pemberton ordered Loring to have Tilghman deploy his brigade in line of battle but quickly countermanded the order. Concluding that the position was untenable,

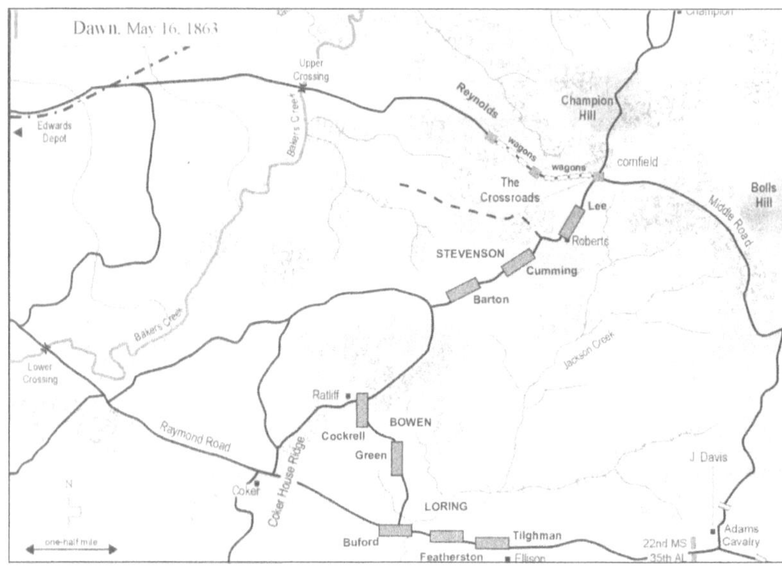

Champion Hill: dawn, May 16, 1863. Courtesy of Timothy B. Smith, from his book *Champion Hill: Decisive Battle for Vicksburg* (2004), 134.

Pemberton had Loring move his division west about three-quarters of a mile to a ridge just east of a small creek. Before the troops could settle in, however, Pemberton ordered Loring to fall back to the next ridge to the west. There Loring's men deployed in line of battle, with Tilghman's Brigade forming the extreme right of the Confederate line and his batteries on both sides of the road leading to Baldwin's Ferry. The gunners of Company G had a clear field of fire all the way to Mrs. Ellison's house.[4]

Loring's Division had been the vanguard in the march the preceding day. Aware of Jackson's fall on the fourteenth and the presence of Grant's army in his front, Pemberton determined to march his army to Edwards. While the balance of the army marched north, Loring's Division, the rearguard, could only watch and wait. Pemberton's withdrawal went smoothly until 11 a.m., when the Federals struck his left flank at Champion Hill. To save his army, Pemberton had to hurry units from his center to his left, and Loring had to stretch his line northward to fill the gap.[5]

Small arms fire dissipated on Loring's front in the morning, as the Union infantry failed to advance. But the opposing artillerymen started an incessant duel in the morning that continued throughout the day.[6] By mid-afternoon, only Tilghman's Brigade, posted along

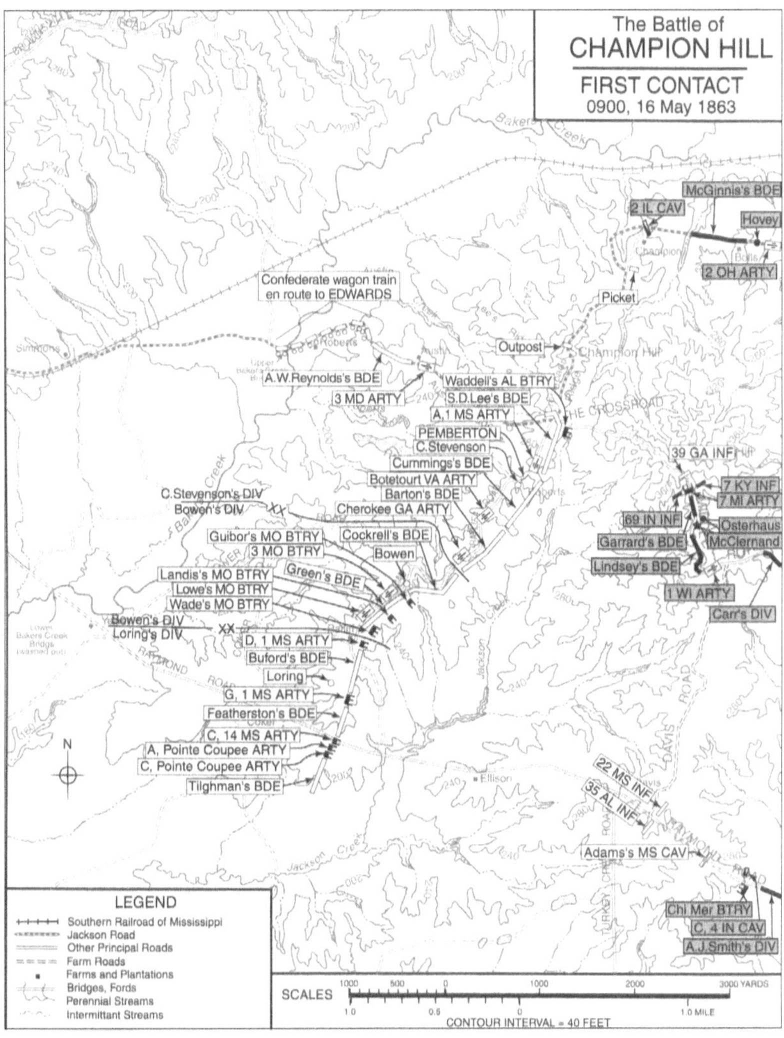

Battle of Champion Hill: first contact, 9 a.m., May 16, 1863. From Warren E. Grabau, *Ninety-eight Days: A Geographer's View of the Vicksburg Campaign* (2000), 585. Used by permission.

a ridge about six hundred yards west of the H. B. Coker house, continued to guard the Raymond Road.[7] Before departing, Loring had informed the brigadier that Pemberton "had directed him to maintain his position at all hazards until sundown." Though Union infantry outnumbered Tilghman's by more than four to one, the Federals failed to advance,[8] their timidity, no doubt, enhanced by the performance of Company G, 1st Mississippi Light Artillery.

Interlude

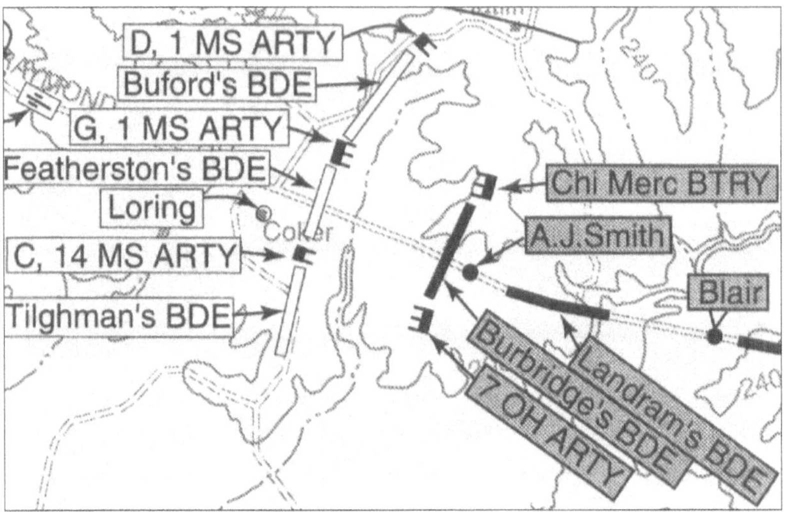

Detail of Battle of Champion Hill: the Crossroads is lost, 1:30 p.m., May 16, 1863. From Warren E. Grabau, *Ninety-eight Days: A Geographer's View of the Vicksburg Campaign* (2000), 587. Used by permission.

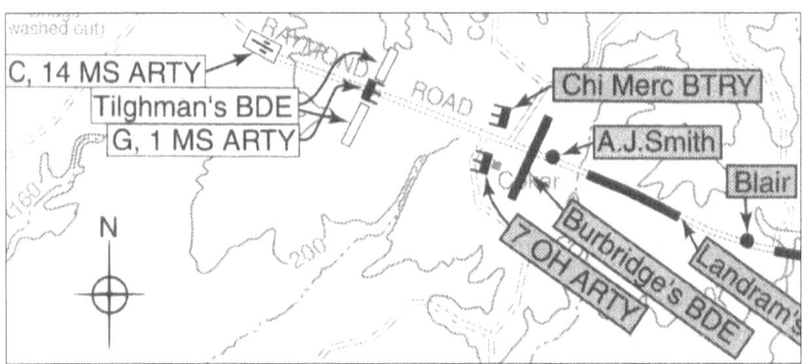

Detail of Battle of Champion Hill: Union counteroffensive, 3:15 p.m., May 16, 1863. From Warren E. Grabau, *Ninety-eight Days: A Geographer's View of the Vicksburg Campaign* (2000), 589. Used by permission.

Though they had been subjected to long range bombardment in the past, Cowan's men now had their first chance to shoot back. Equipped with four 6-pounders and two 12-pounder howitzers, the green Mississippians found themselves facing a formidable challenge. Though assisted by four other cannon in the morning, by early afternoon only two guns of Captain Jacob Culbertson's Company C, 14th Mississippi Artillery Battalion, remained with them.[9] The Confederate smoothbores were no match for the four 10-pounder Parrotts of the 17th Battery Ohio Light Artillery and the two 3-inch rifles—not to mention its four 6-pounder smoothbores—of the Chicago Mercantile Exchange Battery. It was "one of the hottest artillery fights I was ever in," recalled Captain Patrick H. White, commander of the Illinois artillerymen. "I was deaf and dazed from the bursting shells; I could hardly hear myself give an order and one of my ears bled."[10] Supporting infantry on both sides got the worst of the artillery duel, suffering heavier losses than the men serving the guns; **Cowan** had only two men wounded, and White three.[11] Considering that two of Company G's guns were dismounted and a third disabled when a wheel broke during the one-sided contest,[12] it was miraculous that no one was killed. Despite the pounding, Cowan's inexperienced gunners

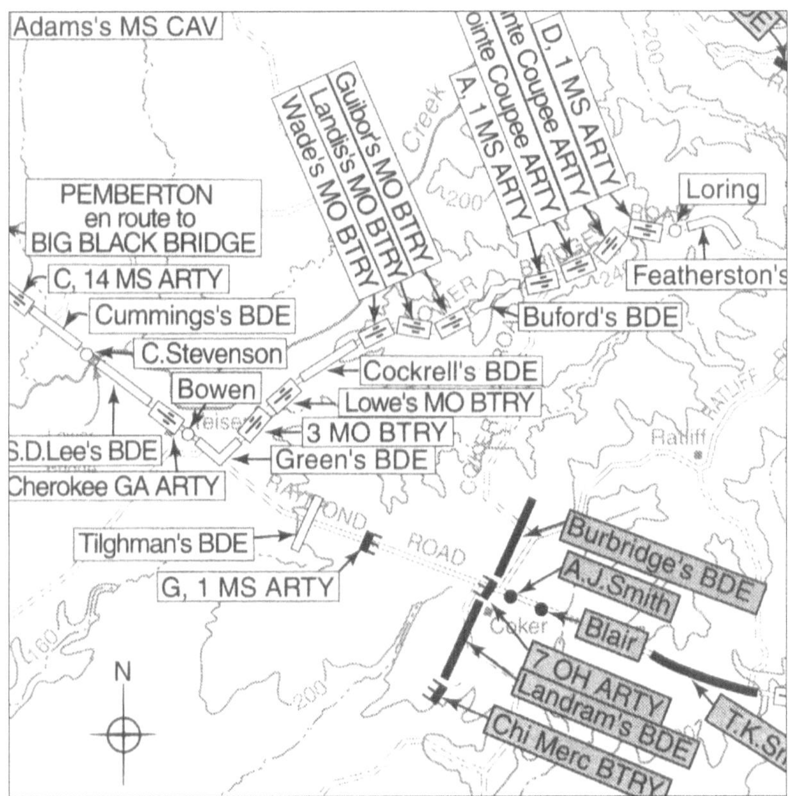

Detail of Battle of Champion Hill: Confederate escape, 5:30 p.m., May 16, 1863. From Warren E. Grabau, *Ninety-eight Days: A Geographer's View of the Vicksburg Campaign* (2000), 591. Used by permission.

Brigadier General Lloyd Tilghman. Courtesy of Lawrence Lee Hewitt.

stayed at their guns. They enabled Tilghman to successfully carry out Pemberton's order, albeit at the cost of his life.

Several eyewitness accounts of Tilghman's death vary widely about the particulars. Edmund T. Eggleston wrote one of them; his "Scenes Where General Tilghman was Killed" appeared in the first volume of *Confederate Veteran*:

Dear Sir—"F. W. M.'s" article on the "Career and Fate of Gen. Lloyd Tilghman," in the September *Veteran*, revived the battle of Baker's Creek, and my memory was freshened regarding the death of the lamented Tilghman. I was an eye-witness to his death. I believe I was the last person he spoke to before he was killed. I was Orderly Sergeant of Capt. James Cowan's Battery, Company G, Col. W. T. Withers' Regiment of Artillery. General Tilghman came to our position, in an open field, on foot. He was in a particularly good humor. He wore a new fatigue uniform. When he arrived near our guns our officers were mounted, and were in position prescribed for dress parade, each Lieutenant, **Geo. H. Tompkins** and **Thos. J. Hanes**, in their positions, and **Captain Cowan** mounted on a large gray horse, making a conspicuous target for the Federal sharpshooters. We were all tyros in war at that time. The General in a pleasant manner said to our **Captain**, "I think you and your Lieutenants had better dismount. They are shooting pretty close to us, and I do not know whether they are shooting at your fine grey horse or my new uniform. They very promptly obeyed the suggestion. Having to go to his headquarters daily with reports, I had become personally acquainted with the affable, gallant and genial officer. Only a few minutes before his death we were sitting on a log near a strip of woodland discussing the line of battle we then held, comparing it with the one we had shortly before occupied. He got up from the log and went to one of our guns, a 12-pound Napoleon, **Corporal "Tommie" Johnson**, gunner, and remarked to him, "I think you are shooting rather too high," and sighted the gun himself. He returned to a little knoll within a few feet of the log on which I was still sitting, and was standing erect, his field glasses to his eyes, watching for the effect of the shot from our gun when he received the fatal wound, not from a "splinter from a shell," however, but from a solid shot. It is true that a horse was killed by the same missile, and I noticed that the horse was dead some time before the General ceased to breathe, though he was unconscious.

It was some little time after the General fell before his son, a youth, could be found, and I shall never forget the touching scene when with grief and lamentations he cast himself on his dying and unconscious father. Those of us who witnessed this distressing scene shed tears of sympathy for the bereaved son and of sorrow for our fallen hero, the chivalrous and beloved Tilghman. His son was thrown from a horse at Mobile sometime afterward and killed. **Captain Cowan** and Lieutenant **Tompkins** are living in Vicksburg. Lieutenant **Hanes** did [until] a few years ago at Vicksburg. He was severely wounded at Nashville—shot though the chest, near the heart—and as he died suddenly, it was thought his wound possibly caused his death after so many years. **Corporal Johnson** was killed at Decatur, Ala., at his post of duty, while preparing a fuse.

Yazoo City, Miss. Sept. 22.
E. T. Eggleston.[13]

"F. W. M."[14] is 1st Lieutenant F. W. Merrin, Company C, 14th Mississippi Artillery Battalion, the other battery serving with Tilghman's Brigade at Champion Hill.[15] Though Merrin's account has generally been accepted by historians, he never claimed to have witnessed the event firsthand or even stated where he was at the time. In fact, Merrin had been ordered to the rear at 1:30 p.m., nearly four hours before Tilghman was hit.[16] Eggleston's account, however, is supported by other sources,[17] including Private **James G. Spencer**, who dictated and signed the following affidavit at the Vicksburg National Military Park:

> Vicksburg, Mississippi, November 25th, 1907, I have this day marked the place where General Lloyd Tilghman was killed in the battle of Champion Hill, May 16th, 1863, by driving an iron pipe into the ground. Said pipe was driven on the ridge first west of the one on which the old Coker House stands and about fifty feet north of the center line of the Raymond Road. I know that the location made is accurate for the following reasons, namely: At the time of the battle I was a private in Capt. Cowan's batter [*sic*] (G, First Mississippi Light Artillery). During the forenoon of the day of the battle, my battery had been in position on the Coker House ridge, but not engaged. About 2 or 2:30 o'clock in the afternoon it was ordered to fall back to the next ridge to the west, the first section went into position on the north side of the road. In taking the new position we were under fire of the Union Sharpshooters and by the time our guns were placed, a Union Battery went into position on the Coker House ridge. General Tilghman went to the north side of the road, probably not more than one hundred feet from the gun that stood first on the north of the road, and first to the left of my gun. I saw him when he fell mortally wounded by a shot from one of the enemy's guns, immediately after he had sighted the said gun of my battery that stood first north of the road and first at the left of my gun.
>
> As heretofore stated, I was probably not more than one hundred feet from the General at the time, and today I had no difficulty in locating the place where he was mortally wounded. The pipe that marks the place where the General fell was driven by me in the presence and with the concurrence of Mr. Sid Thomas, Mr. Z. Wardlaw, Capt. W. T. Ratliff and Capt. William T. Rigby. Mr. Wardlaw said to us while on the ground together that the statement made in his letter of October 23, 1907 to Capt. Ratliff was from common report and not from personal knowledge.[18]

Tilghman fell at 5:20 p.m., according to Colonel Arthur E. Reynolds, who assumed command of the brigade. Shortly thereafter, Reynolds learned that Cowan's battery was nearly out of ammunition, but his orders were to hold. When word finally came to withdraw, Reynolds's eight cannon—Cowan's six and Culbertson's two—stayed behind to cover the retreat. Even then, the Federal infantry failed to press forward, and, when finally allowed to retreat, the artillerymen managed to safely withdraw all their guns.[19]

Eggleston and his comrades had stood toe-to-toe with a superior enemy for more than eight hours; now they had to get out of the way. Shortly before dark, Loring realized his division was cut off. Adopting a circuitous route, Loring attempted to cross Baker's Creek to link up with Pemberton. Unfortunately, the forbidding terrain forced him to abandon all the cannon remaining with his command, including all six of Cowan's guns. Around midnight, he gave up the attempt to rejoin Pemberton and decided his only course dictated a junction with General Joseph E. Johnston. After covering forty miles in twenty-four hours, Loring's Division reached Crystal Springs, twenty-five miles south of Jackson. Two days later it joined Johnston in the capital, minus artillery, wagons, cooking utensils, *and Company G, 1st Mississippi Light Artillery.*[20]

Loring's Division numbered about 7,800 officers and men on the morning of May 16; eight days later the number was 4,862. Casualties suffered at Champion Hill amounted to only 120; obviously the retreat had decimated the division. Colonel Reynolds reported that several men had been wounded in Company G, but official returns listed only two. He also credited **Cowan** with bringing off all his horses, harness, and men, but reported from near Jackson on May 27 that "on the march he and all his men left the command and have not been heard from since."[21] Where did they go?

Eggleston and his comrades were huddled in a creek bottom around midnight on May 16, when Loring's orders arrived to abandon their cannon and that the division would attempt to reach Jackson rather than Vicksburg. After spiking the cannon and sinking them in the swamp, Captain **James J. Cowan** decided, like Nathan Bedford Forrest at Fort Donelson, to ignore his superior's instructions. He and his company struck out for Vicksburg. Though Loring had deemed it impossible, **Cowan** managed to rejoin Pemberton, safely delivering six caissons full of ammunition in the process.[22]

During the siege, Company G manned an 18-pounder, a 30-pounder Parrott, and a Whitworth rifle five hundred yards northwest of the Railroad Redoubt, behind the entrenchments manned by Brigadier General John C. Moore. In addition to supporting the Railroad

Redoubt and Texas Lunette, their field of fire dominated the Baldwin Ferry Road. Company G had two men killed and seven wounded before the garrison's surrender on July 4. The battery members captured and paroled at Vicksburg were eventually assigned to a camp at Enterprise, where they remained for the rest of the year awaiting exchange.[23]

Not all of the members of Company G, however, managed to reach Vicksburg. "We were all in darkness and disorder," Corporal **Lewis M. Spencer** recalled, "and hardly knew what we were doing or who we were following until late the next day."[24] Apparently daylight on May 17 revealed to Senior 1st Lieutenant **George H. Tompkins** that he had been left behind with seventy-eight enlisted men.[25] **Tompkins** and most of the others, including Eggleston, eventually managed to avoid the Yankees and linked up with Colonel Wirt Adams's cavalry during the night of May 20. Learning of the impossibility of reaching Vicksburg and having mounts, most of the artillerymen served the next few days as cavalrymen.[26] Those left afoot joined up with Captain J. A. Hoskins's Brookhaven (Mississippi) Light Artillery, which, long on cannon and short on artillerymen, happened to pass by. Lieutenant **Tompkins** and the rest of Company G, probably including Eggleston, agreed to serve a section of two guns under Hoskins, which they did until June 12, dueling with a battery of Yankee Parrott guns at one point.[27]

By June 13 they had reached Canton,[28] where, on June 18, they became part of a battery newly created by Loring, armed with four 12-pounder Napoleons. Commanded by Captain Jacob Culbertson, the men of the 1st Mississippi Light Artillery Regiment were augmented by a detachment from Captain James T. Smith's Company E, 15th Mississippi Infantry Regiment.[29] Assigned to Featherston's Brigade in Loring's Division, they participated in the abortive attempt to raise the siege of Vicksburg and in the siege of Jackson (July 10–17).[30] Retreating eastward, the ad hoc battery was at Forest on August 10[31] and at Newton eight days later.[32] Sometime after August 31, they moved from Newton to the vicinity of Canton, where they remained for the rest of 1863.[33] **Tompkins** and the men of Company G continued to serve in Culbertson's Battery through October 9,[34] but by then they knew their old unit would be reconstituted once their comrades surrendered at Vicksburg were exchanged. On February 22, 1864, Company G was reorganized as an independent command under **Captain Cowan** at Demopolis, Alabama, where they were equipped with four 12-pounder Napoleons.[35]

Eggleston was listed as present on the return for July–August, but absent sick on the return for September–October.[36] He was released from the General Hospital in Marion and allowed to recuperate at the nearby home of Major Samuel J. Randell,[37] and he was recovering there on November 1, 1863, when Mrs. Sarah A. Fayssoux[38] presented him with a new journal.

Diary of E. T. Eggleston: Volume 2

November 1st 1863

Sun 1: Capt Fayssoux[1] ret'd this AM and says "Thanks to me" he got Merwin's[2] permission to go to see Carlton. I am truly glad I was able to aid him to repay in part the Kindness I have received from his family. He told me he saw Paxton[3] at Enterprise and he said Bryson[4] had a letter for me from my wife. I sent for it and Mr B. has gone to Brandon. I am so disappointed and am afraid he carried the letter with him and will mail it thinking I'm with the Brigade. The Capt. brought some Oysters and we had them for dinner They were very nice I wrote **Tompkins** to day.

Mon 2d: Rode to Meridian to day and saw Gill[5] the man who has Selvin Was very much fatigued by the trip

Tue 3d: Wrote Merwin again sent copy Paxtons certificate

Wed 4th: November 1863: I went to Marion Station to day and went before the Examining board for the purpose of obtaining their certificate as to my condition, but they refused to give one upon the ground that they were only allowed to give such, an one as I wanted to men who were permanently disabled and unfit for service and that they could not say by what I would be well enough for duty in a month. I had to register my name on the hospital books and enter a ward as a patient before they would examine me

---

This comprises pages 2–67, 85–88, 90–95.

but Dr Davenport[6] whose ward I entered allowed me to return to Maj Randells. He was the only member of the board who wanted to grant me a certificate, he was willing to give me all they could say in writing. Rec'vd a letter from Molly to day dated Oct 24th

Thursday 5th: November 1863: Wrote Molly letter "No 1" reply to hers of 24th Octo. and wrote **Jno. Hicks** at Enterprise. A rainy day__ showery. Wrote Joe Harris[7] & Lt. W. H. Weller.[8]

Frid. 6th: Mailed my letter for Molly to Mrs Jenkins[9] Raymond. Spit blood last night

Sat. 7th: Went to Meridian and got my hair cut. Learned that Armstrong had forwarded my letter to Molly. Got $150. from Ball[10] for sight draft on Joe Harris. Saw Bryson and Geo Lawrence[11] & learned from the latter that Mrs. M. A. Cooke[12] is in Brandon. Wrote Molly *No 2* & Geo Lawrence will send it to Mrs Cooke at Brandon. Enclosed in Molly's letter, a letter for Mrs Leiper in Pennsylvania, and one for Mrs McLellan in New Orleans

Sun 8th: Sent Molly's letter to Geo Lawrence by Capt Fayssoux

Mon 9th: November 1863: Wrote Merwin, Barnes and **De Moss**. Molly my darling wife arrived to day from VBurg with dear little John. She heard I was very ill and came to me. My poor little boy is nothing but skin and bones after his long illness.

Wed 11th: Molly suffered very much through the night with slow and sporadic pains Wrote Mother yesterday telling her of Molly's arrival and enclosing a letter for Mrs Leiper and Mrs McLellan. Molly had a bouncing girl at 5 O'clock this evening and her name is Martha Randell after the lady[13] whose hospitality I have been enjoying since the 4th Octo. All is well with my darling wife.

Frid 13th: Wrote Jos. L. H. to LaGrange [Georgia]

Sat 14th: Wrote Jos. L. H. & cousin Belle[14] to LaGrange Capt Fayssoux & his mother[15] left for South Carolina to night.

Sund. 15th: November 1863: Wrote **Van De Moss** & Merwin. Molly & baby doing well. Beautiful weather. clear & cold at night, pleasant though the day. Johnny much improved.

Mond 16th: Wrote Mother and Aunt Sophi[16] ~~and sent to Mrs Jenkins at Raymond~~ and sent to Genl Tappan[17] to hand Mrs Cooke.

Wed. 18th: Our little Martha is one week old to day. She is squalling at an awful rate. She and her mother are doing well.

Frid 20th: Wrote Barnes to pay me the $20 he lost in Gold, for Molly to carry to V. with her. Raining this morning. Wrote Presdt [Jefferson] Davis.[18] [letter appears in Appendix C]

Benjamin S. Tappan. [http://www.tnportraits.org/
tappan-benjamin-s-ml.htm]

Mon 23: *Wrote* Snodgrass,[19] Madison, **Tompkins**[,] Mrs Sthreshley,
Mrs Jenkins & Merwin

Tues 24: *Mailed* letter for **Bigelow, King,**[20] and two Kings in Virginia[21] at Marion Station

Thurs 26: Wrote J L Harris, B. W. Henry[22] and Mrs Jenkins

Sun 29th: November 1863: Rained yesterday turned very cold last
night, clear to day and the coldest weather we have had this fall.

December

Tues. 1st: Winter commenced with a clear and cold day. I am still at
Major Sam J. Randell's in Lauderdale Co. near Meridian, with
Molly, Johnny and Matty. Will rejoin my command as soon as
Molly is able to leave here.

Wed 2d: Went to Meridian and met Merwin & Derbyshire.[23] The latter
was just from our Battery near Canton. Says they have built winter

President Jefferson Davis. Library of Congress.

quarters and are quite comfortable, get good beef and buy sweet potatoes at $2.00 per bushel. Wrote J. L. Harris

Friday 4th: Went to Meridian, bought a Haversack, recvd a letter from Mother dated 23d Nov and also got one from her for Molly. All were well with her and at Woodfield, and they were comfortable out there. Geo Queen and Wm Hunter supply them abundantly with wood.

Sat. 5th: Wrote Tom Roach enclosing his Mother's[24] letter to him and Molly wrote Mrs Martha Hicks[25] to Canton Miss

Sunday 6th: Wrote Mother and sent to Gen Tappan to forward. Molly wrote her also.

Mon. 7th: Wrote Sam Barnes[26] at Enterprise.

Frid. 11th: Wrote Barnes, Harris & Snodgrass.

Sun. 13th: Wrote Roach, **Tompkins** & Snodgrass

Tues 15th: Went to Marion and reported to the Hospital and found I had been reported to Dept. Hd. Qrs. as a deserter from the 8th inst.

Thurs 17th: Went to Marion and obtained my discharge from the Hospital

Frid 18th: Left Maj. Randells & put up at Ragsdale's[27] in Meridian.

Sat 19th: December 1863: Left Meridian at 7 O'clock for Brandon and arrived there at 3 O'clock. Came to Gen Tappan's and was hospitably & kindly received. H. E. Barnes & Ned Porter[28] are here on a visit.

Mon 21: Got a 15 days furlough from Genl Johnston.[29] Wrote Damas[30] & Presdt. Davis Wrote **Tompkins**

Wed. 23: Wrote **Van De Moss** to day.

Frid 25: Went to church to day in Brandon and heard Mr Elwell[31] preach. A lot of lawless solders broke into Genl Tappan's store last night, and robbed him of a bbl. brandy, much smoking tobacco and other things.

Sun 27th: Had Mattie baptized at Gen Tappans by the Revd. Mr Elwell. Miss Margaret Tappan[32] was her god-mother.

Tues 29th: Applied for an extension of furlough. Wrote **A. W. Daniel** and sent draft on **A. A. Folkes** for Twenty five dollars.

Wed. 30th: Wrote Genl L. Polk[33] to Meridian [letter appears in Appendix C]

January 1864.

Sat. 2d: Wrote F. W. Damas

Wed. 6th: Wrote Sam W. Tappan[34]

Sat. 9th: Took my first degree in Masonry.[35]

Sun. 10th: Lt. **Tompkins** arrived this evening en route for Ala. on 20 day furlough.

Mon 11th: Sent application to **Lt Cowan** for extension of furlough to be forwarded through regular channels. Wrote S. W. Tappan Bought 80½ pds Smoking Tobacco @ 2.77 from S. B. Marye[36] amt. $224.37. chrgd one on Henry[37] & Tappan's books.[38] 161 plugs.

Wed 13: Took the Fellow crafts degree in Masonry.

Thur 14: Wrote Mother and sent by Dr Newman.[39] Wrote Damas.

Sat 16th: Passed to a Master-Mason's degree.

Sat 16th: January 1864: Wrote D.O. Merwin

Sun 17th: Wrote **L. B. Cowan** & E. H. Porter

Mon 18th: Recvd a letter from Mother dated Jan 13th and containing news that all were well. Wrote Tom Roach, and enclosed letter from Mother, wrote Mrs. Randell and enclosed letter for Mrs Fayssoux, and sent it to Meridian by S. W. Tappan. Mailed a letter to Philip Gill; and one to Armstrong. Forwarded application for transfer to Jennings Co in Millers cavalry regiment.[40] Mailed Molly's letter to Belle.

Fri 22: Sent **Levy** 79½ pds Smoking Tobacco by Mr Doyle care **A. A. Folkes**. Sent my descriptive list to **Lt Cowan**.

Sun 24: Wrote J. L Harris

Frid 29: Wrote Aunt Sophi to Brownsville care Mrs Messinger.[41]

Sat 30: Wrote **Levy** & sent dft on **A A Folkes** for $25.

February 1864

Mon 1st: Wrote **Lt Tompkins** & D. S. Snodgrass. Wrote **W. V. McCray**.

Wed 3d: do J. M. Robb & J. L. Harris.

Thurs 4th: do Mother to send by Molly.

Sat 6th: Left Brandon and went to Meridian in charge of $2,470,000, government funds.[42]

Sund 7th: Retd to Morton this morning and met our boys who had just arrived from Canton. Recvd letter from Mrs Fayssoux.

Mon 8th: Joined Capt. E. H. Porter with his train[43] at Morton and started with him on the retreat. Yankees advancing upon Morton.[44] Came down from Meridian Sunday with Col. Clark[45] and made his acquaintance, found him a very nice gentleman.

Thurs. 11th: Reached Meridian to night and camped a mile from town. Got a letter from Mother dated 17th Decr.

Frid 12th: Went by Maj. Randell's and took dinner. They appeared glad to see me. Mrs Mills[46] from S.o. Ca. was there. Wrote Molly by Charley Petrie.[47]

Sat 13th: Camped near Old Marion to day. Moved late in the evening towards Lauderdale Springs

Sund. 14th: Passed through Livingston Ala. to day and camped 20 miles from Demopolis. Cloudy & a slight sprinkle to day. Have had beautiful weather since we left Morton.

Mon 15th: Had a terrific rain & wind on the road to day. Traveling was very bad after the rain. Reached our camping ground two miles from the Tombigbee by five o'clock. Dined with Mr Pharis[48] to day on turkey, souces [head cheese], bacon & greens, sausages, butter milk &c *free of charge*. Was pleased with Ala. hospitality.

Tue 16th: Crossed the Tombigbee at 12 O'clock to night, a freezing cold night. Camped near Demopolis until Wed. morning.

Wed 17th: Everything frozen up this morning. Capt Porter and I ~~dined~~ breakfasted with Mrs Hayden[49] this A.M. and had a sumptuous meal, coffee, sausages, eggs, biscuit-egg bread souce, butter & butter milk in profusion. Camped near Demopolis. Wrote cousin Belle to LaGrange Georgia.

Thurs 18th: Still near Demopolis_ snowing slightly.

Frid 19th: Started for Macon Miss but the order was countermanded and we retd to camp. Met all the boys belonging to the battery.

Sat 20th: Wrote Molly and sent by Patterson. Mended the pockets in my coat_ surprised myself sewing as expertly as I did.

Sun 21st: Spent the day in camp reading &c. Major A. M. Paxton dined with us to day. My letter was not sent to Molly by Patterson but was sent by a gentleman to day. Gen Hardee[50] arrived in Demopolis to day.[51] My hopes are more buoyant. He is a general of merit.[52]

Tues 23d: Recrossed the Tombigbee[53] this morning on a pontoon bridge. Wrote Molly and Belle. Went to Demopolis to see Joe Harris and he had left on cars for Selma.

Wednes 24th: Camped within five miles of Livingston Ala. on our way back to Mississippi

Thur 25th: Passed through Livingston this morning. A beautiful young lady gave me a bunch of hyacinths. We are en route for Macon Miss.[54] Camped near Gainesville on the Noxubee river

Frid 26th: Camped near Cooksville in Noxubee Co Miss. Reentered Miss to day at 1 O'clock. Are having charming weather and fine roads for our trip.

Sat. 27th: Reached Macon Miss at 1 o'clock to day. Camped on Noxubee river. We passed a Texan to day who was drunk and evidently imagined himself a General. He was drilling an immense army and arranging it in His order of battle. As we passed he gave the command "Attention World! By nations right wheel_ March! Gen Ross you will command the left. Gen Ferguson, you will command the right. Gen Lee you will command the center; and Wirt Adams you will go to the rear for by G-d you Know you wont fight"!![55]

Sund 28th: Camped near Macon to day.

Mon 29th: Still encamped near Macon Mississippi. Very dull _ no papers, no news_ and no acquaintances in Macon. Fortunately. Lt Huddleston[56] has a few books and with those I managed to amuse myself. Am reading "Chambers Information for the People"_ a fine work.[57] The last day of the winter of 1863–1864! Oh! that our political troubles may be ended before this day twelve months!

March 1864.

Tues 1st: Commenced raining this morning before day. Rained all day. Still camped near Macon Miss.

Weday 2d: Near Macon yet. Clear & pleasant. Wrote Molly to send by courier to Canton care Judge A H Handy.[58]

Thurs 3d: Near Macon still. Clear & pleasant

Frid 4th: Camped near Macon Miss Cloudy & threatening rain. one year from to day I trust may end Lincoln's unhappy and disastrous reign.

Sat 5th: Still near Macon. A Locomotive passed up the road to day from Gainesville, the first since the Yankee raid to Meridian.[59]

Sund 6th: Camped near Macon. orders recvd to start for Canton to join the command.

Mond 7th: Started from Macon to Canton this morning.[60] Rained on us to day. Camped 9 miles from Louisville in Winston Co.

Tues 8th: Paxton & I left the train to day & started for Brandon. Passed through Louisville and met Dr. Scott and Wm J. Cowan.[61] The Dr is living near there. Stayed all night with Dr. Lee, 23 miles from Louisville making 32 miles we traveled to day.

Wed 9th: Traveled 38 miles to day. Reached Hillsboro at 5 o'clock and stayed with Mrs. Wilkens.[62] Rained on us nearly all day. The Yankees burned nearly every house in Hillsboro.

Thurs 10th: Left Hillsboro at 6 & ¾ o'clock. arrived at Brandon at 5 O'clock and found my wife had started home on Saturday. Found all well at Gen Tappan's & that they had lost nothing by the Yankees.

Frid 11th: Carried to Clinton to day to see Molly & found she left for home on Tuesday. Stayed at Mrs. Careys[63] with her sister Miss Gillespie.[64] Wrote Molly and sent by Miss Belle Lawrence[65] to day.

Sat. 12th: Remained in Clinton to day. Met Mr McRaven and Mrs Fisher who saw Molly inside the Feds lines. Mrs F. saw her at the bridge.[66] So she has reached home in safety.

Sund 13th: Joined Capt Porter to day at or near Madison Station. Wrote Molly to send by Mrs Carey.

Monday 14th: Wrote **Capt. Cowan** and **Lt. Tompkins** & sent the former my transfer papers for approval. Sent the letter through Hd. Qrs. brigade to Demopolis by **Geo. Marshall**. Major Wm Paxton[67] arrived to day and brought me letter No 4 from Molly. Letter No 2 also recvd.

Wednes 16th: Started back to Macon, passed through Canton & Sharon. Learned to night that the order for moving to Macon has been countermanded & we will retrace our steps tomorrow. Wrote Molly & Miss Mag T on yesterday. A Very cold & blustering day.

Thurs 17th: Retraced our journey towards Madison Station. Camped two miles from Canton. Very Cold.

Frid 18th: Camped four miles from Calhouns station on the Miss Central Railroad. Quite cold.

Sat 19th: Rained very hard to day. Capt Porter retd from Brandon this evening and brought me letters from Mother sister and from Molly to the Tappans. My letter No 9 to Molly was sent in to day by Mrs. Moody.[68]

Sund 20th: Moved Camp to Calhoun Station this A.M. Wrote Tommy Roach to Mobile and enclosed letters from Sister & Mother. Raining this P.M.

Mon 21st: Wrote Molly No 10 & sent to Lt Coffey by Lt. Wilfong.[69] Cloudy & Cold.

Tues 22d: Snowed a little this morning. Cleared off about 10 O'clock. Will Paxton went to Brandon to day. Capt Porter to Canton. Sent my letter to Molly by Lt Wilfong

Wed 23d: A clear pleasant day. Quiet in camp near Calhoun Station.

Thurs 24th: Raining to day. A hail storm this morning. Still near Calhoun Station.

Frid 25th: Capt P recvd a letter from Brandon brought out by Petrie. Mine sent at the same time not yet to hand. A disagreeable blustering day.

Sat 26th: A beautiful day, calm, clear and sirene Wrote Miss Mary Tappan[70] per Capt McInnis[71] Saw the Mobile News of the 21st; no conformation about our recognition, though it is alluded to as being in the papers in Europe.[72]

Sund 27th: A lovely day. Wrote Belle Harris

Mond. 28th: A hard rain this morning & then clear and windy the balance of the day.

Tuesd 29th: Gen Lee[73] and Armstrong[74] reviewed[75] our Brigade this morning. A cold windy day.

Still near Calhoun Station. Recvd Molly's letter No 3 drafted 17th Feb.

Wed. 30th: Wrote Molly "No 11" to day. A beautiful day.

Thurs 31st: Handed Adjt Marshall[76] my letter to send Lt Coffey for Molly. A hail storm this evening and a hard rain. The last of March 1864.

April 1864.

Frid 1st: A cold windy cloudy day more like a winter day than the opening of the 2d month of spring. At Calhoun Station. Recvd a letter from Mother dated 15th March. All were well & Molly had gone to W_d [Woodfield] to join Aunt & my little girls.

Sat 2d: Cloudy this evening. Still at Calhoun Station.

Sund 3d: Went to Canton to day after my tobacco Dined with Maj. Quaite[77] at his Hd. Qrs. Warm, windy & showerey.

Mon 4th: Moved from Calhoun Station towards Macon & camped 6 miles from Canton.[78] Saw Dr Fitzhugh[79] in Canton and sent messages home by him. He goes to Warren Co next week. Clool [*sic*] & cloudy

Tues 5th: Crossed the Ochnochonee to day and camped. Unusually cold this morning. Cleared off. bright and warm. Met **L. B. Cowan** who handed me my application for transfer disapproved. My luck. Am heartsick and sorely disappointed. Will persevere though for the sake of my family. The Battery has gone to North Ala.

Wed 6th: Passed through Carthage to day. Met Mr. Sam B. Wall[80] there and went to his house and dined with him. Was cordially met and hospitably treated. Miss Martha Stith (Mrs. Bay)[81] put two pockets in my coat. Cloudy. Recvd letter No 1 from Molly to day (dated 12th Feb.)

Thurs 7th: Rained on us all the evening. Camped near Dutchman's store.

Friday 8th: Dreadful roads to traveled over to day. We only came about Eight miles were bogging & stalling continually. Could not catch up with the command and had to camp 5 miles from Philadelphia in a swamp.

Sat. 9th: Crossed a very bad swamp to day and passed through Philadelphia, a dreary dilapidated place Cold and windy. Command has gone on towards Macon via "Skillet" or Winstonville

Sund 10th: Traveled 30 miles to day and passed through Winstonville. another desolate woe begone hamlet. The command had gone on to Macon. Clear & cool to day.

Mon 11th: Passed through Mashulasville[82] and Macon to day. Met Messenger[83] at Macon Got a lady to put two pockets in my coat. A charming spring day. Capt Porter joined us at Macon and brought me a letter from Mother dated 24th March.

Tues 12th: Passed through Fairfield to day and reached the Tombigbee river. Crossed the Bigbee & camped near Bridgeville in Ala.

Wed. 13th: Camped within 19 miles of Tuscaloosa. A beautiful spring day.

Thurs 14th: Reached camp one mile from Tuscaloosa on the Black Warrior at 4 o'clock. Cloudy.

Frid 15th: Camped near Tuscaloosa. A dinner was given to the Brigade in Tuscaloosa. I did not attend. Wrote Mr. B. H. Craig,[84] Gen Polk and Joe Porter.[85]

Sat. 16th: Went to Tuscaloosa this morning and "saw the town". Quite a flourishing place with a number of large factories and many pretty ladies

Sund 17th: Wrote Molly, Mother & Gen Tappan & Presdt Davis to day.

Mond 18th: Started for Elyton to day. Rained last night Capt [Edward H.] Porter left us to day.

Tuesd. 19th: Came 30 miles and camped within 13 miles of Elyton. An unreasonably cold day for April.

Wed. 20th: Passed through Elyton to day and camped in three miles of town. A beautiful day.

Thurs 21st: Passed the day in Camp near Elyton. Wrote Molly No 13 and sent to Mr Tom Marshall[86] via Enterprise care D. O. Merwin. Cloudy.

Frid. 22d: Moved Camp to day. Still near Elyton. Col Miller[87] left to day on furlough 25 days.

Sat. 23d: Camped near Elyton. Cloudy & sprinkling.

Sund. 24th: Rained in showers throughout last night. Cleared off this A.M. and we retd. to withdraw two miles of Jonesboro. and ten miles from Elyton.

Mond 25th: Camped to day ten miles from Elyton at the front of a small mountain. I ascended it this morning and saw a variety of beautiful wild flowers, the wild flag, violet, pink and verbena. I could have culled a pretty boquet. One of the most delightful days I ever beheld. Oh! how I longed for home in such charming weather.

Tues. 26th: Started for Centreville[88] this A.M. and traveled 23 miles over tolerable good roads. Passed through a rich iron country and close to the government iron works.[89] A real warm spring day.

Wed. 27th: Reached Centreville to day and camped on the Cahawba river.

Thurs 28th: **Marshall** left to day and Comd went on duty as Adjt.[90] Wrote Molly and sent by **Marshall**.

Frid 29th: A slight April shower late yesterday evening Wrote Jos A. Porter about transfer.

Sat 30: Wrote Belle Harris to day Camped near Centreville Ala. Wrote Capt [Edward H.] Porter to Selma Ala. Maj. Steede[91] arrived yesterday.

May 1864.

Sund 1st: Left Centreville to day in a shower for Montevallo. Reached Montevallo this evening.

Mond 2d: Recvd. my recent application for transfer "disapproved" and rejoined the battery at Montevallo.

May 3d Tuesday: Wrote Molly and sent by Mrs. Kelley. Was to day reinstated as Orderly Sergeant of the Battery. An unusually cold day for May.

Wed. 4th: In Camp near Montevallo.

Thurs 5th: Recvd a letter from Molly, Mother, Miss Mary Tappan, Mr Snodgrass, Uncle Frank[92] & Capt [Edward H.] Porter. Expect to start for Georgia tomorrow or soon[93]

Frid 6th: Wrote No 16 & to E H Porter & Snodgrass

Sat 7th: Started from Montevallo to day for Rome Ga or Blue Mountain station. Came to the Station by Rail.

Sund 8th: Left Blue Mountain Station for Rome this morning. Made about 16 miles and camped near a fine creek. Elegant water through this poor country.

Monday 9th: Came 33 miles and camped within 14 miles of Rome. Crossed into Georgia this evening.

Tues 10th: Came 14 miles to day and reached Rome Ga on the Coosa river. Started to Resaca but was turned back[,] the enemy who were threatening that place having been repulsed. Camped near Rome waiting developments.[94] We hear glorious news from Dalton, [Georgia,] Virginia and the Trans-Mississippi Department.[95]

Wed. 11th: Rained very hard last night. Ordered to the depot at Rome to await transportation to Resaca Dalton or the front.

Thursday 12th: Reached Resaca at 2 O'clock this morning.[96] Johnston commenced evacuating Dalton to day.[97]

Frid 13th: Skirmishing commenced to day at 2 O'clock and artillery firing at 3 o'clock. Brisk skirmishing throughout the evening.[98] Saw several wounded men. Three were killed by a shell at the depot.

Sat 14th: Heavy firing on the right. Hardee repulsed two assaults of the enemy with great slaughter. The enemy advanced in our front in the evening, driving in our pickets and obtaining possession

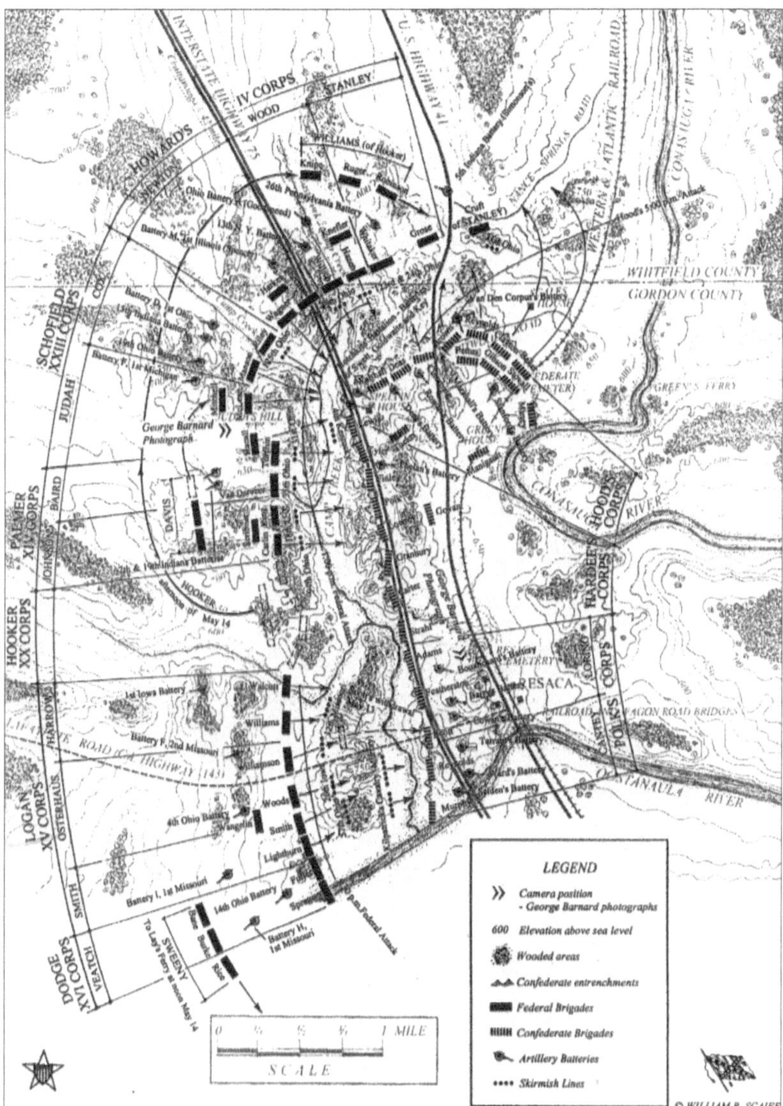

Battle of Resaca: first day, May 14, 1864. Courtesy of the Kennesaw Mountain Historical Association.

of a ridge about five hundred yards in our immediate front. The skirmishing lasted until ten O'clock. **Wm Dancy** was shot through the heart and was instantly Killed. **E H Young** slightly wounded by a ball from a shrapnel in the head.

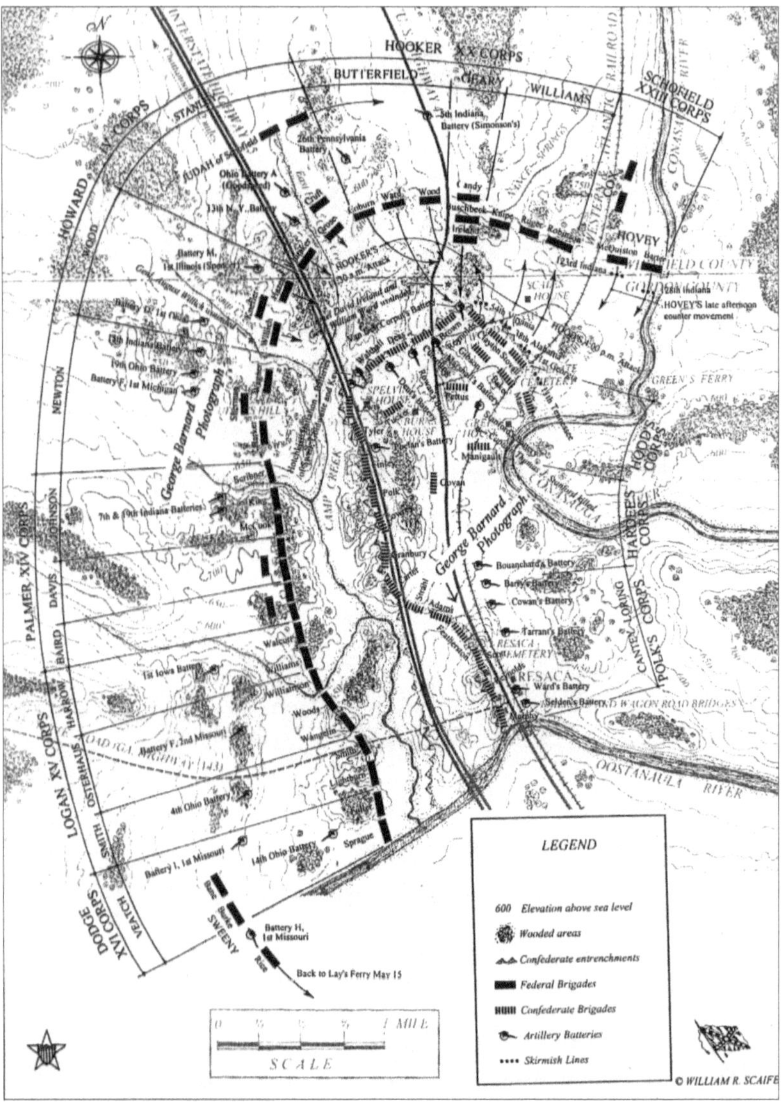

Battle of Resaca: second day, May 15, 1864. Courtesy of the Kennesaw Mountain Historical Association.

Sund 15th: Heavy skirmishing on our right all day, but little in front of our position and on the left. **Cushman** wounded in the calf of his leg to day and his horse was Killed by the same shot.

Monday 16th: Evacuated Resaca at 1 o'clock last night[99] and fell back towards Adairsville. The Yankees pursued us and we made a stand three miles south of Calhoun. Recvd letter "No 10" from my wife per Lt. **L B Cowan** dated April 27th. All were well at home. Nine men from McClendon's Battery temporarily assigned to our Batt. joined us to day.[100] Our cavalry skirmishes with the enemy all day at and near Calhoun. We have a large body of Cavalry with us.[101]

Tuesda 17th: Our Battery and Featherston's brigade[102] were sent near Calhoun last night to picket. Retd to our position on the line about midnight leaving a cavalry picket in front. Met Jim Hunt to day and Jim Fox yesterday. I arrested a man last night for suspicious conduct & carried him to Gen Johnston's Hd. qrs. by order of Genl Featherston.[103] He proved to be Genl Shoupe's[104] chief Surgeon[105] and was identified by Dr Ford[106] of Johnston's staff. Reached Adairsville at 2 O'clock. The enemy followed us closely, skirmishing over the whole road with our Cavalry. They commenced skirmishing with our skirmishers at the outer-lines at 3 O'clock. Rained on us this evening. We left Adairsville at 11 O'clock to night.[107]

Wed 18th: Marched all night last night and reached Cassville about daylight this morning. **Jno McQuaide** fell off a gun carriage and was run over by the carriage on the 16th and seriously injured. My horse was wounded in the thigh at Resaca on the 14th but not severely. Met Lt Weller this morning.

Thursday 19th: Formed line of battle at Cassville at 9 O'clock this morning. The enemy advancing. Skirmishing in front. Changed position and formed new line in rear of Cassville.[108]

Friday 20th: Fell back last night[109] and crossed the Etowah river, fell back towards Atlanta, the enemy having crossed the Etowah at Rome. There seems to be a race between Johnston & Sherman as to which shall reach Atlanta first. The day and night marches are very trying on the men but as yet no evidences of demoralization are exhibited.[110]

Sat. 21st: In Camp all day two miles from Allatoona. The enemy reported crossing the river at Etowah

Sund. 22nd: Recvd letter "No 9" from my dear wife dated 19th April. Still in camp near Allatoona

Mond 23rd: Moved about 14 miles on the Atlanta road.[111]

Tues 24th: March this morning at 5 & ½ O'clock towards "Lost Mountain" on the Atlanta road.

Wed. 25th: Rained yesterday evening. Started on our march at 7 O'clock this morning supposed to be going into position in line of battle.

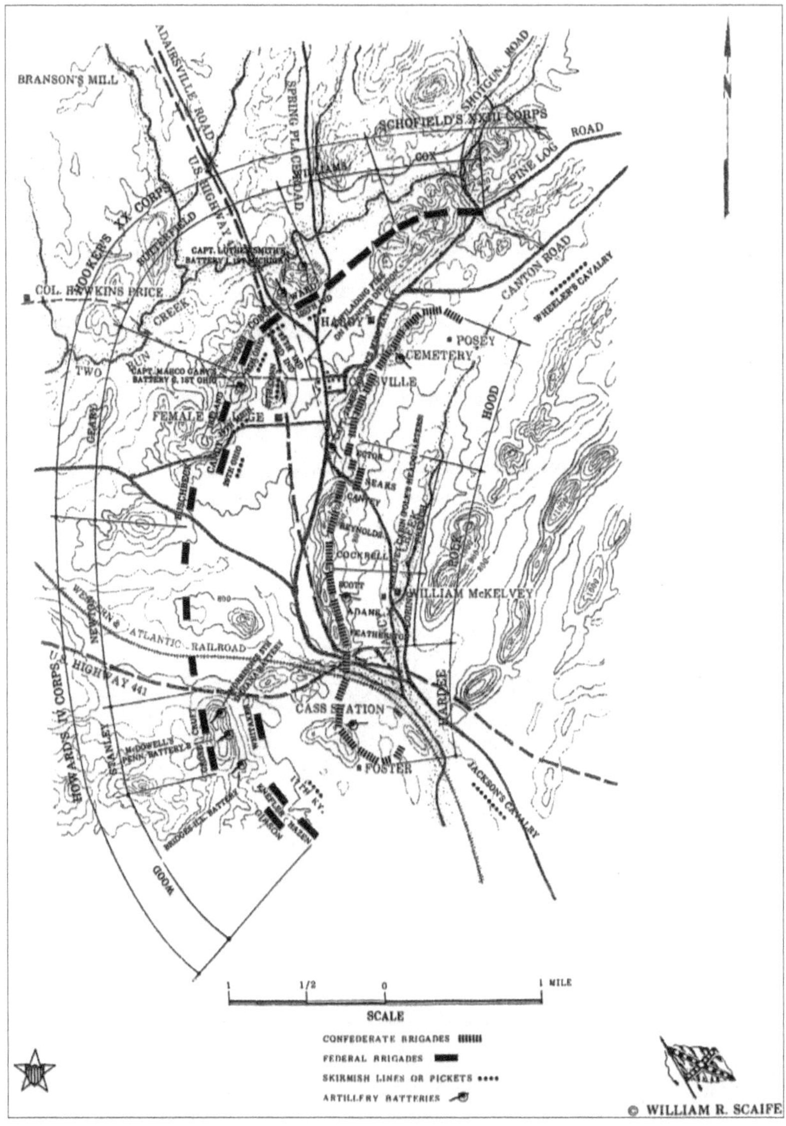

Affair at Cassville: evening of May 19, 1864. Courtesy of the Kennesaw Mountain Historical Association.

Skirmishing commenced at 5 O'clock this evening Heavy firing on our right just at dark. Loss reported heavy on both sides.[112] We were held in reserve. Rained on us again to night.

Thurs 26th: We moved into position near New Hope Church at 1 O'clock last night

Diary of E. T. Eggleston

Friday 27th: Sharpshooters were firing all night. *Jessee Bass* was painfully wounded in the left Knee just at 9 O'clock while he was sleeping. I witnessed a sad sight this morning, the burial of some of our poor fellows who were Killed yesterday. I saw four from the 36th Ala. buried in one grave, stiff and rigid in death and their bodies in the attitudes they were in when their breath left them. **Bass** sent to the Hospital this morning. It was necessary to amputate poor **Bass** leg. Wrote No 17 to day. Heavy firing along the line all evening.

Sat. 28th: Our forces were moving to the right all night.[113] The Enemy could be distinctly heard moving too. Our Battery left in yesterday's position. Gen Johnston has massed his forces on the enemy's left. The enemy charged our lines in front of Cleburne's Division and Gen Hardee was heard to say they must have lost between 4000 and 5000 Killed.[114] That they were piled up in greater numbers than they were at Murfreesboro[115] where the heaviest firing was done. Incessant skirmishing along the whole line throughout the day. one gun from the 1st sec. detached from the batty and moved three hundred yards to our left under command Lt. **Tompkins.**

Sunday 29th: Skirmishing along the lines throughout the day. Very heavy firing tonight at half past ten O'clock. The Enemy made a night attack upon our right, which we repulsed. Heavy cannonading on our extreme left supposed to be an attempt on the part of the enemy to get possession of an important gap[116]

Mond 30th: The most quiet day we have had since we took position here. little firing from sharpshooters. The enemy supposed to be moving on our right flank. Our suspense grows more trying daily.

Tues. 31st: Moderately quiet to day. Regular and continuous sharpshooting. Our battery has not fired a gun since we left Resaca.[117] We changed our position to night at 11 O'clock and moved to the right on Gen Loring's line.

Wednesday June 1st: Constant sharpshooting along the lines. The enemy discovered moving to the right.[118] In position on the line with Featherston's brigade. Quite sick to day.

Thurs 2d: Heavy rain to day at noon. The first good rain we have had for several weeks. Skirmishing continues. No charge or assault has been made on our works for a day or two. Heavy cannonading & musketry on our right at 5 O'clock this evening. **Herring** wounded to night in the breast by spent ball. only bruised severely not penetrated.

Frid 3d: Rained this morning. Wrote "No 18" from Battle field and sent to Thos R. Holloman[119] at Canton. Skirmishing rather more rapid to day. No prospect of a general engagement evident.

Sat. 4th: Rained this morning. The enemy charged our skirmishers in front of French's[120] line and drove them in, we reinforced our men and regained our position. The first charge which has been made in our vicinity for several days. Changed our left line to night. We moved to Lost Mountain at 8 O'clock.[121] Had a terrible time of it; were rained on all night and the roads were in a terrible condition.

Sund 5th: Reached lost Mountain at 5 O'clock, went into park and rested until night when we moved near the village of Lost Mountain and parked for the night. Saw Maj. Steede riding one of 35 grey horses captured recently from the Philadelphia greys by Miller's Regiment.

Mond 6th: Came into position at the foot of Lost-Mountain at 10 O'clock A.M. Rained on us again to day. Replied to Miss Mag Tappan's letter of the 12th ulto. No enemy appeared in our front yet. They can be seen from the top of Lost Mountain moving to our right.

Tues 7th: Rained on us again to day. Changed position to day moved to our right to check a counter movement on the part of the enemy. Recvd letters "No 12 & 13" from my wife and the *first letter* from my dear boy. My friend Joe Porter had me detailed yesterday for Capt Morris'[122] office. As it was only a temporary detail I did not want it; and told **Capt C.** so, and he endorsed on the order that my services "were indispensable to the Efficency of the battery at this time." The detail was made out for Priv. F. Egleston instead of Sgt Eggleston. Tom Folkes[123] was dangerously wounded to day in a skirmish on our right wing.

Wed 8th: Formed line of battle to day near the Railroad and Marietta.

Thurs. 9th: Moved our position to the right at 4 O'clock this evening. Wrote "No 19" and letters to Johnny and Annie & Bob and mailed to W. A Barbour[124] at Jackson Miss. Rained again to day. Rained every day for a week.

Friday 10th: Moved farther to the right and went into position on Scott's line.[125] Rained again today. Rained very hard to day. Heard of the death of Abe Feltus[126] and Jno Lea [Lee][127] in Va. Killed in the recent battles.[128] The Southrons[129] went in with 23 and had 11 Killed and wounded.

Lt Bullock[130] & Sgt_ Maj. Jas. Crump[131] are missing. Skirmishing more brisk to day than for several days, some cannonading on our left four or five miles off.[132] Tom Folkes died last night.

Saturday 11th: A very hard rain again to day. The enemy advancing. Skirmishing on our right and left with some artillery firing on the left.

Sunday 12th: Rained all to day. Tenth day of rain. Impassible for artillery and wagon trains to move. A train of cars from Chattanooga came to within two miles of our lines yesterday.[133] It is stated Blair has reinforced Sherman with the 17th Army Corps.[134] Our battery was reinforced this morning by two men from the hospital.

Mond 13th: Rained nearly all day and turned quite cold. Wrote "No 20" to day and sent to Miss Yoste[135] at Demopolis care H. Gwinner[136] care Maj. W. S. Harris.[137]

Tues 14th: Gen Leonidas Polk was Killed to day by a solid shot which struck him on the right side and passed through him.[138] Gen Loring assumed command of the corps and Gen. Featherston of our Division. Enemy reported advancing in three lines of battle and every thing on our line was called to attention and our guns promptly placed in position. *Did not rain to day.*

Wed 15th: Wrote Sister and Joe Harris to day. Brisk firing on the right and left to day. Two lines of our skirmishers driven in and the enemy advanced his lines.

Thur 16th: Wrote Mr C. K. Marshall[139] and Tom Folkes obituary for the Appeal by request **Gus.**[140] Acting Caisson Lieut., **Lt Edwards** having been assigned to **Lt Hanes** detacht. he having taken command of **Lt. Tompkins'.**

Frid. 17th: Heavy cannonading on our right and left. Yankee Skirmishers charged ours and were repulsed. Dined on Sardines, Lightbread, ginger cake & molasses.

Saturday 18th: Commenced raining at day-break this A.M. & rained very hard for several hours. Rained all day. Moved to night into new lines beyond Kenesaw mountain.[141]

Sunday 19th: Had a miserable time last night; traveled all night through mud and rain, teams baulked and all together it was the worst night I ever Experienced in the army. Rained very hard to day. Took us until night to get all our guns and caissons up to our position.

Monday 20th: Rained all day. Heavy firing on our left his evening. Got a set Wheel Harness to day from Ord. dpt.

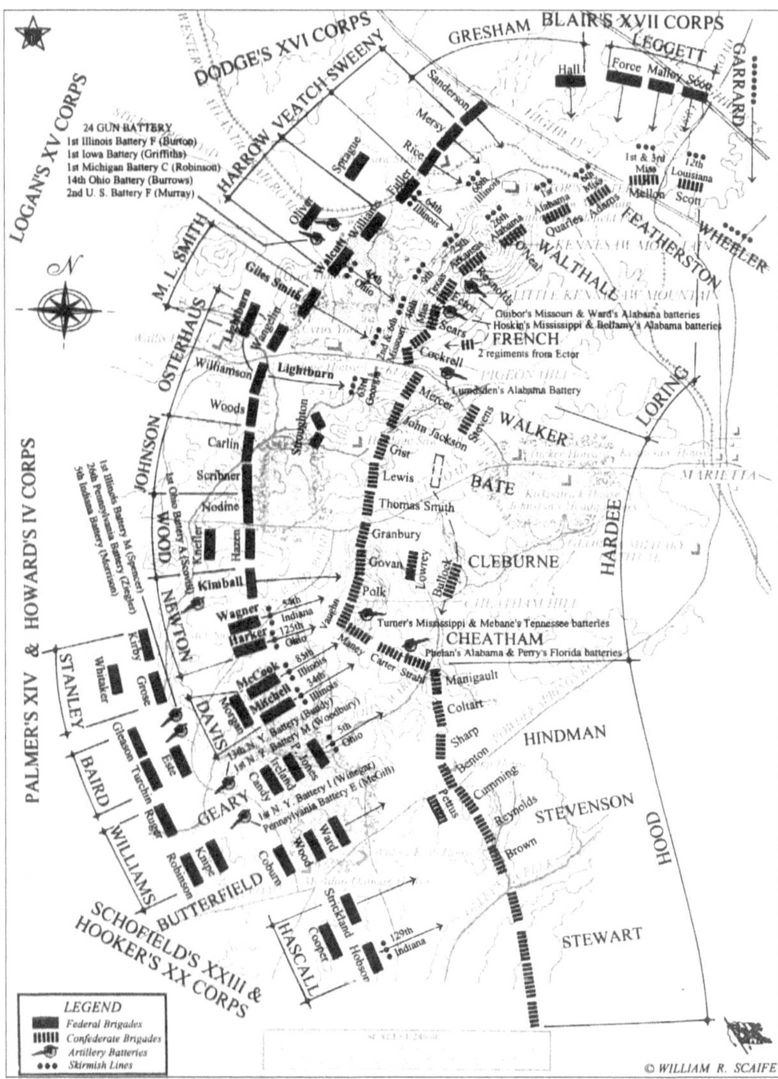

Battle of Kennesaw Mountain: June 27, 1864. Courtesy of the Kennesaw Mountain Historical Association.

Tuesday 21st: A continuation of rainy weather. *Wrote "No 21"* per Miss Yoste who starts for home to day. Our videttes captured Capt Foster of Blair's staff to day. He was drinking and came into our line unsuspectingly.

Wed 22d: Paid **Cummings** $50 in Confed. Fives for $20 in Federal currency. No rain to day. Skirmishing continues along the lines.

Diary of E. T. Eggleston

Thurs 23d: Wrote No 22 and sent per **Bigelow.** Sent **Chas E. Thomas** and **Corp Spencer** their descriptive lists. Very heavy cannonading on our left this evening commencing at 4½ O'clock. A battery in our front opened on us and shelled us for a while.[142] Clear & warm

Frid 24th: Heavy firing to day from our guns on Kennesaw mountains and the enemy's guns they were engaging. Clear & warm

Sat. 25th: Things as usual, weather clear & warm.

Sund 26th: Comparatively quiet. Wrote Tom Roach.

Mon 27th: Heavy skirmishing this evening in our immediate front. The enemy ran Scotts pickets in this A.M They afterwards went out and retook their position without firing a gun. The Enemy having fallen back after driving them in. The 1st Section of our battery shelled the woods for several hours at regular intervals. I went out this evening and examined the ground in front of our battery. We did considerable Execution, Killed 25 Yanks[143] and it is thought wounded many more. I saw two of them—a ghastly spectacle

Tues 28th: Unusually quiet to day. The enemy made an attack along our line yesterday principally on our left and it is Estimated that they lost between 5000 & 6000.[144] Recvd Nora's[145] letter to day.

Wed 29th: Slight skirmishing to day. Warm & cloudy.

Thurs 30th: The enemy attacked our left at 1½ O'clock this morning and were repulsed after a sharp engagement in which but little artillery was used. The rattle of musketry was incessant for nearly three quarters of an hour. A good rain to day. Battery was mustered for pay for May & June. Recvd Sister's letter to day.

July 1st Friday: Wrote Sister & Nora at Brandon. Heavy Art. duel this P.M. between our Kennesaw Batteries and the guns opposing them. Expect a fight tomorrow.

Sat 2d: The enemy opened a furious cannonading along our line at day-break this morning and continued it for an hour. I thought they would assault us, but They did not, and the firing gradually subsided and continued at intervals throughout the day. Fell back to night at dusk.[146] Threatening rain. Recvd letter No 14 from Molly dated 22d ult.

Sund 3d: Traveled all night last night and reached our new lines at day-break. The enemy pursued us very closely and lively Skirmishing has been going on since noon. We are rapidly throwing up fortifications along our line.[147]

Mond 4th: Sgt **Granville Hicks** wounded thorough the right hand to day and lost his first finger. A minnie ball passed through **Sgt.**

Willis' hat this evening while it was on his head without hurting him. We expected a fight to day but nothing was done Except the usual shelling & skirmishing.[148]

Tues. 5th: Fell back last night at 1 O'clock and crossed the Chatta-hoochie this morning at 5 O'clock. Traveled all night last night. The Yankees were celebrating the 4th last night. We could hear them speaking, huzzaing & laughing and their magnificent bands discoursing eloquent strains of music. Recrossed the Chattahoochie and formed line of battle. The enemy shelling us this evening.

Wednes 6th: Comparatively quiet to day. It is reported that a cavalry scouting party came near capturing Gen Sherman to day. He escaped but three of his aids were "taken in out of the wet".[149] I wrote up the clothing Yesterday.

Thurs 7th: All quiet to day little or no picketing firing

Friday 8th: Quiet continued to day. Wrote Molly "No 24" And also wrote Mother.

Sat. 9th: Fell back to night across the Chattahoochie and parked at 1 O'clock on the Pace's ferry road.[150] Recvd letter from Sister and Tommy [Roach].

Sund 10th: Had a hard rain on us to day. Our battery went into position to night on a high hill near the rail-road bridge to assist Scott's brigade and Bauanchaud's battery in guarding the river and preventing the enemy from crossing.

Mond. 11th: The enemy are about 1000 yards from us on the opposite side of the Chattahoochee. They can be seen distinctly moving about in our abandoned works, and an occasional shot is fired from their sharpshooters behind them. Wrote Joe Harris to LaGrange [Georgia]. Recvd. Carpetbag of clothing &c from Brandon. Some two or three hundred of our men and Yankees were bathing together to day in the Chattahoochee and trading Canteens, Knives and whisky &c for tobacco. This is demoralizing and Gen Johnston has issued a stringent order against a repetition of it.[151]

Tues 12th: Rained to day. Recvd a letter from Nora to day.

Wed. 13th: Nice & hot. Wrote **Jessee Bass.**

Thurs 14th: Quiet to day. Had a hard rain and wind to night.

Frid. 15th: Quiet to day. Wrote Nora to Brandon.

Sat. 16th: The enemy opened on us this evening with a battery of Parrott guns; and got our range in 5 Shots.

Sund 17th: We experienced the severest shelling to day I ever underwent. One Section of our battery and Bouanchauds replied to the batty, and did some good shooting. An ambulance was seen carrying off wounded from the Y. battery & two of their embrasures were Knocked to pieces.[152] We changed position to night.

Mond 18th: Went into position last night to guard a ford and moved onto the line this P.M.

Tues 19th: All quiet to day. Gen Johnston relieved from command of the army on the 16th[153] inst and Genl. J. B. Hood placed in command, by order of the War Department.[154]

Civil War Atlanta, summer of 1864. Courtesy of the Kennesaw Mountain Historical Association.

Wed. 20th: We went out and attacked the enemy this evening and drove them from their front lines and some distance beyond. We captured quite a number prisoners Had a great many wounded and am afraid the attack was barren of result to compensate us for our losses, as we fell back to our fortifications after dark.[155] It is reported that we lost several field officers.[156]

Thurs 21st: The enemy advanced their skirmishers in front of our position to day driving our skirmishers from their line. The first section of the battery opened upon them and fired 86 Rds. We fell back into Atlanta tonight.[157]

Frid 22d: Our battery was engaged yesterday and fired 103 Rounds. No casualties. Gen Hardee attacked the enemy this evening on their left and captured 2800 prisoners took 28 ps Artillery and drove them five miles. Wheeler captured and burned 900 wagons.[158] Fired 85 Rds.

Sat 23d: Nothing done to day Except the usual cannonading and skirmishing. Our battery fired 53 Rounds

Sund 24th: A good deal of Artillery practice to day on both sides. Our battery fired 206 rounds from morning until 10 O'clock to night.

Mond 25th: Nothing of any importance transpired to day. We were shelled severely for an hour or so. Wrote Molly "No 25" to day.

Tuesd 26th: Moderately quiet to day. No firing from our battery.

Wed. 27th: Rained this evening. Wrote "No 26" to day. Some heavy skirmishing in our front to day. Featherston's skirmishers repulsed two lines of battle. Scott's were driven in.

Thurs 28th: We had a considerable artillery duel to day. Hardee & Hood's corps had a fight on the left to day. Gens Loring & Stewart[159] were both wounded the one in the breast the other in the forehead.[160] We had one horse Killed, five disabled and two slightly wounded.

Frid 29th: Very quiet along the line until this evening when skirmishing became quite brisk on our right. The enemy continue to shell the city frightening the women & children and battering houses.

Sat 30th: The enemy drove in our pickets in front of Barry's battery, our 4th gun and a parrott battery opened an enfilading fire upon them and drove them back. I was struck on the right leg with a ps of shell while acting No 4 for the 2d ps and slightly bruised. We were severely shelled to day.

Sun 31st: Unusually quiet to day. The enemy seems to be observing the sabbath. Had a very hard rain this evening.

Mond Aug. 1st: We were shelled to day very rapidly for a short time **Warren Cowan** was slightly wounded in the thigh[161] and H. P. Powers[162] was struck in the head with a ball from a shrapnel and Killed.

Tues 2d: Quite to day. Wrote Molly "No 27"

Wed 3d: Several shells bursted over our works this evening and two ps. passed through my [tent] fly. Recvd letters from Mother, Wife, Tom [Roach] and Sister. Thank God my dear ones were well.

Thurs 4th: Remarkably quiet on our front throughout the day but heavy skirmishing and cannonading on the left which continued until 8 O'clock P.M.

Frid 5th: Had a brief duel this evening. **Talt. Cowan** wounded this P.M. in the thigh with a minnie Recvd Letter No 17 from Molly to night. Wrote Mother to day.

Sat 6th: Rained this evening and at night. The enemy fired at us a few times in the evening.

Sund 7th: A quiet day. Rained this evening. Wrote Bob and Molly "No 29".

Mond 8th: Raining throughout the day. All quiet on the line. Not a gun fired at us to day.

Tues 9th: Rainy day. The enemy shelled us all day and Exploded their shells in & around our works but fortunately hurt no one.

Wed 10th: Rained to day. Quiet on our line

Thurs 11th: The enemy shelled Atlanta all night

Frid 12th: Quiet in our front. The enemy continue to shell the city at long range.

Sat. 13th: Quiet in our front and but little cannonading or skirmishing near us on the line.

Sund 14th: Quiet to day. A shower again. The enemy fired three shots at us which fell short. Wrote No 30 to my wife. Our drivers who were armed with rifles sent to man three 6 pdr guns to night.

Mon 15th: Our boys retd. to the fort & rifles. The enemy threw a few shells at us to day. **Williams**[163] arrived to day with my hat and handkchfs.

Tues 16th: The enemy fired a few shots at us to day.

Wed 17th: Quiet to day. Wrote Miss Mag Tappan.

Thurs 18th: Our artillery opened on the enemy this morning at day-light and attempted to learn the changes that had made in the positions of their guns if any. They replied to our batty with a few guns, doing no damage.

Frid 19th: The enemy opened a fierce cannonading upon us at 4 O'clock A.M. and a number of ———— [?] shells burst in and around our works. One dropped in a foot of me while I was in bed and fortunately it did not burst. The third Caisson was blown up to day by the batty on our right. Rained to night.

Sat. 20th: The enemy continue to shell the city at regular intervals throughout the day. They also shell our works with the guns on our right but thus far have hurt no one. Rained to night.

Sund 21st: Rained to day. Twice to day did I come near being struck with fragments of shells once a piece weighing several pounds fell in a few feet of me and the musket balls dropped thick around me, and again one bursted over my head in the works and a fragment cut off a rail and passed closed to me. God preserved me.

Mond 22d: The enemy continue to shell the city.

Tuesd. 23d: Recvd No 18 from Molly dated 12th Aug. and a letter from Mother dated 7th. Thank God all were well.

Wed 24th: Quiet to day **Bigelow** retd to day. Very warm.

Thurs 25: All quiet to day. We heard the enemy moving Art[iller]y this morning.

Frid 26th: The enemy evacuated their works in our front last night. I visited their abandoned line to day. Their works are greatly inferior to ours. Wrote Molly to day.

Sat 27th: The enemy have abandoned their works and are supposed to be retreating or massing on our left to flank us out of Atlanta.[164] Recvd marching orders to night.

Sund 28th: We left Fort Hood to day and moved to the left to join our division. Now occupy the works vacated by Cobb's battery. Met Peyton Eggleston[165] this morning.

Mon 29th: No enemy in our front. Made out muster rolls to day.

Tues 30th: Recvd No 20 from Molly, dated 28th inst. Our Co mustered to day for July & August.

Wed 31st: Recvd No 19 from Molly. Mailed her letter to the Presdt. and gave her letter to Col Clarke[166] to Raymond Burke[167] to deliver. Went into position to day on the inner line of defenses. Hardee & Lee were ordered by Hood to charge the enemy on our left and run them to the river.[168] Hardee dispatched Hood he was about to attempt to carry out his command when Hood recvd the dispatch he requested all who were present at His Hdqrs to unite with him in prayer for the success of the undertaking. What a sublime spectacle! How I should like to have been there and participated in the exercises. It would have been a scene to remember in after years.[169] Very cool for the season.

Thurs 1st Sept.: The battery went out with Walthalls Division[170] one and a half miles on Marietta road to meet an advancing column of the enemy. The column 400 or 500 strong had come up as far as their old works and returned about the time we started after them. We failed to dislodge the enemy from his new position on the Macon road to day. Atlanta after our heroic struggle to save it was evacuated to night and the army is falling back to McDonough. I pity the true citizens who have fallen under the Yankee yokes; though reports say there are not many such in the place.[171]

Frid 2d: We marched all night last night and until dark to day. A trying march on our gallant fellows, but they endured it with characteristic fortitude.

Sat 3d: Reached Lovejoy Station to day and parked in an old field near our new line. Rained on us to night.

Sund 4th: Remained in park to day. Wrote No 32 to Molly. Moved into position to night. We are in a salient and can be enfiladed.

Mond 5th: Some little firing on the line

Tuesd 6th: The enemy disappeared from our front last night and rumors say they are falling back to Atlanta, others again that they are flanking.

Wed. 7th: Went into Camp about ten miles from Griffin and near Lovejoy Station. The enemy have fallen back to Atlanta, to reorganize &c. Sherman says the campaign is ended And *he Knows.*[172] Cloudy & cool.

Thurs 8th: In Camp_ all quiet_ Cool and cloudy.

Friday 9th: **Reid**s train joined us to day.

Sat 10th: Wrote No 33 and sent to Jackson care Col N G Watts[173] by Lt Hudson[174] Hoskin's Battery.

Sund 11th: Wrote Mother to day.

Mond 12th: My birth day. Wrote No 34 to day and sent to Jackson care Col. Watts A ten days truce between the two armies commenced to day to enable Sherman to remove the banished citizens of Atlanta into our lines.[175]

Tues 13th: Recvd a letter from Tommy Roach enclosing one from his Mother dated 25th Aug. Game of Cat & Rat.

Wed 14th: **Van De Moss** went to Columbus to day in a 5 days leave of absence commencing tomorrow. Recvd a letter from Alice Petrie[176] dated Sept 2d. Frenchs & Walthal's Divisions were reviewed to day by Lt Gen Stewart.

Thurs 15th: We are enjoying beautiful weather, rather too cool for the season, but propitious for the exodus of the banished inhabitants of Atlanta. We were paid for 2 Mos to day.

Frid 16th: Had a corps review to day. Gen Hood reviewed Stewarts corps. Gens Lee, Loring Stewart French and Walthall were with him. Wrote Alice Petrie.

Sat 17th: All quiet to day. We anticipate moving soon as preparations are on foot looking to a change of base.

Sund 18th: Recvd orders last night to cook two days ration at 4 O'clock this morning Left camp at 9 O'clock destination unknown._ Gen Hood has exercised much reticence. Rained last night. Rained on us nearly all day. Camped near Fayetteville.

Monday 19th: Ordered to march at 3 O'clock. Up at 2 O'clock and commenced the march at 5 O'clock. Passed through Fayetteville and Palmetto to day and camped near Petersburg.

Tues 20th: Left camp at 5 O'clock and parked on a small creek at 9 O'clock having passed through Petersburg *a large* inland city of *two houses.* one section (the 1st) detached from the Batty. and ordered to report to Gen Featherston on the Pumpkintown road. Lt **Hanes** comdng it. A drizzling rain set in during the evening and continued through the day.

Wed 21st: Drizzled all last night, and this morning. We are having the equinoctial show. Rained very hard this evening.

Thurs 22d: Rainy to day. Weather Exceedingly unpleasant.

Friday 23d: Wrote No 35 to day. Raining throughout the day. **Herring** retd.

Sat. 24th: Wrote Tommy Roach to day and sent his application for transfer to our battery.

Sund 25th: Cleared off yesterday evening, turned cold last night. A beautiful morning! Recvd "No 22" from Molly and letters from Joe [Harris], Belle [Harris] Tom R[oach] and [Edward H.] Ned Porter. Van retd this evening. Lovely weather we are now enjoying after a week of rain.

Mond 26th: Wrote No 36 per mail. The army was reviewed by Presdt. Davis to day. **Dr Harris** relieved **Dr Thornton** to day.

Tues 27th: Wrote Joe & Belle [Harris], E. H. Porter & **Geo. Marshall.**

Wed 28th: Slight rain to day. Cool and pleasant.

Thurs 29th: Recvd orders last night to cook rations[177] and be ready to march at 10 A.M. Left Camp at 11 A.M. Crossed the Chattahoochee at 4 O'clock P.M. Made about 6 miles to day.

Frid 30th: Started on our march at 6 A.M. made about 15 miles and camped at 12 O.

Saturday Octo 1st: Rained on us last night and still cloudy & threatening this morning. One horse died last night_Snagged._ Recvd. orders to March in the morning. Raining through the day.

Sund 2d: Marched at 7 O'clock A.M. Camped at 1½ P.M. Made about 8 miles.

Mond 3d: Reported to Walthall's Division at 7 A.M. **Duke Askew** left on the road sick. abandoned one Horse broken down. Rained on us all day. Reached Big Shanty at 5 O'clock. The Head of the column struck the rail-road at 4 P.M. Captured some sixty odd men at Big Shanty, Killing one and a negro & wounding two or three. The boys commenced the destruction of the railroad with a hearty good will. Made 8 Miles to day.

Tuesd 4th: Raining through the night. Our boys were engaged all night in destroying the road. We have felled trees and brush and obstructed the cuts on the road, and I think it will give Mr Sherman considerable trouble to "clear the track". Started to Acworth 3½ P.M. Acworth captured last night by Lorings Div. 250 Prisoners captured Total prisoners captured at Big Shanty, Moon Station & Acworth 316.[178] Reached Acworth at 6 P M

Wed 5th Made 10 Miles: Marched all night reaching Alatoona heights at 5 A.M. with French's Division. Planted our guns En Barbette not having time to throw up works. Skirmishing commenced before daylight; and art[iller]y firing as soon as it was light. At 9½ A M Gen French[179] sent in flag of truce demanding a surrender of the garrison. The enemy procrastinated giving an answer, when our troops stormed the works carrying two lines and taking two forts, and capturing 70 odd prisoners. The gallant Missourians and Texians did their work in splendid style. Sears' brigade failed to come to time.[180] The enemy reported advancing from Atlanta in heavy force we withdrew at 1 P.M. Our batty fired 202 rounds and tho we were in an Exposed position, thanks to God escaped without a casualty to anyone. Two wheels and one chest of 4th Caisson damaged. We would certainly have obtained possession of the works but for the advance of reinforcements not withstanding a brigade had arrived from Rome last night to increase the garrison.[181]

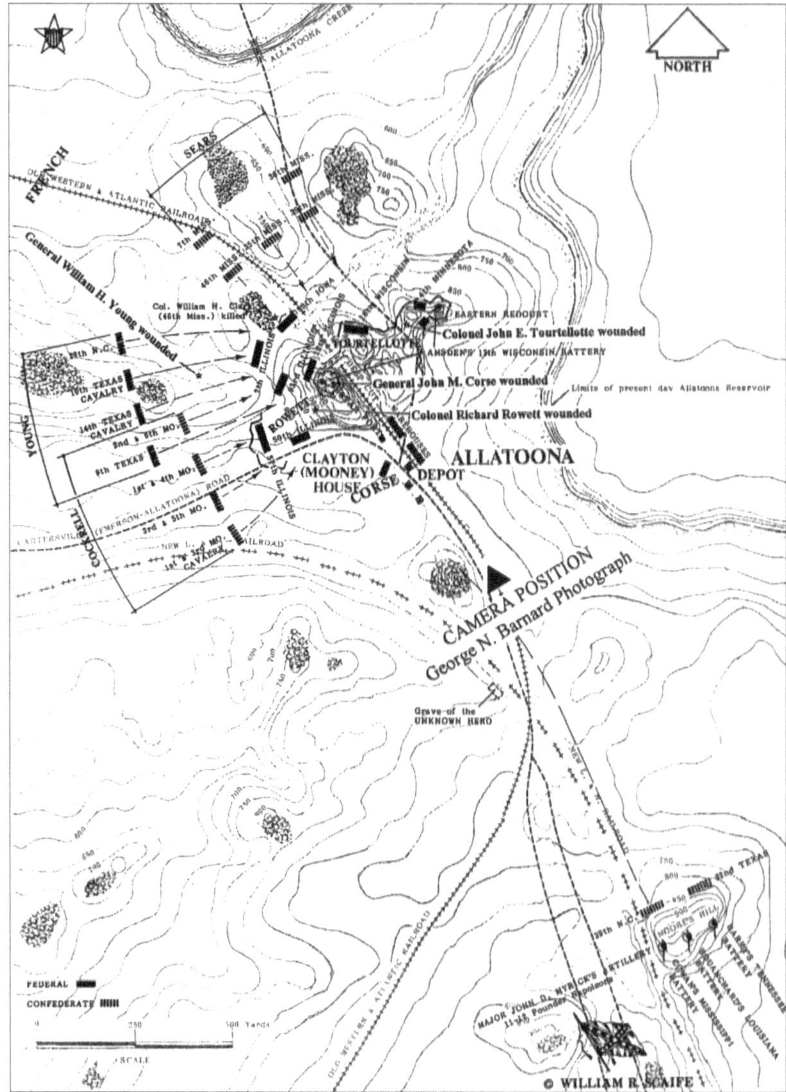

Battle of Allatoona: October 5, 1864. Courtesy of the Kennesaw Mountain Historical Association.

Thurs 6th: Made 7 miles: Bivouacked near Altoona last night. Rained on us all night. We got drenching wet. Joined Walthall & Loring this A.M. at New Hope. Passed over the battles fields of 25th & 27th May[182] and saw acres of timber Killed by minnie balls. Started towards Blue Mountain to day.

Friday 7th: Recvd letter yesterday from Miss Mag Tappan. A beautiful clear day. Marched 14 miles in the direction of Rome through a barren & mountainous country. Camped near Van Wert.

Satur 8th: Turned very cold last night. Clear and windy & cold to day. Marched 13 miles and camped near Cedar_town.

Sund 9th: Heavy frost last night. Camped all day at Cedar town. Turned over 4th Caisson, team of 6 horses & contents of caisson, harness &c, also one ord. wagon 4 mules and mule harness. The army has started on an Expedition[183] taking one batty with Each Division leaving the bal. of the art[iller]y. and trains behind.[184]

Mond 10th: Passed through Cedar-town and Cave Spring. Marched 15 miles to day. Learned that Gen Beauregard has assumed command of the army of Tenn.[185] We are en route for Centre Ala. Crossed that state line and entered Ala at dark.

Tuesd 11th: Traveled over miserable roads in a poor barren piney woods country. Made 16 miles to day & camped near the Coosa river.

Wed 12th: Moved Camp about 1½ miles to day. Rained this evening. Wrote No 37.

Thurs 13th: Wrote No 38. **Capt. Cowan** rejoined us to day.

Friday 14th: Went to centre last night with some of the boys to a frolic. Owing to reports circulated as to the advance of the enemy it did not come off. Ordered at 1½ A.M. to be ready to move. Left camp at 8½ A.M. and marched 15 miles on the Jacksonville road.

Sat 15th: Marched at 6 A.M. made 13 miles and camped near Jacksonville. **Frank Templeton** and **Ben Hicks** retd to day.

Sund 16th: Wrote No 38 & sent by **Reid** to Meridian. Lt. **Tompkins** left on 20 days furlough and **Reid** on 30 days. **Lt Cowan** and **Vaughan** retd to day.

Mond. 17th: Recvd letters No 24 & 25 from home.

Tues 18th: In camp near Jacksonville Ala.

Wed 19th: Finished quarterly ord report to day and handed it in at Ord office.

Thurs 20th: Left camp at 9½ A.M. and marched towards Gadsden and the Coosa river. Recvd a letter from Sister dated 10th inst. Made 10 miles and camped at 4½ P.M. on Gadsden road.

Frid 21st: Up at 3½ A.M. Started on our march at 5½ A.M. Crossed the Coosa at 12½ A.M. passed through Gadsden and camped at 4 P.M. Gens Hood & Beauregard are in Gadsden. Marched 15 miles.

Satur 22d: Recvd letter from Mother dated 7th Sept. Rejoined Loring's Division this A.M. and marched at 8 A.M. Were Kept

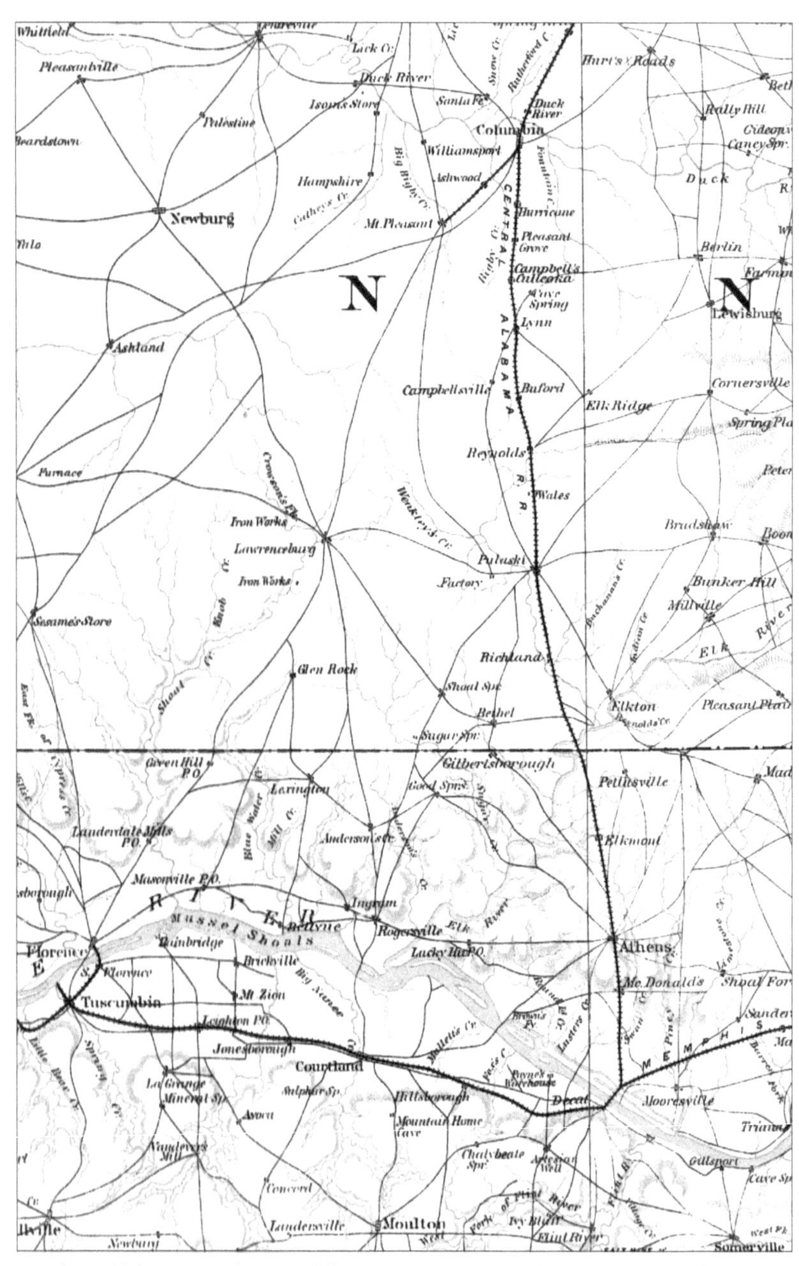

Northern Alabama–southern Middle Tennessee. From *Atlas to Accompany the Official Records of the Union and Confederate Armies* (1891–95), plate CXLIX.

up nearly all night by Maj. Myricks[186] foolishness. Crossed the Head waters of the Black Warrior. Marched 15 miles and camped at "Cross Roads".

Sund 23d: Up at 4 A.M. Marched at 6½ A.M. Crossed the Black Warrior. Camped at 5 P.M. Marched through Summit on the top of the mountain, have traveled all day through a mountainous rocky country. Came 16 miles

Mond 24th: Up at 5 A.M. Marched at 7 A.M. Came 16 miles on the Decatur road.

Tues 25th: Up at 6 A.M. Marched at 9¼ A.M. Passed through Summerville and camped at 5 P.M. Came 12 Miles.

Wed 26th Came 15 miles, raining all day: Up at 4 A.M. marched at 6 A.M. Commenced raining last night and rained on us all day to day. Crossed Flint River and approached Decatur. Attacked Decatur at 2 P.M. with arty and Loring's Division as a support. The enemys arty replied and our battery suffered severely.[187] **Tom Johnsen** [*sic*] was instantly Killed. **Gordon & E H Young** mortally wounded. **Auter,**[188] **Beard, Crimmins** ["E E" inserted in margin] **Ferrell, J W Harris, Kelton Rabb, Sproule, Treanor Yoste** all wounded, and all but **Auter** Seriously. **Trible** [*sic*] **Conklin** and **Wadsworth** slightly wounded.

Thurs 27th: **Stephen Gordon** and **Ebenezer H. Young** died last night. Remained in camp to day. Raining throughout the day. Forces skirmishing all day.

Frid. 28th: Cleared off last night. Went into position at 9 A.M. on the Tennessee river to engage any gun boats that may pass. Engaged two gun boats at 4 P.M. fired 32 rds. striking them several times. No one hurt. Withdrew the Batty at dark and retd to our camp of the 27th.

Sat. 29th: Left Decatur at 7½ A.M. Marched 15 miles on the Courtland road and camped at 5 P.M. Cloudy at night.

Sund 30th: Marched at 6½ A.M. Passed through Courtland & Leetown and camped at latter place at 3½ P.M. Came 15 miles. Cloudy and warm.

Mond 31st: Marched at 6 A.M. on Tuscumbia road, Reached Tuscumbia at 10½ A.M. & camped. Came 10 miles. Have traveled miles since 1st Septem. We have been traveling through a magnificent country from Decatur to this place but the destroyers have been through the country and desolation marks their track. Beautiful residences and highly improved plantations have been burned and laid waste.

Nov 1 Tuesday: Camped at Tuscumbia preparing to go into Tennessee. Cloudy and warm.

Wed 2d: Wrote Miss Mag Tappan and sent her my package of letters per **Herring**, also wrote Joe Harris. Rained last night. Raining and cold to day. Muddy and disagreeable.

Thurs 3d: Camped at Tuscumbia. Cleared off cold this P.M.

Frid 4th: Cloudy windy and disagreeable to day.

Sat 5th: Cleared off last night, White frost this A.M. Wrote Mother to day. Suffered all day with tooth ache. Issued clothing to Co. this P.M.

Sund 6th: Wrote No 41 and mailed at Tuscumbia. Cloudy.

Mondy 7th: Very hard rain fell last night. We were snug in our fly. Cloudy all day.

Tues. 8th: Rained again last night. An official telegram from Gen Forrest was read to the Command this morning dated at Johnstonville Tenn. announcing that he had captured the place and destroyed three gun boats, ~~thirteen~~ Eleven steamers and ~~Eleven~~ fifteen barges and from 75, to 120,000 tons of Q.M. & Comsy stores, and the fire was still raging. His expedition has resulted in the destruction of 4 gun boats 8 guns Each, 14 steamers, ~~and~~ 17 barges and from 75000 to 120000 tons Q.M. & Comsy stores.[189] Rainy all day. Ordered to move in the A.M. and the order afterwards countermanded.

Wed 9th: Rained all day. Cleared off at night & turned cold.

Thur 10th: Wrote No 42 and to Joe Harris. Clouded up this evening.

Frid 11th: One year to day since my Matty was born and one year on the 9th since dear Molly came out to Meridian to see me when I was sick at Maj. Randell's.

Sat 12th: Clear & cold. Stewart's corps was reviewed to day by Gen Beauregard.

Sund 13: Ordered to march at 12 O'clock to day. Got ready to do so and the order was countermanded. Lt **Tompkins** retd. This evening.

Mond 14th: Moved camp at 8 O'clock this A.M. Marched towards Florence and camped a mile from the river having made 5 miles by 10½ A.M. Sent Mississippian a list of casualties at Decatur on 26th. Went to the river and had a fine view of Florence on the opposite bank and the pontoon bridge. The Tennessee is a pretty river at this point. Warm & cloudy.

Tues 15th: Rained last night. Raining through the day

Wed 16th: A disagreeable rainy day. In Camp near Florence.

Thurs 17th: Showering throughout the day. Company was pd. to day to 30th April 1864.

Frid 18th: Rainy day. "Wrote No 43". Recvd orders to cross the Tennessee, packed up, waited several hours and then the order was countermanded.

Sat 19th: Up at 12½ O'clock. Left camp at 3 O'clock, crossed the Tennessee at 7 A.M. ~~and~~ passed through Florence and camped one mile from town, at 11 A.M. having come two miles. A miserable day, has rained slowly all day long.

Sund 20th: A drizzly disagreeable day.

Mond 21st: Move on the Savannah road at 8 A.M. this morning. Commenced snowing just as we started and snowed on us for 2 hours. Came 8 miles and camped at 3 O'clock. **Reid** retd and brought **Bob Wilkins**[190] with him. Very cold to day. Recvd No 28 Nov 12th from dear wife. Aunt was well again.

Tuesd 22d: Marched at 11 A.M. in a snow storm, our teams are nearly used up. Made 15 miles by 11 O'clock P.M. with some of the pieces, but one or two did not get up until 4 A.M. We suffered very much with the cold but it was clear and our sufferings would have greater had it been windy & snowy.

Wed 23d: Entered Tenn. Yesterday evening. Made 10 miles to day & camped at 8 P.M. Clear & cold to day.

Thurs 24th: Came 9 miles and camped at 7½ o'clock P.M. on the Lawrenceburg road.

Frid 25th: Was up till 3 O'clock this A.M. drawing & issuing rations. Left camp at 9 A.M. Made 10 miles and camped at 6½ P.M.

Sat. 26th: Left camp at 8 A.M. passed through Mount Pleasant, a pretty little place; made 18 miles on an excellent turnpike road through a steady rain and camped at dark

Sund 27th: Came through the finest and most beautiful country I ever beheld, passed by the residences of Gen Pillow[191] and Wm Polk[192] brother to the late Lt Gen Polk,[193] two magnificent structures. Sprinkling and sultry to day. Reached Columbia at 2 P.M. and heard skirmishing between the enemy & Lee or Cheatham's corps.[194] 12 miles to day.

Mond 28th: Columbia was evacuated last night and taken possession of by our troops. Three or four hundred yankee prisoners with hang dog countenances and ragged dirty clothes passed our camp this A.M. I rode into the town this P.M. and saw many pretty ladys who seemed glad to see us. The enemy were on the opposite side of Duck river and were shelling the town occasionally and skirmishing across the river.

Tues 29th: **Capt Cowan** left to day with Sgt. **Conklin** ["Lt Hanes" inserted in margin] **Corps Bolls** & **Spencer Beane**, [David] **Donovan Ferrell Greene, Jno Hickman Irwin, Loomis, Stewart** & **Whitman** and a detachment from Darden & Bouanchaud's Batteries[195] to accompany the army on an Expedition.[196] Moved nearer Columbia and camped.

Wed 30th: Left Columbia at 9 A.M. passed through Poplar Ridge and ~~Pleasant~~ Spring Hill made 25 miles and reached Franklin at 8 P.M.

[December] Thurs 1st: A terrific fight took place yesterday evening and throughout the night. The loss was heavy on both sides but heavier on ours. Gens Adams and Cleburne were Killed and Gens. Cockrell and Scott severely wounded. We lost in killed and wounded many brave and valuable field officers.[197] We were not engaged.[198] The Yankees evacuated the place last night. Left camp at 3 P.M. Crossed the Harpeth at 6 P.M. and camped a mile from river.

Frid 2d: Marched at 8 A.M. towards Nashville. Came 13 miles and camped in front of the enemy's works 5 miles from the city

Sat 3d: Rained last night. We invested Nashville to day with our forces, drove in the enemy's pickets & advanced our line. The enemy opened on us with artillery. We did not take position Turned off cold & clear. **Lt Edwards** & Sgt **De Moss** went out to press horses

Sund 4th: In camp in front of Nashville. Had a fine turkey for dinner.

Mond 5th: In camp in front of Nashville

Tues 6th: Went into position tonight.[199] Cloudy & warm.

Wed 7th: Cloudy windy & showery turning cold. Quiet

Thurs 8th: Very cold and cloudy. Remarkably quiet.

Frid 9th: Sleeting to day. Everything covered with sleet to night. Not very cold. My eyes are very sore from smoke.

Sat. 10th: Cloudy and threatening rain. Changed position to night to new line in rear of the one occupied to day.[200]

Sund 11th: A pinching cold day, a sharp cutting wind from the northwest blew all day. We slept on the frozen ground last night, but had plenty of blankets and were warm and comfortable.

Mon 12th: Bitter cold last night. Slept in the open air again on the frozen ground. The wind lulled at dark and it became more pleasant. Moderated considerably to day. Clouding up.

Tues 13th: Much warmer than it has been for several days past. Cloudy & threatening rain.

Wed 14th: Cloudy and warm. Fourth piece left the picket line and joined the bal[ance] of the batty to night.

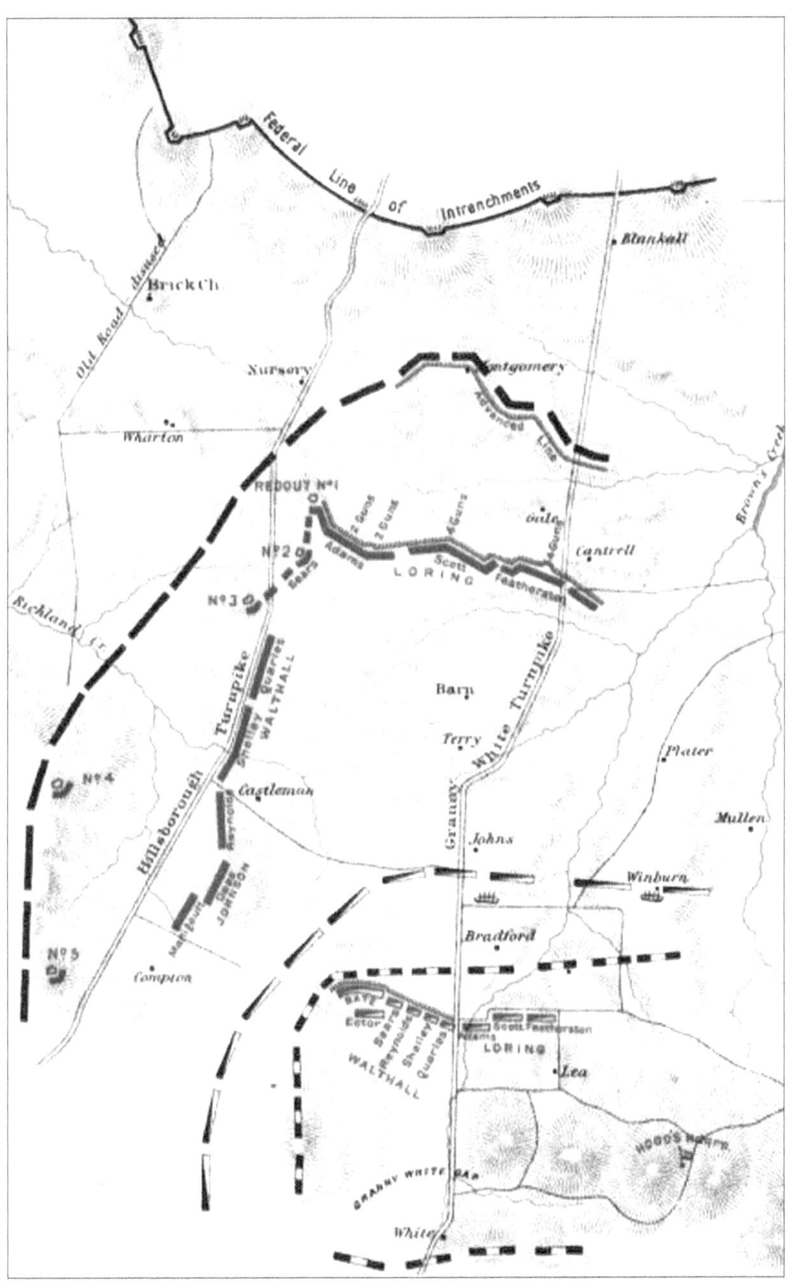

Battle of Nashville: December 15–16, 1864. From *Atlas to Accompany the Official Records of the Union and Confederate Armies* (1891–95), plate LXXIII, no. 2.

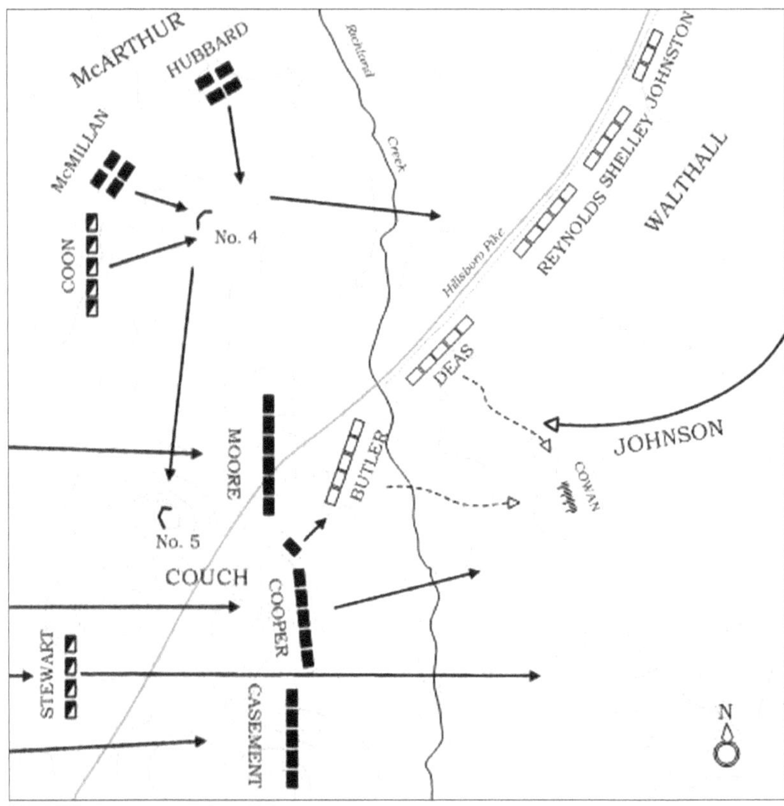

Capture of Cowan's Battery: December 15, 1864. Cartography by Stuart Salling.

Thurs 15th: Heavy skirmishing on our left this morning. We went to the left this evening and lost our guns & horses. The infantry ran like cowards and the miserable wretches who were to have supported us refused to fight and ran like a herd of stampeded cattle.[201] I blush for my countrymen and despair of the independence of the Confederacy if her reliance is placed in the army of Tennessee to accomplish it. There are ten men from the batty missing supposed to be killed or captured among them my dear friend and messmate Sergt **Bentley**. God grant that his life has been spared to his family. We took a section of Hoskins Batty. to night.[202] All of the Co. papers and records were lost, and all of my blankets and rations. Expect to freeze this winter.

Frid 16th: We were on the battle field to day but not engaged. Our army was flanked and badly whipped to day. We feel back to night in a rain.[203]

Sat 17th: Marched all day towards Columbia passed through Spring Hill and camped. Rained all day.[204]

Sund 18th: Reported this A.M. to Gen Cheatham to form line at Spring Hill. Fell back to Columbia and took position on the north of Duck river.

Mond 19th: In line at Columbia. Raining all day. Crossed Duck river to night. It is bitter cold and awfully unpleasant.[205]

Tuesd 20th: Rained on us all day. Freezing cold. Marched till 8 P.M. on the Pulaski road

Wed. 21st: Passed through Pulaski. Raining all the morning and snowing in the evening. Left the pike this P.M. and struck miserable roads.

Thurs 22d: Slept on the frozen ground last night with two thin blankets to cover me. Snowed on us through the night. Our poor troops are suffering terribly. The sun shone out to day for the first time in several days. Bitter cold & clear to night

Frid 23d: A beautiful clear day very cold moving on towards the Tenn river.

Sat 24th: A beautiful winter morning. Moderated somewhat. Crossed the line and passed through Lexington a deserted hamlet. Cloudy this P.M.

Sund 25th: What a christmas! Running from the Yankees through an incessant rain. Crossed shoal creek a wide and rapid stream and joined our cook train and camped.

Mond 26th: A part of the Co. went to Florence to fight gun boats,[206] the bal[ance] crossed the Tenn river at 4 P.M. on a Yankee pontoon.[207]

Tuesd 27th: Reached cousin Jno. L. Eggleston's[208] to day and was affectionately received and hospitably entertained. **Warren Cowan** is with me.

Wed 28th: Left cousin Jno's this morning and went to his bro's (cousin Overton).[209] They too were Kind & cordial and made me stay all night with them. There visits are the bright spots to revert to in the Tenn Campaign; so disastrous to our cause.

Thurs 29th: Left cousin Overton's this A.M. passed through Tuscumbia and stayed at Mr. Carlos's[210] near where the command was encamped[211] Very cold.

Frid 30th: **Jno Ferrill**[212] was Killed at Florence on 27th and Lt **Tompkins** and Mr **Whatley** dangerously wounded. Saw Lt **T** & Mr **W** on the cars to day. Rained on us to night & turned cold.

Sat 31st: Left camp at 2½ P.M. and moved towards Iuka Camped at 8 P.M. a mile from Iuka. A very cold evening. The last of the eventful and disastrous year 1864! May a merciful Father vouchsafe that the coming year may be more propitious to our cause and may he grant us peace and independence ere were are again called upon to record the departure of another year. We have met many reverses and have lost many brave and gallant souls but our Cause is not hopeless, we can yet achieve our nationality with the aid of the All powerful God of battle_ we must bear our reverses with the fortitude of heroes, buckle on our armor and calling on the God of Truth to be our ally resolve to succeed or perish.

Diary of E. T. Eggleston

Epilogue

On January 3, 1865, Stewart's Corps was ordered to depart Burnsville and march to Tupelo. The men had to "work the road where it was bad on their march." Upon reaching Tupelo on the ninth, they were allowed to encamp. When General Beauregard arrived on the fourteenth, he quickly realized that the Army of Tennessee was "no longer an army." Half of the artillery had been lost, and countless horses had been killed or starved to death. Unable to replace the missing guns, a drastic reorganization could not be avoided. Of the twenty-seven batteries assigned to the three infantry corps, six were ordered to North Carolina, five to Demopolis, Alabama, and the balance to Mobile, Alabama.[1] Eggleston found himself in the latter group.

Cowan's Battery arrived in Mobile about 9 a.m. on February 5. The men bivouacked in a cotton shed on Water Street that night and remained there until 3 p.m. on the ninth, when they moved two miles out of town and went into the fortifications in rear of Battery E. They were now one of four batteries assigned to Captain John B. Grayson's Battalion, which was one of four under Colonel Melancthon Smith, commander of the Artillery Reserves, Left Wing, Defenses of Mobile.[2]

Between March 10–27, Cowan's Company was transferred to Fort Blakely, on the eastern shore of Mobile Bay. At least some of Cowan's men were assigned to handle siege cannon, but some may have joined the members of other companies of the 1st Mississippi Light Artillery Regiment who had previously been converted to infantry manning the center of the line of entrenchments; Ector's Brigade was on their left and Thomas' Brigade on their right. Union Major General Frederick Steele advanced his corps from the direction of Pollard, Alabama, and deployed before Fort Blakely on March 26. The Federals began siege operations against the bastion on April 1.[3]

Defenses of the city of Mobile, 1865. From *Atlas to Accompany the Official Records of the Union and Confederate Armies* (1891–95), plate LXXI, no. 13.

The quiet that reigned over Fort Blakely on April 9 was no different from that at Appomattox Court House, Virginia, that Palm Sunday. But at 3 p.m. the Federals began bombarding the bastion and followed up with a furious assault. The Confederates beat back wave after wave but were finally overwhelmed about 6:45 p.m. No more than 150 of the of the 2,300 infantry and 350 cannoneers managed to escape.[4] For Cowan's Battery the war was over, as it soon would be for all Confederates.

Initially held on Ship Island, Eggleston's comrades captured at Fort Blakely were transferred to Vicksburg on May 1. Already paroled when they disembarked there on May 6, they were incarcerated at Camp Townsend. In all probability while visiting his friends, Eggleston obtained his parole. He was allowed to return home, however, but the rest were not released for another ten days.[5]

Sergeant Edmund T. Eggleston managed to miss the inglorious finale. All that is known of his activities during the final months of the war is found in three entries from his diary, his ledger, and three forms issued by the U.S. Army. Eggleston remained with the battery through January, but on February 12 the mess fund was apparently divided, leaving him with $254. Three days later wrote from an unidentified location, "Got a squab for a pet and call him 'John' after my boy." On the eighteenth, he "Drew 4 days rations of rice and pork for 16 men at Demopolis." Regardless of the reason for his being in that town, he was undoubtedly placed in charge of taking these men, whether conscripts or recovered sick and wounded, to Mobile. Then, a month later, he turns up in Vicksburg.

CITY PAROLE.

I, *E. T. Eggleston,* do hereby give my solemn Parole of Honor that I will not convey or divulge any information, which, if known, might in any way be detrimental to the Government of the United States, and that I will remain within the limits of the city of Vicksburg, and report in person to the Provost Marshal *Each day between the hours of 4 Oclock AM & 5 PM (Except Sunday)* until I am released from this obligation by the proper military authority.

E. T. Eggleston,

Subscribed to before me in Vicksburg, Miss., *this 26the day of March, A.D. 1865.*

E F Stafford Capt 124 III[6]
1st Asst Provost Marshal[7]

Epilogue

Because other documents that should have survived did not, the only explanation for Federal authorities allowing Eggleston within their lines and giving him the freedom to roam the city is that he was seriously incapacitated. And possibly those same officials were being unusually kind because of the kindnesses his mother had shown to Union prisoners during the siege of Vicksburg. Had Eggleston deserted, he would have been required to take the oath of allegiance to avoid being sent to a northern prison. In his case, the Federal authorities did not even make him take the oath in return for allowing him to remain in Vicksburg. And any Rebel soldier who continued to believe that Confederate independence could be achieved after Hood's disastrous campaign in Tennessee was unlikely to desert, or to reside among his former comrades after the war if he had deserted.

It is unknown if Eggleston received permission before leaving the city, but his final diary entry, dated April 10, has him "At Winstonville," a town one hundred miles north of Vicksburg. And he was transacting business with Confederate funds between April 6–23. A month later he was back in Vicksburg.

OFFICE EXCHANGE OF PRISONERS,

Vicksburg, Miss.—May 6, 1865.

Edmund T. Eggleston, Orderly Sergeant Cowan's Company *Light Artillery* Regiment, a Paroled Prisoner of War, is hereby furloughed until exchanged, with permission to remain at his home, performing no military duty whatever, and paying proper respect to the authorities in his locality.

By order of Colonel N. G. Watts,
Agent of Exchange, C.S.A.
H. A. M. Henderson,[8]
Lieut. Col, Asst. Agent of Exchange, C.S.A.

Approved
By order of
Brig Genl M. L. Smith.[9]
    A. C. Fisk[10]
    a.a.g.[11]

The following day Eggleston began spending his remaining Confederate currency, managing to unload $130 in eight days, leaving him with $164 in worthless paper. Once the war ended and he free of all restrictions, Eggleston quickly rearmed.

Head Quarters District of Vicksburg,

Vicksburg, Miss., *June 19th, 1865*

Mr. *E T Eggleston,* of *Warren Co. Miss.,* is hereby permitted to keep in his possession *one Shot-gun, one Miss Rifle, one Revolver, and ammunition for self-protection and hunting*

If it is ever ascertained that he has abused or taken advantage of this permission, the weapons will be subject to confiscation, and the offender to arrest and punishment. Good for________days.

By Order of Brig. Gen'l Morgan L. Smith:

A. C. Fisk.

Assistant Adjutant General.[12]

Eggleston remained in Vicksburg, his family residing with his mother. He worked as a clerk for Johnson & Lamkin Wharf Boat Agents in 1866.[13] Later he became partners with D. W. Lamkin.[14] Initially, Lamkin & Eggleston dealt in groceries, liquors, and provisions for steamboats. In 1876, they expanded into cotton, but on May 5,

Elizabeth Stark Gildart Eggleston. Courtesy of Andrew Stevens.

Epilogue

1877, the two men dissolved the company "by mutual consent." Lamkin became a fulltime cotton factor, while E. T. Eggleston & Company carried on providing supplies to vessels plying the Mississippi. Eggleston was also a member of the Cotton Exchange, represented Vicksburg in commercial planning with neighboring communities, and supported the arts.[15]

In 1880, Annie and Mattie still resided with their parents, the latter attending school with her younger sister, Mary "Mamie" Read, who had been born on June 11, 1866. Harris Trent, born on November 28, 1874, rounded out the family. Edmund Trent Jr., born on July 7, 1871, died the following May. Bob had died on August 24, 1878, and John a week later, both of yellow fever. Elizabeth had moved out following her marriage to Eugene Conway on February 5, 1880.[16]

After the city surrendered in 1863, legend has it that Vicksburg did not celebrate July 4 until 1945. At least one of its citizens, however, celebrated in 1879. While Eggleston was being driven through town in a buggy, a bunch of firecrackers exploded and frightened the horse. Before the driver could gain control, the buggy overturned, throwing Eggleston and the driver to the ground. Eggleston was severely injured, the driver only slightly, but "the buggy was a total wreck." Despite pain, Eggleston returned to work about a week later,[17] but more tumult lay ahead.

Eggleston was out of business by the summer of 1881. The 1870s had taken a heavy toll on him. The economic Panic of 1873, the dissolution of his business partnership, the loss of two sons in the 1878 yellow fever epidemic, and his buggy accident had broken him financially. Leaving his family in Vicksburg, he found work first as a clerk and then as a sales representative in Yazoo City. Near the end of the year, he moved his family there, but in 1882 either he or his former company was the defendant in at least four lawsuits.[18] Mattie married A. Miller Payne on May 15, 1884. Mary died on September 25, 1886. Anne married Samuel Gibson Montgomery on April 7, 1891, and Mamie married Samuel N. Sample on February 26, 1892. Edmund Trent Eggleston, Sr., died in Yazoo City on July 21, 1896, and was buried beside his wife in Cedar Hill Cemetery, Vicksburg.[19]

Appendix A

Accounts (pages 68–84, 96, 98 [unnumbered])

The following financial entries not only enhance the diary but fill in gaps that exist in Eggleston's accounts of his daily activities January 1, 1864-May 19, 1865. While some readers may have a cursory interest in the cost or availability of goods at a given time and place in the Confederacy, the following financial entries tell a more significant story that should be of interest to serious scholars, even social historians. It is common knowledge that Civil War soldiers formed their own messes. Such organizations enabled a handful of individuals to share cooking duties and supplement their rations by joint purchases. Usually these groups were segregated, consisting only of officers or enlisted men. Eggleston's, however, did not discriminate, including enlisted men, non-commissioned officers, and officers.

Unfortunately, the following entries are a combination of Eggleston's personal transactions as well as those of his mess. These cash, and occasionally trade, activities are divided between receipts and acquisitions. Specific details of how the mess operated, however, are missing. Even if they understood it, no certified public accountant would approve Eggleston's unorthodox method of calculating. Possibly there was another ledger and what appears in the diary reflects his formula for double checking the accuracy of his math. For that reason, Eggleston's calculations made at the bottom of each page and at end of each month have been omitted, and month and day abbreviations have been standardized. Eggleston changed his bookkeeping method on February 12, 1865, probably as a result of the breakup of the mess because no transactions after that date refer to that account. Going forward receipts and expenditures were listed in a single column, and he listed the types of bills being exchanged rather than what was purchased or sold. He still possessed $164.00 in Confederate money when it became worthless.

Cash Receipts

1864 Jan 1	To Balance on hand	2,681.35
	Short on 31st Decr $24.55	
21	" Smoking Tobacco	4.00
31	" Amt forwarded to Feb	365.67
Feb 1	Short Feb 1st $24.18	
4	To **A. A. Folkes** retd	25.00
18	To **Bentley & Levy** bet deposited	10.00
April 3	To Smoking Tobacco 2 pds	10.00
	" do do 1 pd	5.00
5	" do do 1 "	7.00
6	To Smoking Tobacco	14.00
	" do do	56.00
15	" do do	25.00
17	" do do	5.00
20	" do do	10.00
21	" do do	11.50
23	" do do	25.00
	" do do	5.00
26	" do do	1.00
28	" do do	36.50
June 30	" **Capt. Cowan** Milk 4@ & on Jug 10@	1.75
	" **Jas G. Spencer** on Jug.	1.25
	" Profits on purchases	18.55
July 9	" **G. H. Tompkins** on a/c	15.00
25	" Profits	.25
26	" **Bolls** advanced	.50
Aug 4	" **De Moss** borrowed	10.00
31	" do do	1.00
Sept 1	" **Van De Moss**	15.00
	" **Wadsworth** retd	1.50
15	" Pay from 30th June to 31 Decr	126.00

27	" Lt. **Tompkins** Postage Stamps	5.00
Nov 10	" **J. W. Conklin** retd	3.25
17	" Government to 30. April 1864	84.00
24	" one pr govrnt. Drawers	3.00
Dec 5	" **Geo. H. Tompkins** bal a/c	35.00
	" **L. R. Reid** on a/c	22.00
16	" **T. J. Hanes** on mess a/c	50.00
	" **S. A. Bentley** from **Hanes**	5.00

Cash Expenditures

1864 Jan 4	By telegram to S.W.T.[1]	1.00
6	" 4 pds. Sugar @ 2 1/2.	10.00
9	" Invitations for Masonic order	11.00
11	" Telegram to S. W. Tappan	1.00
	" Gave Genl Tappan's Tom	5.00
13	" Fellow crafts degree	10.00
14	" E. H. Porter for Cotton Yarns	15.00
15	" 1 Doz. Eggs for Nogg	2.50
16	" Master-Mason's degree @ 10.00	
	Tyler's Fees 2.00	12.00
19	" **Geo. Marshall** loaned	50.00
21	" Cutting Suit	10.00
26	" Pd Henry & Tappan for 81 pds Tobacco	224.37
	" Smoking Tobacco telegram	.30
27	do do do	1.00
	" Cutting Hair	1.00
30	" Pd for Washing	6.50
31	" do for do @ 3.00 Polly 2.00	5.00
Feb 1	" Telegram to Mrs. Bobb	1.00
6	" B. S. Tappan[2] paid Tom & Ikes passage to	
	Meridian	9.00
7	" Gave Tom 2.00 Ike 2.00	4.00
	" Gave Molly	41.00
	" Smoking Tobacco pd **Dan Levy**	10.00
	" Gloves	5.00
9	" Breakfast 2.00	2.00
	" Express Charge paid on letter	1.50
12	" Whisky	8.00
13	" Caping Boots	5.00
14	" 1 & 1/2 Doz. Eggs @ 2.00	3.00

15	" Squabs 5 @ 20¢	1.00
17	" Eggs @ 4	4.00
20	" Provisions	3.00
22	" Newspapers	.30
23	" Dinner	1.00
Mar 8	" pd McLemore for Eggs & basket	8.00
	" whisky on E.H.P's[3] quart	1.00
16	" Fodder	5.00
17	" Telegram E. H. Porter at Brandon	1.00
9[4]	" Lodgings Paxton[5] & **I** at Dr Lees	5.00
22	" Mess in Battery due me on a/c (balance)	20.68
25	" Cutting Hair	1.00
26	" Washing Flannel Shirts	1.00
Apr 7	" Dinner **Boone** & **I**	2.00
10	" Eggs @ 4. Chicken 1.50	5.50
	" whisky @ 24. Pipes 70¢	24.70
11	" Repairing Watch	7.00
13	" Potatoes	1.00
15	" W. G. Paxton loaned 2@10.5 46@5.5	00.00
16	" Pipe	8.00
19	" Dinner	1.00
20	" Repairing Boots	1.50
23	" 1/2 Doz. Fodder	1.50
26	" Washing drawers &1 pr Socks	.50
	" Dinner	1.00
27	" Charity	6.60
May 3	" Newspapers	.50
5	" Pd **Lawson**[6] barbering	3.00
6	" **Conklin** paid postage	.30
7	" Whiskey	25.00
8	" Mess a/c whisky 37.50 & Eggs 1.00	38.50
	" Mess a/c _ with Millers Regt	12.00
9	" Mess a/c Molasses	5.00
	" **Capt Cowan** Butter Milk	.50
	" Butter Milk	.10
11	" Mess a/c Biscuit & Bacon	60.00
	" Breakfast **Tompkins Reid** & **I**	9.00
14	" **Van De Moss** loaned retd	00.00
21	" Repairing Bridle	1.00
30	" Sent Joe by **Reid**	10.00
	" **L. R. Reid** loaned	10.00

June 4	" Molasses Lt Allen[7]	00.00
6	" **L. R. Reid** loaned	10.00
9	" Envelopes	2.50
11	" Postage Stamps	2.50
12	" Newspaper	.50
	" Bread	1.25
14	" **Geo. Tompkins** loaned bread	2.50
15	" Newspaper	.50
	" **Geo Tompkins** bread	3.75
	" Bread	3.75
17	" Joe Dyson	10.00
	" **Sam Bentley** loaned	10.00
18	" Bread 1.50 S. Tobacco 2.50	4.00
19	" Joe Dyson for purchases	10.00
21	" Bread & Smoking Tobacco	13.00
22	" Loss on $20 in Green backs got from **J. W. Cummings**	30.00
23	" M. S. Eggleston[8] per **Bigelow** in Green backs	20.00
25	" **S. A Bentley** Bread & cake	2.00
	" **Geo Tompkins** Bread	1.00
	" Bread & cakes	5.00
	" Loss in discounting Confed. issue	16.40
27	" **H. Hills** due on bread	3.75
	" **Geo Tompkins** 1 Plug Tobacco	3.00
	" Bread & Cakes	5.00
	" **Sam Bentley** Cakes	2.00
	" Tin Bucket	1.50
	" **D S Bolls** bread bal due	.50
29	" **Geo H Tompkins** loaned	16.65
	" do Cake Bread	3.00
	" **Sam Bentley** 1 Cake	1.00
	" G. P. Rice[9] 1 Bread	0.00
	" Cake & Bread	2.00
	" **Geo Tompkins** 1/2 qt. Molasses	3.00
	" Molasses ~~& Jug~~	3.00
	" Ink	2.00
	" **H. Hills** bal on 4 Loaves Bread	2.75
30	" **Geo Tompkins** 1 pkge Envelopes	1.50
	" Tobacco, Bread & Peas	4.50
July 3	" Collards	1.50
5	" Molasses 1 pint	2.50

	" **Geo H. Tompkins** do 1 pint	2.50
8	" **Tompkins & Eggleston** bread & onion	3.00
9	" do + do Molasses & Bread	9.00
	" **J. W. Conklin** loaned	3.25
	" **W. R. Wadsworth** do (retd.)	1.50
10	" **Tompkins & E.** Honey 3 pints	7.00
17	" **D. M. Legg** loaned	10.00
18	" Newspapers	.75
20	" do	.25
	" Cakes **McCray & I**	2.00
21	" Paper	.25
23	" Cakes @1.00 Yankee tent @2.00	3.00
24	" Smoking Tobacco	3.00
27	By **Eggleston** & **Tompkins** Pepper	5.00
28	" Matches	1.00
30	" Newspaper	.25
31	" do	.25
	" Cakes	2.00
	" **Eggleston** & **Tompkins** Rice	1.50
	" Toilet Soap	1.00
Aug 9	" **Tompkins** & **E.** onions	1.00
11	" Sharpening Razor @2 & Cutting Hair @2	4.00
18	" Cake 1.00 Newspapers 50¢	1.50
22	" **Tompkins** & **E.** Rice	2.00
26	" **Tompkins** & **E.** onions & Crackers	1.25
31	" **E.T. Eggleston** bread	2.00
	" **Tompkins** & **E.** do	3.00
Sept 1	" Tobacco @4.00 apples 50¢	4.50
8	" Newspaper	.25
13	" Matches pd **A. A. Folkes**	.50
19	" Sorghum **E.**, **Tompkins**, **Green**[10] & co	2.50
	" **Bentley** & **Levy** Sorghum	0.00
	" **Tompkins** & co. Potatoes	2.50
22	" **Tompkins** & co 2 chickens	4.00
28	" Postage Stamps	5.00
29	" Tobacco for Joe	1.25
30	" **Tompkins** & co 1 bus S. Potatoes	6.00
	" Apples	1.50
30	" Pies	1.50
	" Postage Stamps	.50
Oct 6	" Difference in trading overcoats with	

	Fed. Prisoner	40.00
7	" **De Moss** & co **R.E.T.L.B De M.**[11]	
	Molasses	1.00
10	" Apples 2.00 Cake 1.50	3.50
10	" **G. H. Tompkins** Apples	1.00
11	" **Tompkins** & co (6) Sirup	10.00
12	" Smoking Tobacco	5.00
13	" Pies	3.00
15	" **Tompkins** & co Dried Fruit	3.00
18	" Pies	3.00
20	" **Tompkins** & co (6) Potatoes	4.00
	" Saddle Bags from **Dove** (15th)	20.00
25	" **D. Donovan** pd for Pencil	2.00
	" Apples 1.00 Peaches 2.00	3.00
	" Smoking Tobacco	5.00
Nov 7	" Cobbling Shoe	1.50
10	" Putting Slides on Bucket	1.25
	" Tompkins & co (Salt) 6 men	1.00
	" **Van De Moss** - Postage one letter	1.00
12	" Smoking Tobacco	1.00
	" CS notes deposited at Montgomery to be funded in bonds (February)	1,950.00
25	" **Tompkins** & co dried fruit	2.50
28	" The Cabinet	1.00
29	" Apples	5.00
Dec 5	" Mess a/c **G.H.T**[12] & I	15.00
5	" do a/c **G.HT & I**	10.00
8	" 1 pr Shoes	10.00
10	" poker	18.00
14	" do	21.00
18	" Dickens "Short Stories"	2.00
20	" **G H Tompkins** Tobacco	3.00
21	" Pies	10.00
23	" Cooking Breads	2.00
29	" Boy at cousin Overton's	5.00
30	" Saddle Bags	10.00
1865 Jany	By gave Joe	10.00
	" Tobacco	.50
7	" Sorghum **LBC, W.C, B.I.H.**[,] **L R R & ETE**[13]	5.00
	" Breakfast **LRR & I**	1.00
10	" Smoking Tobacco	5.00

13	" Cakes 3@. Repairing Shoes 2@. Fair @1.00		6.00
17	" Pants @60. Cakes @1.00		61.00
19	" Telegram to J. D. Harris		3.00
26	" Supper @4.00 Horse Feed @2.00 Cakes @2.00		8.00
	" **L R Reid** Horse Feed		2.00
29	" Chicken @3.00 Mess a/c 20.32		23.30

Cash Transactions

Feb 12	Reserved Funds Forward	254.00
13	1 V out	249.00
17	1 X out	239.00
Mar 9	4 Vs out	219.00
22	Cotton Money 128.00	
	Confed Fives (18) 90.00	
	Ala ones (6) 6.00	224.00
Apr 6	out 3@ cot. Money	221.00
12	Out @66 Cot. Money	155.00
	Confed & Ala. +66	221.00
13	Out in small notes @27	194.00
15	In in Vs $45	239.00
23	In Vs $50	289.00
	In Cotton Money $5.	294.00
23	Cotton Money 64.00	
	Confed Vs 230.00	294.00
May 7	Out in Cotton Money $20	274.00
11	Out in Fives $60	214.00
14	Out in Fives $50	164.00
19	[last entry]	

Appendix B

Miscellaneous Material in Volume 2*

In order to include the entire second volume of Eggleston's dairy in this book, the following items have been included here. As noted above, the ledger entries begin on June 20, 1863, even though, as made clear below, he did not receive the diary until November 1 of that year. In addition to being referenced in the preceding text, Eggleston's memorandum of letters sent coupled with his diary tell us much about mail delivery in the Confederacy, particularly when one of the parties is behind enemy lines. Given that both parties were literate, at first glance one might think it odd that a husband would write more letters from the front than his wife would from home, which was the case with the Egglestons. The reason was that Edmund had easier access to individuals traveling to his wife's vicinity than she had to people heading in the opposite direction. The remaining items deal with his philosophical views and practical matters of daily life.

[Written sideways]
Sergt. E. T. Eggleston Co G 1st Miss Regiment of Light Artillery
Presented By Mrs Sarah Fayssoux Nov 1st 1863
[Written on very top of page]
Co B 1st Miss Lt. A. Regt.

---

*This material comprises nine unnumbered pages and pages 89 and 97.

[Written on very bottom of page]
April 3d 1864 F.F. May 1st 1864 F.F. July 29th 1864

Memorandum of Letters to Molly

Nov 5th wrote Molly letter No 1
" 7th do do do No 2
" 10th do Mother 16th wrote Mother
" 16th do Aunt Decr 6th do Mother
Feb 12th Wrote Molly by C[harles W.] Petrie No 3
" 20th Wrote do by Patterson No 4
" 23rd No 5 to Molly—Mar 2d do No 6
Mar 11th No 7 from Clinton by Miss Belle Lawrence
Mar 13th No 8 from Clinton by Mrs Carey
Mar 15th No 9 to Miss Mag Tappan to forward
Mar 21st "No 10" to Lt Coffey Scout at Edwards Depot.
April 1st "No 11" to Lt Coffey through Capt Nugent[1]
April 17th No 12 from Tuscaloosa via Capt [Edward H.] Porter to
    Demopolis
April 17th Wrote Mother
" 21st Wrote Molly No 13 from Elyton Ala via Enterprise and sent by
    Mr D O M[erwin]
" 28th "No 14" from Centerville by **Geo M[arshall]** to Newton Miss
" 29th Wrote Joe Porter at Demopolis Ala
" 30th Ed Porter at Selma Ala
" 30th Belle Harris at LaGrange Ga

Memorandum of Letters Written
to Molly & Others

May 3d No 15 from Montevallo Ala per Mrs Kelly[2]
" 5th Wrote E H Porter & Miss Mag Tappan
" 6th No 16 from Montevallo Ala per Mail to Gen B. O. T.[3]
" 6th Wrote E H Porter and D. S. Snodgrass
" 27th No 17 from Lost Mountain battle field
" 29th Wrote Belle Harris from New Hope church.
June 3d No 18 from line of battle near New Hope church, care Thos R
    Holloman Canton Miss.
June 6th Wrote Miss Mag Tappan.

June 7th Recvd letters No12 & 13
June 9th Wrote No 19 from Line of Battle to care W. A. Barbour
" 9th Wrote Johnny and Annie
" 10th Recvd Letter from Belle Harris
" 13 Wrote "No 20" for Miss Yoste & sent to Demopolis Ala.
" 15th Wrote Sister to day at Jackson Miss care Mr Wharton.
" " Wrote Joe Harris to Mobile.
" 16th Wrote C. K. Marshall Atlanta Ga.
" 21st Wrote No 21 for Miss Yoste from near Marietta
June 23d Wrote No 22 and sent by **Bigelow** with @ 20.
" " Sent **Charley Thomas** descriptive list also sent **Corp Spencer** his
    Recvd letters
No 8 & 11 to day and letter from Tommy Roach
26th Wrote Tom Roach to LaGrange
30th Recvd letter from Mahala [Roach]
July 1st Wrote Sister & Nora to Brandon
" 2nd Recvd letter No 14 June 22d from dear Molly
" 4 & 5 Wrote No 23d & sent to Mrs R. at Brandon
" 8th Wrote "No 24" and Mother per Mail.
" " Recvd No 15 from Molly
" 9th Recvd letter from Sister & Tom [Roach] from Brandon dated 2
    & 5 inst
" 11th Wrote Joe Harris
" 12th Recvd a letter from Nora to day
" 13th Wrote **Jessee Bass**
" 15th Wrote Nora Roach to Brandon
" 18th Recvd a letter from Sister
" 25th Wrote "No 25"& sent to care Col Watts
July 27th Wrote "No 26" & sent per Crump to Col Watts at Jackson
Aug 2nd do "No 27"& sent per Mr Howard per do at do
Aug 3d Rec'vd letter from Molly dated 17th July one from Sister 15th
    July one from Mother 10th ult and one from June 16th ult
Aug 4th Wrote No 28. 5th Wrote Mother
Aug 5th Rec'vd No 17th from Molly 7th Wrote Bob
Aug 8th Wrote "No 29" care Col Watts or W. A. Barbour
Aug 14th "Wrote No 30" care Col Watts or W A. Barbour
Aug 26 Wrote No 31 Care Col Watts or Barbour
Sept 4th Wrote No 32 do do at Jackson
" 9th Wrote "No 33" & sent to Col. Watts per Lt Hudson of Hoskins
    Battery

" 11th Wrote Mother to day care Col Watts

" 12th Wrote No 34 care Col Watts [at] Jackson

" 16th Wrote Alice Petrie 14th Wrote Jos. L. Harris

" 23d Wrote No 35 Sent to Brandon per Negro in 15th Miss Regt.[4]

" 24th Wrote Tom Roach at Mobile Ala

" 26th Wrote "No 36" to day & sent per mail care Watts

" 27th Wrote Joe [&] Belle E H Porter & **Geo. Marshall**

Oct 12th Wrote No 37 & sent to Watts via Blue Mountain per Capt Hoskins courrier

Oct 13th Wrote "No 38" and sent to Blue Mountain by a man in Fenner's Batty[5]

" 25th Wrote No 39 & on 29th Wrote addition to it & mailed at Courtland.

Nov 2d Wrote "No 40" and mailed at Tuscumbia Ala.

Nov 3d Wrote Miss Mag Tappan & Joe Harris per **Herring**

" 5th Wrote Mother to day care Col Watts [at] Jackson

" 6th Wrote No 41 and mailed to Jackson care Col. Watts.

"10th Wrote Joe Harris to Mobile Ala & wrote *"No 42"* and sent to Jackson per man in Hoskins Battery

" 18th Wrote "No 43" per mail to Watts

Decr 1st Wrote No 44 from Franklin Tenn & sent to Florence

Jan 12th Wrote No 45 from Columbus Miss

" 19th Wrote No 46 do do do. 22d No 47 per Warren Co

" 26th No 48.

"Persecution may make martyrs or hypocrites but can never produce conviction

Acquire honesty, seek humility practice economy love fidelity"

"Persecution may make martyrs or hypocrites but can never produce conviction"

Acquire honesty seek humility practice economy love fidelity

"A man who is in ernest in his endeavor after the happiness of a future state has in this respect an advantage over all the world For he has constantly before eyes an object of supreme importance, productive of perpetual engagements and activity, and of which the pursuit of which can be said of the pursuit besides lasts him to his life's end"

The four Cardinal Virtues are: *Prudence, Fortitude, Temperance* and *Justice.*

Health, in this sense, is one thing needful. Therefore No pains, expense, self-denial, or restraint, to which we subject ourselves, for the sake of health, is too Much. Whether it requires us to relinquish lucrative situations, to abstain from favorite indulgences, to Control intemperate passions, or undergo tedious regimens; whatever difficulties it lays us under, a man who pursues his happiness rationally and resolutely; will be content to submit to it.

Cassell & Bond—Canton have my Tobacco
    Contents Saddle Bags.
straped: shoe strings. Grey Flannel Shirt. Flannel U. Shirt.
    Tea. Dagurreotype Cravat Drawers.
    over Shirt. Soaps. Matches Mustard.
    Blue Mass
        Unstrapped
    New Pants. H. Wife 3 prs Socks. Wash Rag
    Domes U. Shirts Letters Jeans Pants. Towells
    HdKfs. Razor Strap

    B. H. Craig Cahaba Alabama
    Lt Geo Hunter[6] Co B. 13th Iowa regt. 4th Div. 17th Army Corps[7]
    Col Peters[8] 4th Iowa Cav. Regt. Crockers Brigade[9]

Names of my children and dates of their births
Robert Read Eggleston   Octo 11th 1855
Elizabeth S. G. Eggleston   Jan 6th 1857
———. [?] Eggleston (dead)   Aug 6th 1858
John Fox Eggleston   Aug 6th 1858
Anne Eliza Egglesto   June 9th 1860
Martha R. Eggleston   Nov 11th 1863

Dick H. Eggleston died   Sept 30th 1859

Mrs R. A Fayssoux Chester S.C.
care Maj. Jas Pagan[10]

To Boil (Wash) Flannel Make a lather of suds (hot) and wash your garments then rinse them in warm water

Appendix C

Other Documents of E. T. Eggleston

Of the scores of letters written by Eggleston during the war, the following two, located in the National Archives, are the only known to have survived.

Brandon Decr. 21. 1863.

Hon. Jefferson Davis

    Dear Sir;

I hereby respectfully make application for a commission in the Q. M. or C. S. Department. I have been in the field service for nearly two years as a sergeant of Light Artillery and feel that I can be of more benefit to my country as a Q. M. or Commissary than in my present position. It is evident to my mind from what I have heard, from what has come under my personal observation, and from the course our Congress is persuing in regard to the affairs of those departments, that there is great swindling being done by many of the incumbents; and it would be my pride to counteract as far as possible all fraudulent transgressions against the government.

I have had much experience in business and think I could discharge the duties of a Q. M. or Commisy. to the satisfaction of the heads of those departments.

As to my character &c, you sir, who are well acquainted with my family, and have perhaps some recollection of me as a young man, will need no references, but I can safely refer to the Right Revd. M. Green[1]

Bishop of the Diocese of Miss. to the Rev. Dr W. W. Lord,[2] to Gen. B . S. Tappan, and the Rev. F. W. Damas,[3] for such an endorsement of my character and capacity as will be entirely satisfactory to you.

> I am very respectfully
> Your obdt. Servant &c
> E. T. Eggleston.
> Orderly Sergt Capt. Cowan's Battery G,
> 1st Miss Regiment Light Art. now
> attached to Culbertson's Battery,
> Featherston's Brigade
> Loring's Division.

Resply: referred by the Presdt to the Hon: Sec: of War.

> J. C. Ives[4]

Jan' 25   Col. & A.D.C.[5]

When Eggleston wrote the above, he was probably aware that his mother had written to Davis in the spring on his behalf. That letter with Davis's endorsement has not been found, but it generated the following on a separate sheet of paper:

Endorsement: W. H. McCardle,[6] A.A.G., for Lt. Genl. Pemberton, April 2, 1863, HQ, Dept. of Miss & Ea. La., Jackson: "Respectfully returned to Lt Col. Broadwell;[7] if the services of mr Eggleston are absolutely indispensable he will be detached."

Endorsement: Lt. Colonel W. A. Broadwell, April 3, 1863, Jackson: "I cannot say that any mans services are *absolutely indispensable* Respectfully returned to the Commissary Genl. If the President thinks proper to Commission this Gentleman, his services can be rendered available either as Qr. master or Commissary."

Lt. Colonel W. A. Broadwell to Maj. R. W. Memminger,[8] April 7, 1863, Jackson, MS: "I beg leave to enclose an application of Mrs Eggleston, to have her son "Trent" detailed for Commissary Duty_ If in accordance with the views of the Genl. to accede to the wish of the President as shown by his endorsement on the application, the person can be employed by me.

I am not acquainted with him, but learn from Major McCardle, that he has good character and qualifications_

I beg leave to inform the Genl. in this connection, that I have no special Agents or clerks, & have had no assistance of this Kind except such as was obtained thro' the regular bonded & Commissioned officers of the army_ I mention this because the time appears to have come, when I am required to explain everything_ But at the moment I have no favors to ask for myself"

This time, unfortunately for Eggleston, the president did not get his way.[9]

Brandon Jany 1st 1864.
Col. Thos. M. Jack:[10]
    Respected Sir;
        On the 21st ulto. Gen. Jos. E. Johnston granted me direct from his Hd. Quarters, a fifteen days furlough to enable me to accompany my wife to Raymond and to make arrangements to send her to V.Burg whither she is compelled to go as all she possesses and three of our little children are in Warren Co. She came out to see me in Octo when I was sick and has since given birth to an infant. She has with her this infant aged seven weeks & a little boy five years old who has been sick since August last; and she has no servant or any one to aid her.

Owing to the inclemency of the weather and the sickness of our children it has been impossible for me to carry my family to Raymond. In addition to the above grounds upon which I base my application for an extension of furlough. I would mention that I am just out of the hospital at Marion Miss having been discharged from there on the 17th ulto. after a dangerous attack of Pneumonia; that I have a physician's certificate stating it would be dangerous for me to return to field service this winter as the exposure might render me a burden to myself and the country and jeopardize my life. that my command is now in Winter Quarters near Canton Miss; that there are more Sergts. belonging to my Battery than are requisite for its proper organization; that I am assisting Gen. Henry in his office as C.S. Depositary during the indisposition of his partner & clerk, Gen. Tappan, and am therefore still *on duty* though regularly furloughed. _ I call your attention to Gen. Henry's note inclosed herein. In consideration of the foregoing facts I respectfully ask for an extension of furlough from the 6th to the 15th Feb. next to enable me to make arrangements to get my wife to the Federal lines and to secure the restoration of my health.
Respectfully,

Your obdt. Servant &c
E. T. Eggleston orderly Sergt.
Culbertsons Battery
Featherston's Brigade
Loring's Division[11]

Appendix D

Roster of Company G, 1st Mississippi Light Artillery

Because no muster rolls exist for the unit following April 1864, when the battery saw the most action, it was necessary to look beyond official records to compile an accurate roster. The following names were derived from four sources: official Confederate documents, Union prisoner of war records, pension records, and accounts by individuals who either belonged to the company or were associated with it.

When possible, the entries for each individual include their date and place of birth; prewar county of residence and occupation; marital status; slave status (NS means he did not own slaves and did not reside with a slave owner); prior military experience; how and when they joined Company G; changes in rank; instances of being wounded or captured; last known service status; postwar residence and occupation; and date and place of death. All locations are in Mississippi unless otherwise indicated.

With his father, brothers, and brother-in-law deceased and having no sons old enough to serve, it is not surprising that available records indicate that Edmund T. Eggleston had no relatives serving with him. Census records and the wealth of genealogical information now available online, however, indicate the opposite was usually the case for the members of Cowan's Battery. More than just being friends or close neighbors, the original 114 members were united by blood and marriage. They included first cousins, uncles and nephews, and at least nine sets of brothers. Captain **James J. Cowan's** new command included his brother Private **Warren F. Cowan**, his wife's brother Sergeant **Archibald N. Craig**, his sister Martha's son Private **Joseph T. Hicks**, his sister Mary's son Sergeant **Granville Hicks**, two first cousins, brothers Lieutenant **Ludwell B. Cowan** and Private **Tarlton B. Cowan** and **Ludwell's** wife's four brothers, Privates **Charles, Charles H., James,** and **Richard W. Harris**. For these men the war was a family affair.

Abraham, Thomas J.: born c. 1839 in Ireland; railroad hand in Anderson County, TN; single; NS; Company A, 10th Mississippi Infantry Regiment; 9/4/63; private; detailed in Ordnance Depot, Macon, before being paroled at Columbus, 5/18/65.

Adams, Rodolphus: born 5/24/30 in VA; superintendent of City Hospital in Warren County; married; NS; Company A, 3rd Battalion Mississippi Infantry (State Troops); 8/12/62; private; status not stated, roll for Jan.–Feb. 1863; watchman in Warren County; died 3/15/82 and buried in Vicksburg.

Adams, S.: captured at Fort Blakely; released from Camp Townsend on parole 5/16/65.

Aldridge, Alfred D.: born c. 1840 in Madison County; farmer in Hinds County; single; slave owner; Company H, 1st (Percy's) Mississippi Infantry (Army of 10,000); volunteered 5/12/62; private; discharged for disability 8/15/62; merchant in Greenville.

Anderson, Nathaniel R.: born c. 1842 in GA; student in Hinds County; single; NS; 8/12/62; bugler; deserted 7/17/63.

Anderson, William D.: born 11/18/43 in Butts County, GA; farmer in Hinds County; single; family owned slaves; Company B, 22nd Mississippi Infantry Regiment; 2/1/63; private; captured at Fort Blakely; released from Camp Townsend on parole 5/16/65; died 3/19/85 and buried in Hinds County.

Askew, Dukelet: born 7/6/28 in Hertford, NC; farmer in Hinds County; married; slave owner; volunteered 4/26/62; private; captured at Fort Blakely; released from Camp Townsend on parole 6/16/65; lawyer and merchant in Hinds County; died in 1902 and buried in Hinds County.

Askew, Jeremiah Bush: born 4/2/33 in Hertford, NC; clothing merchant in Warren County; single; slave owner; volunteered 4/26/62; corporal; wounded 6/25/63 at Vicksburg; died 6/27/63 buried in Vicksburg.

Auter, Albert F.: born c. 1846 in OH; student in Warren County; single; family owned slaves; volunteered 5/12/62; private; captured at Fort Blakely; released from Camp Townsend on parole 5/16/65.

Auter, Solomon Brecount: born c. 1832 in MS; clerk in Warren County; married; slave owner; volunteered 4/26/62; private; captured at Vicksburg and Fort Blakely; released from Camp Townsend on parole 5/16/65; bookkeeper in Vicksburg; died after 1900 and buried in Vicksburg.

Ayers, George W.: born c. 1834 in TN; day laborer in Poinsette County, AR; single; NS; volunteered 4/26/62; private; captured at Vicksburg; deserted 8/23/63.

Ayers, Jacob: born c. 1838 in TN; clerk in Yalobusha County; single; residing in slave owning household; volunteered 4/26/62; private; captured 5/17/63 at Big Black River; paroled from Fort Delaware (DE) prison 7/2/63; joined Captain Stan Miotkowski's Independent Battery A, Pennsylvania Heavy Artillery, 7/7/63.

Bass, Jessee: born c. 1834 in VA; overseer in Issaquena County; single; slave owner; 12/31/62; private; captured at Vicksburg and Fort Blakely; released from Camp Townsend on parole 5/16/65; Warren County; buried in Warren County.

Beane, Melbourne: born c. 1836 in VA; Warren County; single; residing in slave owning household; volunteered 4/26/62; private; captured at Vicksburg and Fort Blakely; released from Camp Townsend on parole 5/16/65; resided in Vicksburg.

Beard, Parmenas A.: born c. 1847 in NC; student in Madison County; single.

Bell, Jefferson Harris: born c. 1833 in MS; farmer in Warren County; married; NS; 8/2/62; private; status not stated, roll for Jan.–Feb. 1863; farmer in Winn Parish, LA; died before 1900.

Bell, William Tyree: born c. 1835 in MS; clerk in Hinds County; married; NS; 8/2/62; private; status not stated, roll for Jan.–Feb. 1863, but an exchanged prisoner of war 1/9/64; farmer in Warren County; died 12/12/1928 and buried in Warren County.

Bentley, Samuel A.: born October 1831 in MS; married/widower; Company G, Confederate Guards Regiment Louisiana Militia; volunteered 5/12/62; private/sergeant; captured near Nashville, TN, 12/15/64; discharged from Camp Douglas (IL) prison 6/18/65; cotton buyer in Grayson, TX.

Bigelow, Milton Henry: born c. 1837 in NY; architect and builder in Warren County; single; family owned slaves; volunteered 4/26/62; private/corporal; captured at Vicksburg; deserted 8/23/63; paroled at Grenada 5/22/65; Vicksburg; died 10/11/78 and buried in Vicksburg.

Billings, Albert D.: born c. 1839 in MS or PA; Warren County; single; family owned slaves; Company H, 9th and Company F, 10th Mississippi infantry regiments; volunteered 4/26/62; private; at hospital when paroled at Columbus 5/17/65; clerk in Vicksburg.

Billingslea, James E.: born c. 1839 in MS; farmer in Warren County; single; family owned slaves; volunteered 4/26/62; sergeant; captured at Vicksburg; at Lovejoy Station, GA, on 9/18/64.

Billingslea, Taylor (slave): born c. 1848 in MS; belonged to Elijah Young of Madison County; 1/18/64; personal servant of his son, Ebenezer H. Young, who was mortally wounded at Decatur, AL, 10/26/64; after seeing to Ebenezer's burial, Taylor returned to Madison County and delivered Ebenezer's watch, ring, and Bible to his mother; farm laborer in Madison County. Granted a pension by the state of Mississippi after the war for his service.

Boaze, Samuel F.: born c. 1833 in MS or KY; Holmes County; single; NS; private; captured near Vicksburg 5/18/63; paroled at Fort Delaware (DE) prison 7/3/63 and exchanged 7/4/63; farmer in Madison County. Only POW records, and those filed under Booze.

Boggins, L.: claimed to be a private in the company when paroled 5/21–25/65 at Memphis, TN.

Boland, John S.: born c. 1830 in County Mayo, Ireland; married/widower; volunteered 5/12/62; private; captured at Fort Blakely; released from Camp Townsend on parole 5/16/65; cotton broker in New Orleans, LA; died 2/4/84 in New Orleans.

Bolls, David S.: born c. 1838 in MS; farmer in Hinds County; single; slave owner; volunteered 4/26/62; private/corporal; captured at Fort Blakely; released from Camp Townsend on parole 5/16/65.

Boon, H.: claimed to be a resident of Warren County and a private in the company when paroled 7/3–7/10/65 at Alexandria, LA.

Boyle, Owen: volunteered 4/26/62; private; captured 5/17/63 at Big Black River; paroled at Fort Delaware (DE) prison 7/3/63; joined Captain Stan Miotkowski's Independent Battery A, Pennsylvania Heavy Artillery, 7/7/63; invalid in PA in 1881.

Brantley, George Washington: born c. 1835 in AL; brick maker in Warren County; single; NS; 10/6/62; private; status not stated, roll for Jan.–Feb. 1863.

Brick, John E.: born c. 1812 in NJ; brick layer in Warren County; married; NS; Company E, 2nd Mississippi Infantry Battalion (State Troops); substitute for Hal P. Noland 1/8/63; private; captured in Hinds County 7/6/63; took oath of allegiance and released from Camp Morton (IN) prison 1/2/65; brick mason in Vicksburg.

Brown, Charles B.: private; captured at Fort Blakely; released from Camp Townsend on parole 5/16/65; Vicksburg. Only POW records.

Bunker, Jethro: born c. 1833 in NY; farmer in DeKalb County, IL; married; NS volunteered 5/12/62; private; captured near Nashville, TN, 12/15/64; signed oath of Allegiance and released from Camp Douglas (IL) prison 3/7/65; grain clerk in New Orleans, LA.

Burdett, Simeon M.: born c. 1848 in AL; Chambers County, AL; single; NS; volunteered; private; captured at Fort Blakely; released from Camp Townsend on parole 5/16/65. Only POW records.

Butler, William Chaplain: born 8/17/44 in MS; student in Claiborne County; single; family owned slaves; 10/16/62; private; died 12/24/63 in Port Gibson.

Cabaniss, G. M.: private; captured at Fort Blakely; released from Camp Townsend on parole 5/16/65. Only POW records, and those filed under Cabbrett.

Cabaniss, W. W.: private; captured at Fort Blakely; released from Camp Townsend on parole 5/16/65. Only POW records, and those filed under Cabbrett.

Carleton, Samuel M.: private; captured at Fort Blakely; released from Camp Townsend on parole 5/16/65.

Carrabine, Daniel W.: born c. 1842 in Ireland; Warren County; single; slave owner; 9/2/62; private; wounded and captured at Nashville, TN, 12/15/64; died 12/22/64 at Nashville.

Carraway, T. L. H.: born c. 1829 in GA; farmer in Covington County; married; family owned slaves; private; captured at Fort Blakely; released from Camp Townsend on parole 5/16/65; farmer in Covington County.

Cathell, Jonathan: born c. 1839 in MS; farmer in Warren County; married; NS; 9/11/62; private; captured at Big Black River 5/17 or 21/63; paroled from Fort Delaware (DE) prison 7/30/63; exchanged 7/31/63; issued clothing 8/13/63.

Clark, Robert A.: born c. 1825 in NC; lawyer in Hinds County; married; slave owner; 9/8/62; private; wounded and left in Vicksburg 7/8/63; farmer in Warren County.

Clarke, William H.: born c. 1843 in NC: student in Warren County; single; residing with slaveholder; 1/13/63; private; captured at Fort Blakely; released from Camp Townsend on parole 5/16/65; Copiah County.

Clore, Daniel P.: born c. 1827 in MS; convict laborer in Chicot County, AR; residing with slaveholder; volunteered 9/13/62; private; captured at Vicksburg; deserted 8/23/63.

Coleman, J. W.: private; captured at Fort Blakely; released from Camp Townsend on parole 5/16/65. Only POW records.

Conklin, James William: grocer in Vicksburg; volunteered 5/12/62; sergeant; captured at Vicksburg and Fort Blakely; released from Camp Townsend on parole 5/16/65; grocer in Vicksburg.

Cook, Hartwell Harris: born 10/1/46 in MS; student in Warren County; single; family owned slaves; 2/2/64; private; unattached when paroled at Jackson 5/19/65; died 12/30/84 and buried in Copiah County.

Countryman, Columbus S.: born c. 1845 in Perry County, AL; farm worker in Warren County; single; family owned slaves; Company E, 2nd Mississippi Infantry Battalion (State Troops) and Company G, 24th Mississippi Infantry Regiment; 3/14/63; private; received medical discharge 9/10/63.

Countryman, Robert: born c. 1837 in TX; Warren County; single; family owned slaves; 8/12/62; private; captured near Nashville, TN, 12/15/64; discharged from Camp Douglas (IL) prison 6/18/65; farmer in Warren County.

Countryman, William P.: born c. 1842 in AL; Warren County; single; slave owner; Company G, 24th Mississippi Infantry Regiment; volunteered 4/26/62; private; captured at Vicksburg; deserted 8/23/63; farmer in Warren County.

Cowan, James Jones: born 8/5/30 in MS; dry goods merchant in Vicksburg; married; slave owner; volunteered 4/26/62; captain; captured at Vicksburg and Fort Blakely; confined in New Orleans, LA, 4/30/65; exchanged 5/1/65; parole not dated; dry goods merchant in Vicksburg; died 10/1/98 in Knoxville, TN; buried in Vicksburg.

Cowan, Ludwell B.: born 4/19/28 in OH or AL; farmer in Warren County; married; slave owner; 1st Mississippi Infantry Regiment (pre-war); volunteered 4/26/62; junior 2nd lieutenant; captured at Fort Blakely; confined in New Orleans, LA, 4/30/65; exchanged 5/1/65; paroled 5/12 or 15/65 in Jackson; planter in Washington County; died 5/24/92 and buried in Vicksburg.

Cowan, Tarlton B.: born 7/20/26; Company A, 21st Mississippi Infantry Regiment; transferred 2/2/64; private; wounded during Atlanta Campaign; retired and assigned to Invalid Corps 12/7/64; paroled 5/12/65 at Jackson; died 7/16/99 and buried in Washington County.

Cowan, Warren F.: born c. 1839 in MS; lawyer and farmer in Clark County, AR; single; NS; Company A, 21st Mississippi Infantry Regiment; transferred 5/22/62; private/corporal/private; captured at Fort Blakely; released from Camp Townsend on parole 5/16/65; lawyer and judge in Vicksburg; died in 1891.

Cox, George L.: private; captured at Fort Blakely; released from Camp Townsend on parole 5/16/65. Only POW records.

Craig, Archibald N.: born c. 1839 in Scotland; bookkeeper in Jefferson County; single; slave free; Company D, 22nd Mississippi Infantry Regiment; volunteered 4/26/62; sergeant/private/sergeant; captured at Vicksburg; detached as clerk at Jackson; paroled 5/11/65 at Jackson.

Crimmins, Timothy: volunteered 4/25/62; private; paroled 4/22/65 at Greenville, AL.

Crow, A.: Captain Thomas Hightower's Local Defense Company (Calhoun County, MS); private; captured at Fort Blakely; released from Camp Townsend on parole 5/16/65. Only POW records.

Culbertson, Julius: born c. 1839 in LA; planter in Madison Parish, LA; married; slave owner; 5/16/62; private; "in accordance with an Act of Congress authorizing the transfer of any private or non-commissioned officer, who may have enlisted in a State, other than his own, to any regiment or company in his own State, I would respectfully solicit your approval of my application for transfer from your Company to Capt Harper's Co. Col. Pargoud's Regiment of Cavalry,[1] now doing Confederate service in Madison Parish La." submitted 3/9/63; buried in Fort Worth, TX. No record of his having served in any LA unit.

Culbertson, Levi P.: born c. 1836 in MS; planter in Madison Parish, LA; single; slave owner; 5/16/62; private; status not stated, roll for Jan.–Feb. 1863; physician in Fort Worth, TX; died 4/10/68 and buried in Fort Worth.

Cummings, John W.: born c. 1830 in MS; overseer in Warren County; married; NS; 4/3/64; private; captured at Fort Blakely; released from Camp Townsend on parole 5/16/65.

Curtis, E. L. S.: born c. 1848 in LA; student in Madison County; single; family owned slaves; private; captured at Fort Blakely; released from Camp Townsend on parole 5/16/65.

Cushman, Cornelius B.: born c. 1843 in MS; student in Warren County; single; family owned slaves; single; volunteered 4/26/62; private; present on roll for Mar.–Apr. 1864.

Dancy, William D.: born c. 1842 in MS; student in Madison Parish, LA; single; family owned slaves; 5/16/62; private/corporal; killed in action 5/14/64 at Resaca, GA.

Daniel, Athelston W.: born c. 1835 in LA; Orleans Parish, LA; NS; volunteered 5/12/62; private/corporal; detached as clerk in Quartermaster's Department of Featherston's Brigade when paroled 4/26/65 at Greensboro, NC.

Daniels, F. V.: born c. 1837 in VA; bookkeeper in Warren County; married; slave owner; volunteered 4/26/62; private; transferred to Telegraph Company at Vicksburg 3/14/63; clerk in Galveston, TX.

Daugherty, John M.: born c. 1822 in VA; Hinds County; single; slave owner; private; captured at Fort Blakely; released from Camp Townsend on parole 5/16/65; laborer in Hinds County. Only POW records.

Defir, Samuel C.: born c. 1845 in AL; private; captured at Fort Blakely; released from Camp Townsend on parole 5/16/65; farmer in Desha County, AR. Only POW records.

DeMoss, Vanerson: born c. 1836 in MS; Madison Parish, LA; married; family owned slaves; volunteered 4/26/62; sergeant; present, roll for Mar.–Apr. 1864; paroled at Shreveport, LA, 6/7/65.

DeNight, David Wesley: born c. 1844; single; volunteered 4/26/62; private; discharged by Civil Authority under Minority Act of Congress 11/9/62; clerk in Vicksburg.

Donovan, David S.: single; volunteered 4/26/62; private; captured at Fort Blakely; released from Camp Townsend on parole 5/16/65; collector for Merchant's and People's Wharf Boat in Vicksburg; died 6/3/79 in Edwards.

Donovan, Thomas W.: born c. 1842 in MS; laborer in Warren County; single; NS; volunteered 4/26/62; private; captured at Vicksburg; refused to be paroled at Vicksburg and asked to take the Oath of Allegiance and be released.

Dove, Sampson D.: born c. 1826 in IN; overseer in Warren County; married; slave owner; 7/14/62; private; captured at Fort Blakely; released from Camp Townsend on parole 5/16/65.

Drummond, T. W.: volunteered 4/26/62; private; status not stated, roll for Jan.–Feb. 1863.

Drummond, Warren F.: volunteered 4/26/62; private; paroled at Jackson 5/12/65.

Edwards, Benjamin Charles: born 10/11/30 in Warren County; farmer in Warren County; married; slave owner; volunteered 4/26/62; senior 2nd lieutenant; captured at Vicksburg and Fort Blakely; confined in New Orleans, LA, 4/30/65; exchanged 5/1/65; paroled at Jackson 5/12/65; dealer in boat stores in Vicksburg; died 8/2/72 and buried in Warren County.

Edwards, Isaac Newton: born c. 1832 in Claiborne County; Warren County; married; NS; volunteered 4/26/62; private; captured at Vicksburg 10/20/63; in prison at Alton, IL, 7/10/64.

Edwins, Asa W.: born c. 1830 in PA; machinist in Dallas County, AL; single; NS; corporal; captured at Fort Blakely; released from Camp Townsend on parole 5/16/65; engine builder in Indianapolis, IN. Only POW records.

Eggleston, Edmund Trent: born 9/12/33 in MS; farmer in Warren County; married; slave owner; volunteered 4/26/62; sergeant; paroled 3/26/65 at Vicksburg; merchant in Vicksburg; died 7/21/96 in Yazoo City; buried in Vicksburg.

Eldridge, George L.: born c. 1838 in VA; iron molder in Madison County; married; NS; 12/16/62; private; captured at Fort Blakely; released from Camp Townsend on parole 5/16/65; worked in Madison County.

Erdman, William: born c. 1837 in Switzerland; single; NS; volunteered 4/26/62; private; captured at Raymond 5/18/63; signed Oath of Allegiance 2/13/65 at Fort Delaware (DE) prison 2/13/65 and discharged 2/15/65; engineer and machinist in New Orleans.

Ervin, J. H.: private; captured at Fort Blakely; released from Camp Townsend on parole 5/16/65. Only POW records.

Everett, J. C.: private; captured at Fort Blakely; released from Camp Townsend on parole 5/16/65. Only POW records.

Everett, T. J.: private; captured at Fort Blakely; released from Camp Townsend on parole 5/16/65. Only POW records.

Ewing, Jessee H.: 4/14/64; private; present, roll for Mar.–Apr. 1864.

Fairchild, William A.: born 7/12/38 in NY; insurance agent in Warren County; single; NS; volunteered 4/26/62; private/corporal; detached to the Quartermaster Department in the fall of 1862 until paroled 5/12/65 at Meridian; insurance agent in Vicksburg; died 9/28/78 and buried in Vicksburg.

Farmer, Anderson: volunteered 4/26/62; private; deserted 7/19/63.

Fears, Robert L.: born c. 1837 in MS; volunteered 5/12/62; private; captured at Vicksburg; never returned; died 1870.

Ferrell, Ebenezer E.: Warren County; volunteered 4/26/62; private; present, roll for Mar.–Apr. 1864.

Ferrell, John B.: born c. 1841 in MS; student in Warren County; single; family owned slaves; Company H, 21st Mississippi Infantry;

volunteered 4/26/62; private; captured at Vicksburg; killed in action at Florence, AL, 12/27/64.

Flateau, Louis Spence. See **Lewis M. Spencer**.

Fly, John James: born c. 1825 in VA; Warren County; single; NS; 7/30/62; private; captured at Vicksburg; remained in Union lines and imprisoned; released from Camp Morton (IN) prison 11/9/63 on taking Oath of Allegiance.

Folkes, Augustus A.: born c. 1839 in MS; clerk in Warren County; single; NS; volunteered 4/26/62; private/corporal/private; captured at Fort Blakely; released from Camp Townsend on parole 5/16/65; clerk in Vicksburg.

Franklin, Mason: 4/23/63; private; captured at Vicksburg; court-martialed 7/5/64 and sentenced to hard labor.

Freeman, J. W.: private; captured at Fort Blakely; released from Camp Townsend on parole 5/16/65. Only POW records.

Gordon, Stephen: from Camp of Instruction 10/15/62; private; mortally wounded 10/26/65 at Decatur, AL.

Graham, A.: private; captured at Fort Blakely; released from Camp Townsend on parole 5/16/65. Only POW records.

Grant, Robert C.: born 5/3/48 in MS; student in Warren County; single; family owned slaves; 46th Mississippi Infantry Regiment; 2/2/64; private; captured at Fort Blakely; released from Camp Townsend on parole 5/16/65; died 2/20/1904 and buried in Warren County.

Greene, William L.: born c. 1846 in Ireland; student in Warren County; single; family owned slaves; 7/9/63; private; captured at Fort Blakely; released from Camp Townsend on parole 5/16/65; grocer in Vicksburg; buried in Vicksburg.

Gregg, Henry: private; captured at Fort Blakely; released from Camp Townsend on parole 5/16/65. Only POW records.

Grimm, Leon P.: born 1836; volunteered 5/12/62; private; captured at Fort Blakely; released from Camp Townsend on parole 5/16/65; died 1892 and buried in Shreveport, LA.

Guider, Benjamin F.: born 10/9/36 in Bavaria; jeweler and watchmaker in Warren County; single; NS; volunteered 4/26/62; private/musician; detailed in regimental band; captured at Vicksburg; remained within Union lines and supposed to be a deserter; jeweler and watchmaker in Vicksburg; died 5/6/1916 and buried in Vicksburg.

Guinn, J. H.: private; captured at Fort Blakely; released from Camp Townsend on parole 5/16/65. Only POW records.

Hamilton, William C.: born c. 1843 in OH; watchmaker in Warren County; single; NS; 5/11/64; private; present on roll for Mar.–Apr. 1864.

Hamly, A. P.: private; captured at Fort Blakely; released from Camp Townsend on parole 5/16/65. Only POW records.

Hand, John F.: born c. 1828 in MS; farmer in Clarke County; married; volunteered 5/12/62; corporal/private; absent without leave since 7/18/1863.

Hanes, Thomas J.: born c. 1834 in AL; confectionary in Warren County; married; slave owner; volunteered 4/26/62; junior 1st lieutenant; captured at Vicksburg and near Nashville 12/16/64; transferred from Camp Chase (OH) prison to City Point, VA, 3/4/65 for exchange; paroled 5/15/65 at Jackson; confectioner in Vicksburg.

Harris, Dr.: assigned 9/26/64; surgeon.

Harris, Charles: volunteered 4/26/62; private; never present or paid.

Harris, Charles H.: volunteered 3/26/62; private; status not stated, roll for Jan.–Feb. 1863.

Harris, James Watkins: born c. 1844 in MS; student in Warren County; single; family owned slaves; volunteered 4/26/62; private; captured at Fort Blakely; released from Camp Townsend on parole 5/16/65.

Harris, Richard W.: born 10/26/38 in MS; farmer in Warren County; single; family owned slaves; volunteered 3/26/62; private/corporal; captured at Fort Blakely; released from Camp Townsend on parole 5/16/65; farmer in Warren County; died 10/31/95 and buried in Warren County.

Harrison, George: born c. 1836; private; deserted; imprisoned at Memphis, TN, 8/14/64; took Oath of Allegiance 9/14/64. Only POW records.

Harrison, John P.: volunteered 4/26/62; private; captured at Fort Blakely; released from Camp Townsend on parole 5/16/65; carpenter in Vicksburg.

Harrison, L. G. W.: 8/4/62; private; captured at Vicksburg; AWOL 8/23/63.

Haver, Adam: born c. 1837 in MD; butcher in Warren County; married; NS; 8/18/62; private; captured at Vicksburg; never returned to duty; Vicksburg; died in 1897 and buried in Vicksburg.

Haver, Michael: born in 1832 at sea; farmer in Warren County; married; NS; 8/18/62; private; captured at Vicksburg; never returned to duty; buried in Vicksburg.

Herring, Isaac Edwin: 2/18/63; private; AWOL on roll for July–Aug. 1863.

Hewitt, J. A.: private; captured at Fort Blakely; released from Camp Townsend on parole 5/16/65. Only POW records.

Hickman, Jesse Preston: born 6/30/48 in MS; student in Madison County; single; family owned slaves; private; admitted to hospital in West Point 1/10/65; captured at Fort Blakely; released from Camp Townsend on parole 5/16/65; farmer in Madison County.

Hickman, John P. H.: born c. 1846 in MS; student in Madison County; single; NS; private; captured at Fort Blakely; released from Camp Townsend on parole 5/16/65. Only POW records.

Hicks, Benjamin J.: born c. 1846 in MS; student in Warren County; single; family owned slaves; Company A, 21st Mississippi Infantry Regiment; transferred 5/16/62; private; present, roll for Mar.–Apr. 1864; prisoner of war 4/14/65.

Hicks, John R.: born c. 1840 in MS; medical student in Warren County; single; family owned slaves; Company L, 21st Mississippi Infantry Regiment; private; captured at Fort Blakely; released from Camp Townsend on parole 5/16/65; physician in Vicksburg. Only POW records.

Hicks, Joseph Granville: born c. 1841 in MS; student in Warren County; single; NS; volunteered 4/26/62; sergeant; transferred to Invalid Corps; paroled in Jackson in May 1865; resided in Warren County.

Hicks, Joseph T.: born c. 1841 in MS; clerk in Warren County; single; family owned slaves; volunteered 4/26/62; private; died 8/4 or 6/62 near Vicksburg.

Hill, Charles Henry: born c. 1829 in TN; farmer in Warren County; single; slave owner; from camp of instruction 10/15/62; private; took Oath of Allegiance 10/26/64 at Chattanooga, TN.

Hopper, David: born c. 4/23/26 in MS; farmer in Warren County; married; slave owner; 1/14/63; private; wounded and captured at Vicksburg; paroled in hospital 7/4/63; deserted about 6/1/64; court-martialed 6/30/64 and sentenced to hard labor; died 11/17/88 and buried in Warren County.

Horner, John H.: 4/18/83; private; captured at or near Vicksburg 5/29 or 30/63; imprisoned in Alton, IL; exchanged at City Point, VA, by 6/21/63; captured at Fort Blakely; released from Camp Townsend on parole 5/16/65.

Houly, James H.: private; captured near Vicksburg 5/18/63; imprisoned at Fort Delaware (DE); exchanged 7/4/63; received at City Point, VA, 7/6/63. Only POW records.

Howell, Levi: 8/5/62; private; status not stated, roll for Jan.–Feb. 1863.

Howell, M. V.: born c. 1840; married; 8/5/62; private; status not stated, roll for Jan.–Feb. 1863; deserted and took Oath of Allegiance at Memphis, TN, 4/7/65.

Irwin, John Q.: born c. 1825 in KY; physician in Orleans Parish, LA; married; slave owner; 1/8/63; private; captured at Fort Blakely; released from Camp Townsend on parole 5/16/65.

Jett, Samuel E.: born c. 1845 in MS; student in Warren County; single; family owned slaves; 5/16/62; private; captured at Vicksburg; AWOL since 8/23/63.

Johnson, James P.: 8/4/63; private; died 10/1/63 before ever being paid.

Johnson, Thomas G.: born c. 1838 in MS; volunteered 4/26/62; private/corporal; killed in action at Decatur, AL, 10/26/64.

Johnson, William Henry: volunteered 4/26/62; private; captured at Fort Blakely; released from Camp Townsend on parole 5/16/65; surveyor in Warren County.

Jones, Benjamin F.: volunteered 4/26/62; private; received medical discharge at Vicksburg 12/15/62.

Jones, Joseph C.: born c. 1830 in MS; volunteered 5/12/62; private; captured at Fort Blakely; released from Camp Townsend on parole 5/16/65.

Kelly, William W.: born c. 1845 in MS; 5/28 or 6/2/62; private; captured at Vicksburg and Fort Blakely; released from Camp Townsend on parole 5/16/65.

Kelton, John W.: born c. 1838 in Chester County, PA; carpenter; volunteered 4/26/62; private; captured at Big Black River 5/18 or 21/63; imprisoned at Camp Morton (IN) and Fort Delaware (DE); paroled 7/3/63 and exchanged in VA; lost right arm in line of duty prior to 2/24/65 and retired for disability at Selma, AL, 3/14/65; paroled as straggler at Selma 5/25/65.

Kestner, J.: volunteered 4/26/62; private/musician; detached to regimental band; captured at Vicksburg; remained within enemy's lines and supposed to be a deserter.

King, Edwin: born c. 1830 in MS; volunteered 4/26/62; private; roll for Jan.–Feb. 1863, sick in Vicksburg Hospital and medical discharge recommended; laborer in Vicksburg.

King, Horatio N.: born 6/2/39 in MS; clerk in Warren County; single; family owned slaves; volunteered 4/26/62; corporal; present, roll for Mar.–Apr. 1864; unattached when paroled 5/19/65 at Jackson; clerk in Vicksburg; died 8/15/82 and buried in Vicksburg.

Klein, George Marion: born c. 1844 in MS; student in Warren County; single; family owned slaves; Company F, 10th Mississippi Infantry Regiment; volunteered 4/26/62; sergeant; detailed as clerk 2/2/63 until captured at Vicksburg; Vicksburg parole last record of service; banker in Vicksburg.

Kleinman, Euly: born 1/6/32 in Hesse; slave owner; 8/3/62; private; captured at Vicksburg; AWOL since 8/23/63; plasterer in Vicksburg; died 7/22/92 and buried in Vicksburg.

Lakeman, Francis Marion: born c. 1832 in MS; 8/3/62; private; captured at Vicksburg; refused parole and was incarcerated at Camp Morton (IN) prison; died 8/19/63 at Camp Morton and buried in Indianapolis, IN.

Lawson, Houston: born c. 1843 in TN; carpenter in Claiborne County; single; volunteered 4/26/62; private; captured at Vicksburg; AWOL since 8/23/63.

Lawson, Pryor N.: born c. 1841 in TN; volunteered 4/26/62; private; roll for Jan.–Feb. 1863, sick in regimental hospital; farmer in Bolivar County.

Legg, Daniel M.: born c. 1829 in OH; farmer in Warren County; married; NS; volunteered 4/26/62; corporal/private; captured at Vicksburg; appointed hospital steward 12/1/64; farmer in Warren County.

Lemmons, Frederick: volunteered 4/26/62; private; captured at Vicksburg; "Paroled, went outside of the lines with their Command, Deserted and came back"; died of chronic diarrhea at Gratiot Street Prison Hospital, St. Louis, MO, 10/1/63, and buried in Jefferson Barracks National Cemetery, St. Louis.

Lennan, Thomas F.: born c. 1826 in GA; traveling agent in Madison County; married; volunteered 4/26/62; private; captured at Big Black River 5/18/63; paroled from Fort Delaware (DE) prison 7/3/63; joined Captain Stan Miotkowski's Independent Battery A, Pennsylvania Heavy Artillery, 7/7/63.

Levy, Daniel S.: born c. 1826 in Prussia; Issaquena County; single; 5/16/62; private; captured at Fort Blakely; released from Camp Townsend on parole 5/16/65; merchant in Vicksburg; buried in Vicksburg.

Lewis, Thomas V.: born c. 1845 in MS; student in NC; single; slave owner; 4/13/64; private; captured at Nashville, TN, 12/15/64; incarcerated in Camp Douglas (IL) prison; suffered frostbite in both feet; took Oath of Allegiance 6/4/65 and released 6/19/65; Hinds County.

Loomis, Samuel T.: volunteered 4/26/62; private; captured at Vicksburg and near Fort Blakely 4/1/65; released from Camp Townsend on parole 5/16/65.

Lowry, Benjamin: from camp of instruction 10/14/62; private; detached, working in Linen Department of City Hospital, Vicksburg, 4/30/63 last record.

Lyndsey, James: private; captured at Fort Blakely; released from Camp Townsend on parole 5/16/65. Only POW records.

MacGoodridge, J.: private; captured at Champion Hill 5/16/63; incarcerated at Fort Delaware (DE) prison; joined Captain Stan Miotkowski's Independent Battery A, Pennsylvania Heavy Artillery, 7/7/63. Only POW records.

Mackin, Pat: 8/28/62; private; AWOL since 7/18/63.

Malloy, Thomas: born c. 1834 in WI; laborer in Warren County; married; NS; 8/11/62; private; captured near Jackson in July 1863; incarcerated in Camp Morton (IN) prison, where he died 12/16/63; buried in Indianapolis, IN.

Marley, Walter Stephen: born c. 1832 in MS; farmer in Warren County; single; slave owner; Captain Gartley's (Yazoo Rangers) Mississippi Cavalry Company; 1/29/64; private; captured at Fort Blakely; released from Camp Townsend on parole 5/16/65.

Marr, Henry B.: Company E, 1st Mississippi Light Artillery; transferred prior to roll for Mar.–Apr. 1864; private; captured at Fort Blakely; released from Camp Townsend on parole 5/16/65.

Marsh, Josephus: volunteered 4/26/62; private; captured at Vicksburg; AWOL since 7/18/63.

Marshall, George W.: born c. 1817 in NC; farmer in Panola County; married; 5/15/62; private; appointed adjutant 9th Mississippi Cavalry Regiment 12/21/64; paroled 5/14/65 at Meridian.

Martin, Austin M.: born 10/21/38 in MS; day laborer in Calhoun County; married; 4/22/63; private; captured at Vicksburg; AWOL since 8/23/63; farmer in Chickasaw County; died in 1913 and buried in Chickasaw County.

Mathews, W. B.: private; captured at Fort Blakely; released from Camp Townsend on parole 5/16/65. Only POW records.

McCool: private; captured at Fort Blakely; released from Camp Townsend on parole 5/16/65. Only POW records.

McCray, William Vick: born c. 1834 in MS; volunteered 5/12/62; corporal/sergeant; court-martialed 2/14/63 and sentenced to company punishment; captured at Vicksburg and Fort Blakely; released from Camp Townsend on parole 5/16/65; clerk in Vicksburg; died in 1882 and buried in Vicksburg.

McDonald, John: born in December 1833 in Ireland; contractor; single; volunteered 6/12/62; private; captured at Vicksburg and Fort Blakely; released from Camp Townsend on parole 5/16/65; contractor in Jackson; died in Jackson 7/4/1904.

McFarland, Andrew Jackson: born c. 1843; volunteered 5/19/62; private; sick from enlistment through roll for Jan.–Feb. 1863 and never paid; supposedly discharged, later served in the Commissary Department, and surrendered at Gainesville, AL; farmer in Copiah County.

McKelley, John R.: private; sent home sick in August 1862.

McLaughlin, Marion: 8/18/62; private; AWOL since 7/16/63.

McQuaide, John C.: born c. 1842 in New Orleans, LA; railroad clerk in Vicksburg; single; family owned slaves; Company F, 10th Mississippi Infantry Regiment; volunteered 4/26/62; private; present, roll for Mar.–Apr. 1864; paroled at Meridian 5/11/65; employee of Dabney, Vernon, and Searles in Vicksburg; died 8/6/1903 in Vicksburg.

McRae, John R.: born in 1841 in MS; student in Warren County; single; family owned slaves; volunteered 5/12/62; private; detailed to Quartermaster Department 8/19/62; recommended for medical discharge 12/15/62; still on detached service, roll for Jan.–Feb. 1863; operated Ice Cream Saloon in Vicksburg; died in 1885 and buried in Vicksburg.

Miller, Jacob R.: born c. 1835 in Holland; 8/12/62; private; status not stated, roll for Jan.–Feb. 1863; shoemaker in Vicksburg; died 3/27/1912 and buried in Vicksburg.

Minter, A. C.: born c. 1844 in MS; private; lost left arm at shoulder at Decatur, AL, in October 1864; on furlough from 10/26/64 until paroled at Jackson 5/1–20/65; grocery farmer in Madison County. Only POW and pension records.

Murphy, William R.: born c. 1840 in MS; 8/8/62; private; captured at Vicksburg and in front of Fort Blakely 4/2/65; released from Camp Townsend on parole 5/16/65.

Neelly, John W.: born c. 1835 in MS; Claiborne County; single; volunteered 4/26/62; private; captured at Fort Blakely; released from Camp Townsend on parole 5/16/65.

Neely, Samuel C.: born c. 1833 in MS; planter in Yazoo County; married; slave owner; volunteered 4/26/62; private; captured at Fort Blakely; released from Camp Townsend on parole 5/16/65.

Newman, James B.: sergeant; rolls for July–Oct. 1863, temporarily attached to Signal Corps. No other records, but on James Cowan's postwar roster.

Nix, L. B.: private; captured at Fort Blakely; released from Camp Townsend on parole 5/16/65. Only POW records.

Noland, Henry Pearise: born c. 1842 in MS; planter in Warren County; married; slave owner; volunteered 4/26/62; private; furnished a substitute (John E. Brick) and discharged 1/8/63; farmer in Warren County; died 12/27/1935 in Vicksburg.

Noland, Thomas Vaughn: born c. 1835 in Jefferson County; planter in Warren County; single; slave owner; captain, Company H, 21st Mississippi Infantry Regiment; sergeant; discharged for disability 11/13/62; afterward served as a private in Company E, 2nd Mississippi Infantry Battalion (State Troops) and in Company C, 2nd Mississippi Battalion (Harris's State Cavalry); died 5/6/1908 and buried in Gulfport.

Norris, E. S.: private; captured at Fort Blakely; released from Camp Townsend on parole 5/16/65. Only POW records.

O'Conner, Patrick: 3/13/63; private; captured at Fort Blakely; released from Camp Townsend on parole 5/16/65.

O'Reilly, Thomas: 5/3/63; private; captured at Vicksburg.

O'Riley, John R. M.: born 7/12/32 in Mallow, County Cork, Ireland; bookkeeper in Warren County; single; NS; volunteered 4/26/62; private/sergeant/private; captured at Vicksburg and Fort Blakely; released from Camp Townsend on parole 5/16/65.

Pace, L. A. B.: born 4/11/38 in MS; farmer; single; 8/6/62; private; captured at Vicksburg; AWOL since 8/23/63; died 9/25/92 and buried in Lamar County.

Parks, Samuel G.: born c. 1825 in Warren County or Ireland; overseer; single; NS; Company E, 2nd Mississippi Infantry Battalion (State Troops); 9/15 or 17/62; private; captured at Fort Blakely; released from Camp Townsend on parole 5/16/65; Warren County.

Parr, John: born c. 1831 in England; bricklayer; 6/2/62; private; health wrecked supposedly by siege of Vicksburg but no record of parole; because of illness detailed as nurse in Way Hospital, Demopolis, AL; paroled at Meridian 5/14/65; businessman in Demopolis, AL.

Pettway, John Robert: born c. 1836 in TN; farmer in Warren County; single; slave owner; Company I, 18th Mississippi Infantry Regiment; 9/17/62; private; captured near Vicksburg about 5/19/63; incarcerated at Camp Morton (IN) and Fort Delaware (DE); signed Oath of Allegiance and released 6/7/65; justice of the peace in Warren County; buried in Warren County.

Powell, Andrew J.: born 12/30/25 in MS; farmer in Warren County; married; lived with slaveholding family; 8/11/62; private; status not stated, roll for Jan.–Feb. 1863; "killed . . . by a negro" 2/4/64 and buried in Warren County.[2]

Powell, Benjamin T.: born c. 1846 in MS; student in Jasper County, TX; single; 5/25 or 29/62; private; present, roll for Mar.–Apr. 1864.

Powell, Charles W.: born c. 1836 in NC; surveyor in Warren County; slave owner; volunteered 4/26/62; private; died of typhoid fever 9/21/62 in Warren County.

Powell, John F.: born c. 1834 in MS; clerk in Warren County; private; captured in Warren County 5/28/63; sent to Military Prison, Alton, IL; exchanged and sent to City Point, VA, 6/21/63; captured at Vicksburg 5/18 or 27/64; paroled at Camp Morton (IN) prison and forwarded for exchange 3/15/65; received at Boulware's and Cox's Wharf, James River, VA, 3/23/65; admitted to General Hospital, Howard's Grove, Richmond, VA, 3/24/65 with debility and furloughed for thirty days.

Rabb, Asa M.: born c. 1843 in MS; student in Madison County; single; family owned slaves. Only records are Eggleston's diary and James Cowan's postwar roster.

Reid, Luther R.: born c. 1837 in VA; clerk in Warren County; married; lived with slaveholding family; volunteered 4/26/62; private; captured at Vicksburg and Fort Blakely; released from Camp Townsend on parole 5/16/65.

Richards, Joseph C.: residing in Madison County; slave owner; volunteered 4/26/62; private; captured in Warren County 5/18 or 21/63; paroled at Fort Delaware (DE) prison 7/3/63; joined Captain Stan Miotkowski's Independent Battery A, Pennsylvania Heavy Artillery, 7/7/63.

Russell, Frank B.: born c. 1827 in AL; farmer in Calhoun County; married; NS; Company B, 9th Mississippi Infantry Regiment; volunteered 4/26/62; private; status not stated, roll for Jan.–Feb. 1863; buried in Vicksburg.

Ryan, Edward E.: born c. 1823 in MS; laborer in Jackson County; married; NS; volunteered 9/14/62; private; "Coffin and hearse" 8/30/64 last record.

Scott, Edward W.: born c. 1847 in MS; student in Warren County; single; family owned slaves; Company H, 21st Mississippi Infantry Regiment; private; captured at Vicksburg and Fort Blakely; released from Camp Townsend on parole 5/16/65.

Scott, Silas S.: 8/28/62; private; captured at Vicksburg; present, roll for Mar.–Apr. 1864.

Shack, John D.: born in 1843 in AL; 8/2/62; private; status not stated, roll for Jan.–Feb. 1863.

Shearer, Edwin R.: born c. 1846 in AL; student in Dallas County, AL; single; family owned slaves; corporal; captured at Fort Blakely; released from Camp Townsend on parole 5/16/65; bookkeeper in Selma, AL. Only POW records.

Shellers, C. B.: born c. 1832 in OH; machinist in Warren County; single; NS; 8/3/62; private; detached, working in grist mill at Haynes's Bluff, Feb. 1863; died 4/22/86 and buried in Warren County.

Smith, Thomas William: volunteered 4/26/62; private; status not stated, roll for Jan.–Feb. 1863.

Smithart, Calvin Warren: born c. 1841 in MS; Warren County; single; NS; volunteered 4/26/62; private; present, roll for Mar.–Apr. 1864.

Smithart, George Washington: born c. 1840 in MS; Warren County; single; NS; 8/4/62; private; captured at Vicksburg; AWOL since 8/23/63.

Smithart, William Osborne: born 5/12/44 in Redwood; Warren County; single; NS; volunteered 4/26/62; private; captured at Fort Blakely; released from Camp Townsend on parole 5/16/65; died 3/4 or 14/94 at Mechanicsburg and buried in Phoenix.

Spaulding, Thomas B.: born c. 1841 in AL; clerk in De Soto Parish, LA; single; NS; private; captured at Vicksburg; paroled in Hospital No. 3 on 7/16/63; "These Prisoners were Paroled after the surrender of the Garrison of Vicksburg under the agreement of Capitulation but not sent out of our lines until the 24th Nov. 1863." Only POW records.

Spencer, Horatio N.: born in 1842 in MS; 6/1/62; private; admitted to Way Hospital, Meridian, 1/7/65 with wound and furloughed; doctor in St. Louis, MO.

Spencer, James Grafton: born 9/13/44 near Port Gibson; student; single; 5/1/63; private; captured at Fort Blakely; released from Camp Townsend on parole 5/16/65; politician in Port Gibson; U.S. Congress (1895–97); died 2/22/1926 in Port Gibson.

Spencer, Lewis M. (aka Louis Spence Flateau): born c. 1828 in Prussia; volunteered 5/12/62; corporal; paroled 6/7/65 at Shreveport, LA; fur dealer in St. Louis, MO.

Sproule, Robert: born c. 1841 in Ireland; bookbinder in Warren County; single; NS; 8/3/62; private; paroled 5/19/65 at Jackson; died in Warren County.

Stafford, James H.: born c. 1814 in NC; farmer in Warren County; married or widower; private; admitted to hospital at Macon, GA, 5/31/64; returned to duty 6/6/64; farmer in Warren County.

Stafford, Joseph Henry: born 5/28/45 in MS; student in Warren County; single; NS; 4/13/64; private; wounded at Nashville, TN; admitted to Way Hospital, Meridian, 1/13/65 and furloughed; Bolivar County; died 5/30/1922 in Memphis, TN.

Stafford, William Alexander: born c. 1842 in TN; student in Warren County; single; NS; volunteered 4/26/62; private; present, roll for Nov.–Dec. 1863.

Standard, Jesse F.: born c. 1840 in MS; Warren County; single; family owned slaves; volunteered 4/26/62; private; captured at Vicksburg and Fort Blakely; released from Camp Townsend on parole 5/16/65; farmer in Warren County; buried in Warren County.

Steele, Charles Oscar: born c. 1842 in MS; clerk in Vicksburg; single; family owned slaves; volunteered 4/26/62; private; granted sick leave for broken leg 11/1/63; admitted to hospital in Meridian with wound 1/19/65; deemed suitable for discharge having been unfit for field service for eight months because of improperly set broken leg but "fit for service as Clk Transportation Q.M. Dept" 4/11/65; Captain T. C. McMacken, Assistant Quartermaster at Canton, requested Steele be detailed to him as a clerk on 4/15/65; grocer in Vicksburg.

Steenhins, Henry L.: born c. 1846 in KY; 2/23/63; private; captured at Vicksburg; refused parole and sought to take Oath of Allegiance; sent north as a prisoner and incarcerated at Camp Morton (IN) and Camp Douglas (IL) prisons; finally allowed to take Oath of Allegiance and released 12/28/64.

Stewart, Robert: volunteered 4/26/62; private; captured in Warren County 5/18 or 5/21/63; incarcerated at Fort Delaware (DE) prison; exchanged 7/4/63; admitted to hospital in Petersburg, VA, 7/8/63 and returned to duty 7/13/63; admitted to Mississippi Soldiers' Hospital, Richmond, VA, with gunshot wound to the leg 7/14/63; admitted to General Hospital, Camp Winder, Richmond, 7/15/63; returned to duty 7/22/63 and furloughed for forty days; captured at Fort Blakely; released from Camp Townsend on parole 5/16/65.

Templeton, John Frank: born c. 1836 in MS; lawyer in Warren County; single; slave owner; 2/1/63; private; captured at Fort Blakely; released from Camp Townsend on parole 5/16/65.

Terry, John M.: farmer in Hinds County; Company E, 1st Mississippi Infantry Regiment; private; captured at Fort Blakely; released from Camp Townsend on parole 5/16/65. Only POW records.

Thomas, Charles E.: born c. 1828 in Prussia; operated beer saloon in Warren County; married; NS; volunteered 4/26/62; private; captured at Vicksburg; returned to duty from 1st Mississippi C.S.A. Hospital, Jackson, 7/8/64.

Thompson, Benjamin Franklin: private; captured at Fort Blakely; released from Camp Townsend on parole 5/16/65; bookkeeper in Selma, AL. Only POW records.

Thornton, Charles B. C.: born c. 1837 in Baltimore, MD; physician and druggist in Madison County; married; slave owner; a conscript in Brookhaven 12/31/62; examined by Army Medical Board 3/9/63 at Jackson; assigned to duty as assistant surgeon by Lieutenant General Pemberton 3/14/63; appointed assistant surgeon 7/10/63 to rank from 3/9/63, accepted 10/3/63 and confirmed 1/30/64; serving with Culbertson's Battery 10/5/63; serving with Featherston's Brigade, Jan. 1864; serving with Cowan's Battery by 3/7/64; relieved 9/26/64; serving with Myrick's Battalion in Oct. 1864; reported AWOL in Dec. 1864; transferred 2/8/65 from Direction Hospital, Meridian, to Quintard Hospital, Meridian; on duty at Quintard Hospital 3/7/65; paroled as surgeon 6/2/65 at Vicksburg; physician in Holmes County; died 1/26/1917 in Thornton.

Tompkins, George Helm: born in 1834 in Brandenburg, KY; Warren County; married; NS; volunteered 4/26/62; senior 1st lieutenant; paroled 5/12/65 at Jackson; bookkeeper in Vicksburg; died 11/20/1905 in Vicksburg.

Trainer, Thomas C.: born 6/1/36 in Ireland; laborer in Warren County; 6/10/62; private; captured at Fort Blakely; released from Camp Townsend on parole 5/16/65; salesman in Vicksburg; died 1/17/76 and buried in Water Valley, Yalobusha County.

Tribble, John F.: born c. 1847 in MS; student in Madison County; single; family owned slaves; private; captured at Fort Blakely; released from Camp Townsend on parole 5/16/65. Only POW records.

Tribble, Robert E.: born c. 1841 in MS; student in Madison County; single; family owned slaves; Company I, 10th Mississippi Infantry Regiment; volunteered 4/26/62; private/corporal; captured at Fort Blakely; released from Camp Townsend on parole 5/16/65.

Trowbridge, Albert B.: born c. 1842 in MS; apprentice saddler in Warren County; single; family owned slaves; 8/3/62; private; killed in action at Vicksburg 5/22/63 and buried in Vicksburg.

Turnbull, E. H. Bay: born c. 1845 in Charleston, SC; student; single; family owned slaves; 6/22/62; private; captured at Mechanicsburg 6/4/63 and near Vicksburg 6/15/63; transferred from Vicksburg 6/23/63; admitted to Overton U.S. Military Hospital, Memphis, TN, 6/26/63, and treated for gunshot wound; sent to prison 7/3/63; transferred to Military Prison 7/4/63; took Oath of Allegiance; released 7/7/63 "& going North"; claimed he surrendered at Haynes's Bluff 5/22/63 "because I did not want to remain in the Rebel Service any longer, but wanted to get North to my Relatives in Saint Louis and New York City" and that he spent four weeks with the 14th Illinois Cavalry Regiment before being sent to Memphis, TN, where he took the Oath of Allegiance and was released 7/7/63; arrived in St. Louis about 7/11/63; stayed with relatives until well enough to travel to New York City about 8/1/63; returned to St. Louis in November and visited one of his family's plantations at Skipwith Landing, Issaquena County, about 12/1/63; returned to St. Louis, then traveled to New Orleans, LA, to secure funds from his father's agent; returned to St. Louis about 4/6/64 and was arrested 4/18/64 under suspicion he was aiding the Confederacy; claimed to have taken the Oath of Allegiance twice prior to 4/25/64; was released from Gratiot Street Prison after posting $5,000 bond; railroad clerk in Grand Gulf; claimed to be eighteen on 12/4/62 and seventeen on 4/25/64.

Vaughn, James William: born c. 1844 in MS; student in Warren County; single; residing in slave owning household; 12/20/62; private; captured near Vicksburg 5/18/63; incarcerated in Fort Delaware (DE) prison; exchanged in Virginia in July; present, roll for Mar.–Apr. 1864; Warren County.

Wadsworth, William Richard: born c. 1846 in MS; student in Warren County; single; family owned slaves; Captain William P. Maxey's local defense company of mounted infantry (organized at Brandon, MS, 4/26/63); private; captured at Fort Blakely; released from Camp Townsend on parole 5/16/65; clerk in Vicksburg. Only POW and pension records.

Webster, Napoleon Bonaparte: born c. 1841 in MS; laborer in Warren County; single; NS; volunteered 4/26/62; private; captured and paroled near Snyder's Bluff 7/19/63; Warren County; died 2/15/1915 and buried in Warren County.

Welsh, H. George: born c. 1832 in England; blacksmith in Hinds County; single; NS; private; captured at Fort Blakely; released from Camp Townsend on parole 5/16/65. Only POW records.

West, Gabriel J.: 5/26/41 in Claiborne County; planter in Claiborne County; single; slave owner; volunteered 5/12/62; private; promoted and transferred to Trans-Mississippi Department 8/24/63.

Westcott, Edwin Glover: born 1/6/36 in England; tanner; single; 7/11/62; private; captured at Vicksburg; AWOL from Company F, 1st Detachment Paroled Prisoners, at Demopolis, AL, since 2/14/64; tanner in Yazoo County; died 11/28/1910 and buried in Yazoo County.

Whatley, Walton: born c. 1828 in AL; overseer in Warren County; married; slave owner; 7/4/62; private; wounded in the face 12/27/64; furloughed from St. Mary's Hospital, Montgomery, AL, 3/28/65 for sixty days.

Whitaker, John Wesley: born c. 1825 in TN; managed housing for railroad employees; married; NS; 12/31/62; private; captured at Vicksburg and Fort Blakely; released from Camp Townsend on parole 5/16/65; farmer in Hinds County; died 3/21/96 and buried in Jackson.

Whitaker, Warden G.: born 1/14/32 in Warren County; farmer in Warren County; married; slave owner; volunteered 4/25/62; private; captured near Vicksburg 5/16/63; incarcerated at Camp Morton (IN) and Fort Delaware (DE) prisons; paroled and exchanged in Virginia in July 1863; captured at Fort Blakely; released from Camp Townsend on parole 5/16/65; farmer in Warren County; died 11/1/1925 and buried in Warren County.

White, Thomas S.: born c. 1814 in MS; farmer in Rankin County; married; NS; private; captured at Fort Blakely; released from Camp Townsend on parole 5/16/65. Only POW records.

Whitman, John: resident of Warren County; slave owner; volunteered 4/26/62; private; captured near Vicksburg 5/18/63; incarcerated at Camp Morton (IN) and Fort Delaware (DE) prisons; paroled and exchanged in Virginia in July 1863; present, roll for Mar.–Apr. 1864.

Wiggins, Benjamin F.: born c. 1846 in MS; student in Lafayette County; single; volunteered 5/12/62; private/corporal; captured at Fort Blakely; released from Camp Townsend on parole 5/16/65.

Wilkins, John Robert "Bob": born c. 1849 in MS; student in Warren County; single; family owned slaves; 11/21/64; private; Warren County. Only record is Eggleston's diary.

Williams, Elijah B.: born c. 1830 in VA or Ireland; overseer in Warren County; married; 8/4/62; private; captured at Vicksburg; AWOL since 8/23/63; watchman in Vicksburg.

Williams, John T.: born c. 1826 in GA; overseer in Claiborne Parish, LA; single; residing in slave owning household; private; captured near Nashville, TN, 12/16/64; imprisoned at Camp Chase (OH); took Oath of Allegiance 5/10/65. Only POW records.

Willis, David C.: born c. 1837 in MS; law student in Warren County; married; slave owner and residing in slave owning household; volunteered 4/26/62; private; only record, status not listed.

Willis, Joseph B.: born c. 1830 in MS; planter in Claiborne County; single; NS; volunteered 5/12/62; private/corporal/sergeant; captured at Fort Blakely; released from Camp Townsend on parole 5/16/65.

Willis, Thomas D.: born c. 1845 in MS; student in Claiborne County; single; family owned slaves; volunteered 4/26/62; private; captured at Fort Blakely; released from Camp Townsend on parole 5/16/65; farmer in Warren County.

Winger, John D.: born c. 1841 in LA; Warren County; single; family owned slaves; 8/11/62; private; captured at Vicksburg; paroled 7/11/63 (last record).

Woods, James Thomas: born 1/24/33 in KY; overseer in Warren County; married; residing in slave owning household; volunteered 4/26/62; private; captured at Fort Blakely; released from Camp Townsend on parole 5/16/65; barkeeper in Vicksburg; buried in Yazoo County.

Wright, Charles Edwin: born 3/3/41 in Warren County; single; volunteered 4/26/62; private; captured at Big Black River 5/17/63; sent from Camp Morton (IN) prison to Fort Delaware (DE) prison 6/22/63 (last record); editor of *Vicksburg Herald*; died 11/20/1923 and buried in Vicksburg.

Wright, William W.: born c. 1843 in MS; Warren County; single; family owned slaves; 8/4/62; private; captured at Vicksburg; AWOL since 8/23/63; mechanic in Vicksburg.

Yerger, D. D.: private; captured at Fort Blakely; released from Camp Townsend on parole 5/16/65. Only POW records.

Yoste, George W.: born c. 1843 in MS; jeweler in Warren County; single; family owned slaves; volunteered 4/26/62; private; wounded and in City Hospital, Mobile, AL, when captured 4/12/65; on crutches when paroled 5/11/65; watchmaker in Vicksburg.

Young, Ebenezer H.: born c. 1838 in MS; catcher of runaway slaves in Madison Parish, LA; single; residing in slave owning household; 1/18/64; private; mortally wounded at Decatur, AL, 10/26/64.

Young, Henry T.: born c. 1835 in MS; farmer in Warren County; married; slave owner; volunteered 4/26/62; private; captured at Fort Blakely; released from Camp Townsend on parole 5/16/65; lawyer in Vicksburg.

Young, John B.: born c. 1833 in Warren County; planter in Warren County; married; slave owner; volunteered 4/26/62; private; received medical discharge 5/2/63; farmer in Warren County.

Young, William Harrison: born c. 1844 in MS; Warren County; single; family owned slaves; volunteered 4/26/62; private; status not stated, roll for Jan.–Feb. 1863.

NOTES

Some of the information documented here was obtained from subscription websites protected by password and inaccessible to nonsubscribers. In those cases, only part of the web address has been cited. The complete URL is on file with the publisher.

Notes to Preface

1. Larry J. Daniel, *Cannoneers in Gray: The Field Artillery of the Army of Tennessee, 1861–1865* (University: Univ. of Alabama Press, 1984), 225.
2. Edward Noyes, ed., "Excerpts from the Civil War Diary of E. T. Eggleston," in "Notes and Documents," *Tennessee Historical Quarterly* 17, no. 4 (Dec. 1958): 336–58.
3. Joseph T. Glatthaar, *Soldiering in the Army of Northern Virginia: A Statistical Portrait of the Troops Who Served under Robert E. Lee* (Chapel Hill: Univ. of North Carolina Press, 2011).

Notes to Prologue

1. Eggleston's first name appears as both Edmond and Edmund. He left no definitive evidence himself. When identifying himself, as in the diary, or when signing a document, it was either as "E. T.", "Trent", or "E. Trent." Though Edmund appears on his tombstone and an abundance of documents written by others, family records also disagree. His daughter Mary Read Eggleston Sample named her first child for her father, and he went by "Edmond" his entire life. In 1899, however, Mahala P. H. Eggleston Roach, wrote that her brother, "Edmund Trent Eggleston, was named for these two uncles of our father." They were Edmund, "born 17th January, 1773 after midnight of a Sunday evening," and William Trent, "born May 24th, 10. O'clock, 1777." Manuscript of M. P. H. Roach, Mar. 11, 1901, in possession of Andrew Stevens, Dallas, TX.; Tiffany Coyle to Lawrence Hewitt, e-mail, Aug. 6, 2013.
2. Roach-Eggleston Family Pedigree, Roach-Eggleston Family Papers, Old Court House Museum, Vicksburg, MS; Inventory, p. 4, of Eggleston-Roach Papers, Louisiana and Lower Mississippi Valley

Collections, Special Collections, Hill Memorial Library, Louisiana State Univ., Baton Rouge.

3. Robert Eggleston, "The Egglestons of Virginia," http://www.penn laird.com/eggleston/Rframe.html (accessed July 4, 2013); P. Hamilton Baskervill, *Andrew Meade of Ireland and Virginia; his ancestors, and some of his descendants and their connections, including sketches of the following families: Meade, Everard, Hardaway, [Eggleston,] Segar, Pettus, and Overton* (Richmond, VA: Old Dominion Press, Inc., 1921), 120–22; Application for Membership of Lemuel Eggleston Montgomery, descendant of Richard Eggleston of Virginia, to The Mississippi Society of the National Society Sons of the American Revolution, National Number 58272, State Number 98, filed Apr. 24, 1944, and certified May 15, 1944, http://search.ancestry.com/ . . . (accessed July 7, 2013; password protected site). Complete citation available from UTP.

4. Roach-Eggleston Family Pedigree, Roach-Eggleston Family Papers; "British Legion, Gildart's Troop," *The On-Line Institute for Advanced Loyalist Studies,* http://www.royalprovincial.com/military/musters/ britlegn/blgild1.htm (accessed July 4, 2013); "Appendix A," in "Appendices A through E," Mersey Heritage Society, http://www.mersey. ca/RaddallAppendices.html%23APPENDIX%20A (accessed July 4, 2013); Don Gara, "Gildart, Francis," in *Biographical Sketches of the Cavalry Officers of the British Legion,* http:/home.golden.net/~marg/ bansite/odds/bl_cavalry.html (accessed July 4, 2013); "Robert Stark," *lewiscomplete,* http://trees.ancestry.com/ . . . (accessed July 7, 2013; password protected site). Complete citation available from UTP.

5. "Edwards to Feltus," pp. 1, 5, 6, *Mississippi, Wilkinson County Newspaper Slave Ads, 1823–1849,* http://search.ancestry.com/ . . . (accessed July 7, 2013; password protected site). Complete citation available from UTP; D. H. Eggleston, "Wilkinson 1825," *Mississippi State and Territorial Censuses, 1792–1866,* http://interactive.ancestry.com/ . . . (accessed July 7, 2013; password protected site). Complete citation available from UTP; Roach-Eggleston Family Pedigree, Roach-Eggleston Family Papers; D. H. Eggleston, p. 37, 1830 Schedule of Persons, Mississippi, Wilkinson, Not Stated, R01171, Fifth Census of the United States, 1830, M-19, National Archives and Records Service, Washington, DC.

6. "Edwards to Feltus," pp. 1, 5, *Mississippi, Wilkinson County Newspaper Slave Ads, 1823–1849.* It should be noted that according to the 1840 census, Elizabeth Eggleston owned fourteen slaves. E. H. Eggleston, p. 1, 1840 Schedule of persons, Mississippi, Wilkinson, Not Stated, Roll 217, Sixth Census of the United States, 1840, M704, National Archives and Records Service, Washington, DC.

7. Elizabeth S. Eggleston, p. 56, Free Schedules, Mississippi, Warren, Vicksburg, Roll 382, 1850 Federal Population Census, M432, National Archives and Records Service, Washington, DC; Roach-Eggleston Family Pedigree, Roach-Eggleston Family Papers.

8. Elizabeth S. Eggleston, p. 11, Slave Schedules, Mississippi, Warren, Vicksburg, Roll 389, 1850 Federal Population Census, M432, National Archives and Records Service, Washington, DC.

9. Little is known about Mary Susan Read. She was born in Kentucky on May 2, 1835. Her father was born in England and her mother in Kentucky. Application for Membership of Lemuel Eggleston Montgomery; Trent Eggleston, p. 58; 1880 Population Schedule, Mississippi, Warren, Vicksburg, Roll 667, T9, National Archives and Records Service, Washington, DC.

10. See Appendix B, page 91; Roach-Eggleston Family Pedigree, Roach-Eggleston Family Papers.

11. See p. 139n81 and 149n16.

12. T. Eggleston, p. 89, 1860 Free Schedule, Mississippi, Warren, Not Stated, Roll 592, 1860 Federal Population Census, M653, National Archives and Records Service, Washington, DC; T. Eggleston, p. 129, 1860, Slave Schedule, Mississippi, Warren, Not Stated, Roll 603, 1860 Federal Population Census, M653, National Archives and Records Service, Washington, DC.

13. H. C. Clarke, "General Directory for the City of Vicksburg: Containing the Name and Address of Every Professional and Business Man and Resident of the City," http://homepages.rootsweb.ancestry.com/~holler/dir1860.htm%20 (accessed July 5, 2013); Roach-Eggleston Family Pedigree, Roach-Eggleston Family Papers.

14. E. Eggleston, p. 7, 1860 Free Schedule, Mississippi, Warren, Vicksburg, Roll 592, M653; Robt Eggleston, p. 2, 1860 Slave Schedule, Mississippi, Warren, Vicksburg, Roll 603, M653.

15. *Population of The United States in 1860; compiled from the original returns of The Eighth Census, under the direction of the secretary of the interior, By Joseph C. G. Kennedy, superintendent of census.* (Washington, DC: Government Printing Office, 1864), 270–72.

16. Dunbar Rowland, *The Official and Statistical Register of the State of Mississippi, 1908* (Nashville, TN: Brandon Print. Co., 1908), 446, 485, 495, 496, 497, 597, 628, 642, 830, 832, 847, 880.

17. *Population of The United States in 1860,* 264–65, 272.

18. Albert Burton Moore, *Conscription and Conflict in the Confederacy* (1924: repr., New York: Hillary House Publishers Ltd., 1963), 13, 14–15.

Notes to Volume 1

1. William Temple Withers was colonel of the 1st Mississippi Light Artillery Regiment. Born in Harrison County, Kentucky, on January 8, 1825, and educated at Bacon College in his native state, Withers practiced law in Cynthiana, Kentucky, before moving to Jackson. A lawyer and planter by 1846, he served as an officer in the Mexican War and was wounded at the Battle of Buena Vista. In 1860 he owned $75,000 real and $240,000 personal property, including eleven slaves. In the early months of the Civil War, Withers acted as a brigadier general in charge of Camp Boone, a training camp just south of the Tennessee-Kentucky border for Confederate volunteers from the Bluegrass State during Kentucky's period of neutrality. Early in 1862, the secretary of war requested him to raise a regiment of artillery, and on March 22 became captain of Company A, 1st Mississippi Light Artillery. He became colonel of the regiment on May 14 and distinguished himself during the Battle of Chickasaw Bluff, the siege of Vicksburg, and at Mobile, Alabama. Often absent from duty because of the wounds sustained during the Mexican War, Withers was assigned to the Invalid Corps on March 5, 1865. After the cessation of hostilities, he returned to Jackson and resumed his law practice. In 1871, he moved to Lexington, Kentucky, where he bred horses until his death on June 16, 1889. An obituary described him as "a thorough Christian gentleman, a noble and honest man." Bruce S. Allardice, *Confederate Colonels: A Biographical Register* (Columbia: Univ. of Missouri Press, 2008), 404; W. T. Withers, p. 2, 1860 Free Schedule, Mississippi, Hinds, Township 5, Roll 582, M653; W. T. Withers, p. 1, 1860 Slave Schedule, Mississippi, Hinds, Township 5, Roll 597, M653.

2. Cowan's company became Company G, 1st Mississippi Light Artillery Regiment.

3. Mahala Roach, 1862 Diary, May 12, 17 and 20, Roach and Eggleston Family Papers, 1825–1905, in Southern Historical Collection, Louis Round Wilson Special Collections Library, Univ. of North Carolina, Chapel Hill.

4. A native of North Carolina, in 1860 Thomas J. Finney was a 48-year-old merchant living in Warren County with his wife and five children. He owned real estate valued at $50,000 and a like amount of personal property, including fifty slaves. T. J. Finney, p. 37, 1860 Free Schedule, Mississippi, Warren, Not Stated, Roll 592, M653; T. J. Finney, pp. 29–30, 1860 Slave Schedule, Mississippi, Warren, Not Stated, Roll 603, M653. His son, Thomas J. Finney Jr., served as a private in Company C, 28th Mississippi Cavalry Regiment. Service record of Thomas J. Finney, Twenty-eighth Cavalry, Roll 55, Compiled Service Records of Confederate Soldiers Who Served in Organizations from the State

of Mississippi, M-269, War Department Collection of Confederate Records, RG 109, National Archives and Records Service, Washington, D.C. (hereafter cited as CSR MS).

5. Though June 28 is generally given as the start of Union operations against Vicksburg, Flag Officer David G. Farragut arrived below the town on May 24. Before returning to New Orleans, he ordered six gunboats to blockade the Mississippi River below Vicksburg and to occasionally bombard its defenses. Charles Lee Lewis, *David Glasgow Farragut: Our First Admiral* (Annapolis, MD: U.S. Naval Institute, 1943), 87–88.

6. The transcriber of Eggleston's diary appears to have misread the date of this entry and the following. Because Union mortars shelled the town on June 26–27, this entry was probably made for June 25. Lewis, *Farragut,* 97.

7. The "Fort Hill" mentioned by Eggleston is almost certainly what today is called the Third Louisiana Redan, situated on the Jackson road not far from the Illinois Monument. "During the war, what we call today Fort Hill, was known as Fort Nogales, whereas what we call the Third Louisiana Redan was always known as Fort Hill as it is the highest eminence in Vicksburg." Terrence Winschel to Lawrence Hewitt, e-mail, June 11, 2013.

8. The date for this entry is erroneous, probably the result of the transcriber having misread the previous entry. It should be June 28, the day Farragut's fleet ran the batteries. Lewis, *Farragut,* 98.

9. Born in Mississippi about 1826, E. B. Willis had a wife and five children in 1860. A farmer in Warren County, he claimed to own $25,000 real and $9,000 personal property, but the later does not reflect the true value of his fifty-one slaves. Willis enlisted at Kosciusko, Attala County, on September 15, 1863, in Company E, 5th Mississippi Cavalry Regiment. He was made a corporal by October 1 and deserted on October 26. He returned to duty, was reduced in rank to private, and deserted on February 4, 1864. By the time he returned to duty, his unit was reassigned as Company I, 18th Regiment Mississippi Cavalry. On September 1, he was detached and assigned to "Post duty." He was paroled at Gainesville, Alabama, on May 12, 1865. Edwin C. Bearss, *The Vicksburg Campaign,* 3 vols. (Dayton, OH: Morningside House, Inc., 1985–86), 3:748, 1428; E. B. Willis, p. 3, 1860 Free Schedule, Mississippi, Warren, Not Stated, Roll 592, M653; E. B. Willis, p. 2, 1860 Slave Schedule, Mississippi, Warren, Not Stated, Roll 603, M653; Service record of E. B. Willis, Fifth Cavalry, Roll 30, CSR MS; Service record of E. B. Willis, Eighteenth Cavalry, Roll 51, CSR MS.

10. The Willis place was located near the city cemetery (Cedar Hill). From this position, the company could "make a quick movement into the city

to thwart any attempt by the Federal infantry that accompanied Farragut in the summer of 1862 from making a landing." Terrence Winschel to Lawrence Hewitt, e-mail, Apr. 7, 2013.

11. Flag Officer Charles H. Davis's fleet joined Farragut's above Vicksburg on July 1, and his mortar boats began shelling the Confederate defenses late on July 2. Lewis, *Farragut,* 105, 106.

12. Contemporaries also described this site as a ridge known as Magnolia Grove and as Mr. Marshall's property. Special Order 33, Third District Headquarters, Brig. Gen. Martin L. Smith, Aug. 7, 1862, and Lt. B. M. Harrod, A.D.C., to Col. W. T. Withers, Aug. 7, 1862, both in Order Book, 1st Mississippi Light Artillery Regiment, Mississippi Department of Archives and History, Jackson.

13. Based on Eggleston's comments regarding the deaths of other relatives and friends, it is noteworthy that he failed to mention his cousin. A Mississippi native, Harry P. Eggleston was twenty-four, single, and working as a clerk in Vicksburg when he enlisted on February 15, 1862, in Company A, 21st Mississippi Infantry Regiment. He was killed during the Seven Days' Battles near Richmond, Virginia. Mahala Roach, 1862 Diary, July 12, Roach and Eggleston Family Papers; Service record of Harry P. Eggleston, Twenty-first Infantry, Roll 293, CSR MS.

14. Though the *Arkansas* successfully passed through the combined Union fleets above Vicksburg, the Confederate ironclad was badly damaged in the process. Edwin C. Bearss, *Rebel Victory at Vicksburg* (Little Rock, AR: Vicksburg Centennial Commemoration Commission, 1963), 225.

15. Born in Kentucky on May 27, 1817, Isaac N. Brown joined the U.S. Navy in 1834. Resigning his commission as a lieutenant in 1861, he joined the Confederate navy at that rank and was still a lieutenant on July 15, 1862. After the war he tried farming in Coahoma County before moving to Navarro County, Texas, in 1883. He died on September 1, 1899, and is buried in Corsicana, Texas. "Isaac Newton Brown of Navarro County, Texas," *Navarro County Texas: Genealogical and Historical Web Site,* http://www.rootsweb.ancestry.com/~txnavarr/biographies/b/brown_isaac_newton.htm (accessed July 7, 2013).

16. For an excellent account of the naval operations on July 15, see Bearss, *Rebel Victory at Vicksburg,* 204–44.

17. USS *Essex.* Bearss, *Rebel Victory at Vicksburg,* 262.

18. Cowan's company was ordered to relocate so that their campsite could be taken over by the battalions of heavy artillery manning the lower batteries along the Mississippi River. Special Order 33, Third District Headquarters, Brig. Gen. Martin L. Smith, Aug. 7, 1862, in Order Book, 1st Mississippi Light Artillery Regiment.

19. Though the 1860 census lists no real or personal property for Sarah Cowan, she owned eighty-eight slaves. She was the mother of **James Jones Cowan** and **Warren F. Cowan.** Sarah Cowan, p. 62, 1860 Free

Schedule, Mississippi, Warren, Not Stated, Roll 592, M653; Sarah Cowan, pp. 62–64, 1860 Free Schedule, Mississippi, Warren, Not Stated, Roll 592, M653.

20. Mahala Roach, 1862 Diary, Aug. 9 and 11, Roach and Eggleston Family Papers.

21. Sergeant **Thomas Vaughn Noland** suffered from chronic bronchitis and would be discharged for disability at Vicksburg on November 13, 1862.

22. U.S. Navy War Records Office, *Official Records of the Union and Confederate Navies in the War of the Rebellion,* 31 vols. (Washington, DC: Government Printing Office, 1894–1927), series 1, 19:181. Hereafter cited as *ORN;* all references are to series 1 unless otherwise stated.

23. No record of this particular engagement was found, but it was not uncommon for Confederate troops on both banks of the Mississippi River to open fire on passing Federal transports and, in turn, come under fire when a warship steamed within range. Warren E. Grabau, *Ninety-eight Days: A Geographer's View of the Vicksburg Campaign* (Knoxville: Univ. of Tennessee Press, 2000), 31.

24. Mahala Roach, 1862 Diary, Sept. 6, Roach and Eggleston Family Papers.

25. Elizabeth Stark Gildart Eggleston resided at the corner of Fayette and Farmer streets in Vicksburg. H. C. Clarke, "General Directory for the City of Vicksburg: Containing the Name and Address of Every Professional and Business Man and Resident of the City."

26. Apparently Eggleston is referring to having the cheeks cut down. The cheeks, one on each side of the cannon tube, hold the barrel in place. These would need to be cut down in the rear in order to allow the tube to be elevated, if the tube was larger near the breech than the carriage had been designed for. Phillip Faller to Lawrence Hewitt, e-mail, Mar. 2, 2013.

27. He died of typhoid fever.

28. Major General Thomas J. "Stonewall" Jackson actually captured over 12,700 Union troops, 47 pieces of artillery, and 13,000 small arms. National Park Service, "1862 Battle of Harpers Ferry," in *Harpers Ferry: National Historical Park, WV, VA, MD,* http://www.nps.gov/hafe/historyculture/1862-battle-of-harpers-ferry.htm (accessed July 4, 2013).

29. Private **Luther R. Reid** had been sent home on sick leave in August.

30. The election was for county officials: circuit clerk, probate clerk, treasurer, assessor, coroner, ranger, and surveyor. Jason Niles, "October 6, 1862, Monday: *Election Day,*" and "October 7, 1862, Tuesday," both in *Diary of Jason Niles, June 22, 1861–December 31, 1864: Electronic Edition,* Academic Affairs Library, Univ. of North Carolina at Chapel Hill, http://docsouth.unc.edu/imls/niles/niles.html%20 (accessed July 31, 2013).

31. Sergeant **Archibald N. Craig**.
32. Born in Scotland about 1822, Thomas P. Bruce lived with his wife and two children in Warren County in 1860, where he worked as an overseer on the Purvis estate. He owned $20,000 personal property. P. P. Bruce, p. 57, 1860 Free Schedule, Mississippi, Warren, Not Stated, Roll 592, M653.
33. Tennessee-born John Jones Pettus became a planter and politician in Mississippi. A fire-eating secessionist, he served three terms as governor, the first for five days in 1854 and consecutively from 1859–1863. He joined the army after leaving office. Never requesting amnesty, he died a fugitive in 1867. National Park Service, "John Jones Pettus," http://www.nps.gov/resources/person.htm?id=25 (accessed July 4, 2013).
34. Mahala Roach, 1862 Diary, Dec. 20, Roach and Eggleston Family Papers.
35. Ibid., Dec. 21.
36. Mrs. Annie E. Lake's plantation was located between Chickasaw Bayou and the Yazoo River. The Federals, three brigades under Brigadier General George W. Morgan (2nd Division, 13th Corps), actually landed north of Lake's plantation at Johnson's plantation, but the fighting occurred on Lake's plantation. Bearss, *The Vicksburg Campaign*, 1:152, 159.
37. The Confederates lost 58 killed, 117 wounded, and 19 missing; the Union 213 killed, 1,016 wounded, and 561 missing. Ibid., 224–29.
38. Mahala Roach, 1862 Diary, Dec. 29, Roach and Eggleston Family Papers.
39. Brigadier General Louis Hébert's Brigade consisted of the 3rd and 21st Louisiana, 36th , 37th, 38th, and 43rd Mississippi infantry regiments, the 7th Mississippi Infantry Battalion, Appeal Arkansas Battery, Company H, 1st Mississippi Light Artillery, and Tobin's Tennessee Battery. Bearss, *The Vicksburg Campaign*, 1:226.
40. Colonel Wirt Adams's Mississippi Cavalry Regiment. Ibid., 225.
41. General Braxton Bragg fought the indecisive Battle of Murfreesboro, Tennessee, December 31, 1862–January 2, 1863. Confederate cavalry leaders were more successful. Major General Earl Van Dorn destroyed Major General Ulysses S. Grant's supply depot at Holly Springs on December 20, while Brigadier General Nathan Bedford Forrest disrupted Union supply lines farther north in West Tennessee and Brigadier General John Hunt Morgan did the same in central Kentucky.
42. Mary Farrar Stark Gildart Wilkinson was Eggleston's mother's sister. She and her husband, Robert A. Wilkinson Sr., were both Mississippi natives. He operated a sugar plantation in Plaquemines Parish, Louisiana, that apparently belonged to his father, Joseph B. Wilkinson Sr. Robert claimed only $1,200 in personal property in 1860, including one slave. Born on December 16, 1809, Robert died on August 30,

1862; he was survived by his father, who died on November 8, 1865. According to Eggleston's diary, Mary passed through Federal lines at least twice following the fall of New Orleans. "Mary Farrar Stark Gildart (Wilkinson)," *Jefferson College Board of Trustees Members,* http://trees.ancestry.com/pt/RequestTreeAccess.aspx?tid=4272226 6&pid=19918035062%20 (accessed July 7, 2013; password protected site); Robert A. Wilkinson, p. 17, 1860 Free Schedule, Louisiana, Plaquemines, Not Stated, Roll 414, M653; Robert A. Wilkinson, p. 5, 1860 Slave Schedule, Louisiana, Plaquemines, Not Stated, Roll 430, M653; Ben Achee, *1865 Orleans Parish Death Index–O through Z,* http://files.usgwarchives.net/la/orleans/vitals/deaths/index /1865dioz.txt (accessed July 7, 2013); "Robert Andrews Wilkinson," Smolenski Family Tree, http://trees.ancestry.com/tree/22740791/ person/1445777568 (accessed July 23, 2014).

43. Confederate assumptions were correct this time. Union troops landed in Louisiana at Young's Point on January 23 intending to open up the canal across the base of De Soto Point opposite Vicksburg. Popularly known as "Butler's ditch," the canal had been started by Brigadier General Thomas Williams the previous summer. Bearss, *The Vicksburg Campaign,* 1:436–37.

44. At this time, Thomas Railey Markham was serving as chaplain for the 1st Mississippi Light Artillery. Born in Fayette in 1828, he spent his early years in Vicksburg. He entered the Princeton Theological Seminary in 1850 and, in 1856, became the minister of Lafayette Presbyterian Church in New Orleans, Louisiana. After the Civil War, he resumed his duties at that church and continued in that position until 1894. He assisted the Episcopal bishops of Mississippi and Louisiana at the funeral of Jefferson Davis. Receipt for pay, Jan. 15, 1863, papers of Thos. R. Markham, Roll 248, Unfiled Papers and Slips Belonging in Confederate Compiled Service Records, M-347, War Department Collection of Confederate Records, RG 109, National Archives and Records Service, Washington, DC (hereafter cited as UPSBCCSR); Inventory, p. 4, of Markham (Thomas R.) Papers, Louisiana and Lower Mississippi Valley Collections, Special Collections, Hill Memorial Library, Louisiana State Univ., Baton Rouge; Robert Lowry and William H. McCardle, *A History of Mississippi, from the Discovery of the Great River by Hernando De Soto, including the Earliest Settlement made by the French, Under Iberville, to The Death of Jefferson Davis* (Jackson, MS: R. H. Henry & Co., 1891), 644.

45. The *Queen of the West* had steamed downriver to destroy the CSS *City of Vicksburg* with the intention of returning upstream. Damaged during its unsuccessful attempt, the *Queen* continued downriver. For a full account of the operation, see Bearss, *The Vicksburg Campaign,* 1:618–21.

46. The vessel was the ironclad USS *Indianola*. Its captain, Lieutenant Commander George W. Brown, recalled, "The weather was all I could desire." Quoted in ibid., 648.

47. **Thomas Vaughan Noland** had previously served in Company G, 1st Mississippi Light Artillery Regiment. At this time he apparently was a private in Company C, 2nd Mississippi Battalion (Harris's) State Cavalry. H. Grady Howell Jr., *For Dixie Land I'll Take My Stand! A Muster Listing of All Known Mississippi Confederate Soldiers, Sailors and Marines*, 3 vols. ([Madison, MS]: Chickasaw Bayou Press, 1998), 3:2235.

48. W. E. Hall was born in Tennessee about 1832. In 1860, he and his Canadian-born wife A. J. were living with P. A. and A. F. Montgomery. P. [a.k.a. Joseph] A. Montgomery was a major planter in Claiborne County who owned $25,000 real and $200,000 personal property, including 181 slaves. Hall enlisted in Company D, 2nd Mississippi Infantry Battalion (State Troops), at Port Gibson on May 31, 1862. Though listed as having been discharged prior to December 1, 1862, he was listed as "Absent without leave" on the muster roll for Dec. 1, 1862–Mar. 1, 1863. W. E. Hall, p. 11, 1860 Free Schedule, Mississippi, Claiborne, Police District 5, Roll 580, M653; J. A. Montgomery, pp. 25–27, 1860 Slave Schedule, Mississippi, Claiborne, Police District 5, Roll 596, M653; Service record of W. E. Hall, Second Battalion, Infantry (State Troops), Roll 127, CSR MS.

49. Born on September 2, 1811, in Calvert County, Maryland, Benson Heighe Blake was a large planter in Warren County in 1860. He owned $300,000 real and $200,000 personal property, including 169 slaves on three plantations. Though never nominated by President Jefferson Davis, Blake was regarded as a colonel in the Confederate army. Brigadier General Martin L. Smith appointed him provost marshal of Vicksburg on June 26, 1862, and he also served as an aide to Brigadier General John C. Breckinridge. Though his compensation appears to have been limited to feed for two horses for his personal use, Blake profited from the war by selling goods and services to the Confederate government—lumber and tools for the construction of defenses at Snyder's Bluff; cattle, sheep, corn, and pickle pork for soldiers' rations and fodder for their horses and mules—and leasing his steam mill and hands to grind corn and his wagons for hauling. He died at Blakely plantation, Warren County, on July 26, 1873. B. Blake, p. 13, 1860 Free Schedule, Mississippi, Warren, Not Stated, Roll 592, M653; B. Blake, pp. 9–11, 1860 Slave Schedule, Mississippi, Warren, Not Stated, Roll 592, M653; Blake Girl, "Benson Blake," Find A Grave, http://www. findagrave.com/cgi-bin/fg.cgi?page=gr&GSln=BL&GSpartial=1&GS byrel=all&GSst=27&GScntry=4&GSsr=4241&GRid=13610756&" (accessed July 5, 2013); Papers of B. Blake, Roll 29, UPSBCCSR.

50. Louis Hébert was born in Iberville Parish, Louisiana, on March 13, 1820. After graduating third in the West Point class of 1845, he served in the engineers before resigning in 1846 to run his father's sugar plantation. Active in the state militia 1847–1861, he entered the Confederate army as colonel of the 3rd Louisiana Infantry Regiment. He saw action at Wilson's Creek, Missouri, and was captured during the Battle of Pea Ridge, Arkansas. Following his exchange, he was promoted to brigadier general on May 26, 1862, and participated in the Iuka and Corinth campaigns that fall, before being assigned to the Vicksburg defenses. Captured when the town surrendered on July 4, 1863, Hébert was assigned to the Army of Tennessee after being exchanged. He was serving in North Carolina when the war ended. Returning to Louisiana, he worked as a newspaper editor and teacher, dying on January 7, 1901. William C. Davis and Julie Hoffman, eds., *The Confederate General,* 6 vols. (Harrisburg, PA: National Historical Society, 1991), 3:82–83.

51. Horace E. Barnes was born in Pennsylvania about 1829. In 1850 he worked on his father's farm in Susquehanna County, Pennsylvania, but went back to school and in 1860 was working as a civil engineer in Warren County. He owned $1,000 real and $1,000 personal property. On June 3, 1862, he was appointed 1st lieutenant and ordnance officer for the 1st Mississippi Light Artillery Regiment. He served with the unit for the remainder of the war and was captured and paroled at Vicksburg in 1863. Also see p. 152n26. Horace Barnes, p. 11, 1860 Free Schedule, Pennsylvania, Susquehanna, Gibson, Roll 829, M432; H. E. Barns, p. 28, 1860 Free Schedule, Mississippi, Warren, Not Stated, Roll 592, M653; Service record of H. E. Barnes, First Light Artillery, Roll 81, CSR MS.

52. William H. Brown was twenty-two when he enlisted in New Orleans on March 12, 1861, as a private in Company D, 1st Louisiana Heavy Artillery Regiment. Appointed 3rd sergeant April 4, 1861, he was sentenced on February 25, 1863. Service record of William H. Brown, First Heavy Artillery, Roll 35, Compiled Service Records of Confederate Soldiers Who Served in Organizations from the State of Louisiana, M-320, War Department Collection of Confederate Records, RG 109, National Archives and Records Service, Washington, DC (hereafter cited as CSR LA).

53. Fort Jackson was located on the west bank of the Mississippi River below New Orleans. The city surrendered on April 25, 1862, and four days later the garrison of Fort Jackson mutinied, forcing their commander, Brigadier General Johnson K. Duncan, to surrender the fort on April 30.

54. William M. Estelle was captain of Company H, 38th Mississippi Cavalry Regiment. At the time of the execution, he was serving as "Provost

Marshal Post Snyders Mills." Service record of William M. Estelle, Thirty-eighth Cavalry, Roll 63, CSR MS.

55. Dennis Kean was twenty-eight when he enlisted in New Orleans on February 28, 1861, in Company B, 1st Louisiana Heavy Artillery Regiment. Mustered in as a sergeant on March 24, he was demoted to private by April 20, 1861. He was sentenced on February 25, 1863. Service record of Dennis Kean, First Heavy Artillery, Roll 40, CSR LA.

56. At this time Major General Carter L. Stevenson was commanding the 2nd Military District, Department of Mississippi and East Louisiana, with headquarters at Vicksburg. His command included his own division, as well as those of Major Generals Martin Luther Smith and Dabney Maury. As these troops were widely dispersed, it would have been impossible for all of them to witness the execution. Actually, there were at least three separate executions, one for each of the three divisions. U.S. War Department, *The War of the Rebellion: A Compilation of the Official Records of the Union and Confederate Armies,* 128 vols. (Washington, DC: Government Printing Office, 1880–1901), series 1, 24, pt. 3:647 (hereafter cited as *OR;* all references are to series 1 unless otherwise stated); Isaac E. Herring to [wife], Mar. 8, 1863, in Isaac E. Herring Letters, Old Court House Museum, Vicksburg, MS.

57. **Vanerson DeMoss**.

58. No record of this engagement was found. It may have been that the "boat" was a barge loaded with coal, which were periodically allowed to drift downstream unmanned to resupply the Union vessels operating between Vicksburg and Port Hudson, Louisiana. *ORN,* 24:443.

59. Grant's Yazoo Pass Expedition reached Fort Pemberton via the Tallahatchie River on March 11. That Confederate bastion prevented Union vessels from entering the Yazoo River above Vicksburg. The Federals actually had eight gunboats but were in the Tallahatchie rather than the Yazoo River. Bearss, *The Vicksburg Campaign,* 1:520.

60. The USS *Kosciusko,* also called the *Lancaster,* and the USS *Switzerland* were both rams; neither was an ironclad or a transport. *ORN,* ser. 2, 1:123, 218; Bearss, *The Vicksburg Campaign,* 1:520.

61. Though credited to the state of Arkansas, the Appeal Battery was the second artillery unit raised in Memphis, Tennessee. Sponsored by the *Appeal,* ten of its employees enlisted in the unit, half of the newspaper's staff. "Confederate Park, Memphis, TN. getting new cannons," Steen Cannons, Ashland, KY, http://steencannons.com/confederate-park-memphis-tn-getting-new cannons/ (accessed July 4, 2013).

62. 1st Mississippi Sharpshooter Battalion. Bearss, *The Vicksburg Campaign,* 1:573–74.

63. Born in Pennsylvania on August 10, 1814, John C. Pemberton graduated twenty-seventh in the West Point class of 1837. After a varied and distinguished career, he resigned from the U.S. Army in 1861 and

joined the Provisional Army of Virginia, training cavalry in Richmond. Shortly thereafter he entered Confederate service as a colonel and was assigned to train artillery units at Norfolk, Virginia. Promoted to brigadier general on June 17, 1861, he was transferred that fall to South Carolina. When General Robert E. Lee was transferred to Virginia on March 2, 1862, Pemberton, now a major general, was placed in command of the Department of South Carolina, Georgia, and East Florida. In October, he was promoted to lieutenant general and transferred to command the Department of Mississippi and East Louisiana, establishing his headquarters in Jackson. After surrendering Vicksburg on July 4, 1863, Pemberton was unable to secure a command commensurate with his rank and resigned. President Davis immediately appointed him a lieutenant colonel of artillery. Bankrupt at the end of the war, his mother provided him with a farm in Virginia, which he worked from 1866 to 1875. He then moved in with relatives in Pennsylvania, where he died on July 13, 1881. Davis and Hoffman, eds., *The Confederate General,* 5:8–9.

64. Born in Virginia on September 21, 1817, Carter L. Stevenson ranked forty-second out of West Point's 45 graduates in 1838. After fighting in the Mexican War and Indians in both Florida and Texas, he was serving in Utah when the Civil War erupted. He entered the Confederate army in June of 1861 as a major and quickly rose to colonel in command of the 53rd Virginia Infantry Regiment. After serving in Virginia, Stevenson was promoted to brigadier general and transferred to the Department of East Tennessee in the spring of 1862. After capturing Cumberland Gap on the Tennessee-Kentucky border, he was promoted to major general and, with his division, was transferred to the Army of Tennessee and then, in December, to Vicksburg. Captured there on July 4, 1863, Stevenson rejoined the Army of Tennessee following his exchange, serving with that army for the remainder of the war. Returning to Virginia, he worked as an engineer until his death on August 15, 1888. Ibid., 6:8–9.

65. In early 1863, the 1st Mississippi Light Artillery Regiment was officially assigned to Brigadier General Stephen D. Lee's Brigade. Actually, the eleven companies were widely dispersed. Two, including Eggleston's, were at Haynes's Bluff; three at Port Hudson, Louisiana; and the remaining six scattered about Mississippi. Though Eggleston writes "first corps," battalion would be more correct. He views the eight companies in Mississippi as the first, and the three companies at Port Hudson as constituting the second battalion. He assumed, possibly influenced by a desire to be stationed closer to home, that Stevenson could only find use for eight united companies at Vicksburg. *OR*, 24, pt. 3:624, 703–706, 1148.

66. Later designated the 29th Louisiana Infantry Regiment, it was commanded by Colonel Allen Thomas. Though part of Lee's Brigade, it

obviously was left behind when the balance of the brigade moved out on March 24. Also see p. 138n67. Ibid., 704.

67. Eggleston undoubtedly goes on to describe the success of Brigadier General Stephen D. Lee's expedition to Deer Creek (March 24–29), which negated the need for the 28th Louisiana Infantry Regiment to reinforce him. Ibid., pt. 1:461–64.

68. There is no record of a Mark ever serving with the company; **Joseph Granville Hicks**; **Silas Scott**; probably **Charles Harris**.

69. Though Banks removed the majority of his troops from Baton Rouge following Farragut's passage of the Port Hudson batteries on March 14, he left a sizeable garrison in the town. Lawrence Lee Hewitt, *Port Hudson: Confederate Bastion on the Mississippi* (Baton Rouge: Louisiana State Univ. Press, 1987), 108.

70. Along with troops under Lee and Lieutenant Colonel Samuel W. Ferguson, Brigadier General Winfield S. Featherston's Brigade participated in the successful expedition along Deer Creek. Following the Federal withdrawal, Featherston was ordered to return with his brigade to Haynes's Bluff. Also see p. 138n67. Bearss, *The Vicksburg Campaign,* 1:588–89, 595.

71. Rather than Mobile, Union Major General Nathaniel P. Banks, commanding the Department of the Gulf, turned his attention to western Louisiana. Hewitt, *Port Hudson,* 108.

72. It is remarkable that Markham knew this on March 29 because Stevenson did not issue Special Order No. 79 until the following day. The order stated: "The Batteries of the 1st Miss. Reg't Light Art will be concentrated near Haynes Bluff under the command of Col W. T. Withers. All orders &c for this command will as far as practicable go through him." Before the six companies scattered about Mississippi could be relocated to Haynes's Bluff, however, Federal operations brought about a different redeployment of the companies. Order Book, 1st Mississippi Light Artillery Regiment.

73. As soon as Featherston's Brigade reached the Yazoo River the men were loaded aboard steamboats and transported upstream to Fort Pemberton, which protected Greenwood, where they arrived on April 1. Bearss, *The Vicksburg Campaign,* 1:589.

74. Eggleston was right to be skeptical. The Federals had only 12,600 soldiers killed, wounded, or missing at Fredericksburg. National Park Service, "Battle of Fredericksburg," *Fredericksburg & Spotsylvania: National Military Park, Virginia,* http://www.nps.gov/frsp/fredhist. htm (accessed July 4, 2013).

75. The Federal flotilla was personally commanded by Acting Rear Admiral David D. Porter aboard the ironclad *Tuscumbia.* Bearss, *The Vicksburg Campaign,* 2:85.

76. Major General William W. Loring.
77. This is an excellent example of Pemberton's indecisiveness in responding to various Federal operations even before Grant crossed the Mississippi River below Vicksburg on April 30.
78. **Archibald N. Craig** was currently serving as the assistant commissary of subsistence for the regiment.
79. The rumor was false, but it reflects the success of Grant's diversionary tactics, albeit with Porter's aid, to prevent the Confederates from shifting troops south into a better position to counter his impending crossing of the Mississippi below Vicksburg.
80. Robert Andrews Wilkinson Jr. was the son of Eggleston's Aunt Mary Wilkinson. Though Bob, sixteen or seventeen at this time, spent time with Cowan's battery, there is no official record of his ever being enrolled in the unit. Robert A. Wilkinson, p. 17, 1860 Free Schedule, Louisiana, Plaquemines, Not Stated, Roll 414, M653.
81. Apparently Woodfield was the name of Sophia G. Fox's plantation in Warren County.
82. Actually, the entire structure was swept downstream. The elaborate barrier had prevented Federal vessels from passing up the Yazoo River. The raft at Yazoo City was towed downriver and replaced the lost one on April 24. Bearss, *The Vicksburg Campaign*, 2:102–3.
83. The armada consisted of seven gunboats, three transports, and several barges, including one loaded with ammunition. Though the Confederates claimed to have destroyed two transports, only one was destroyed, and one barge loaded with coal was sunk. Ibid., 58–59, 68, 70, 73.
84. A resident of Jackson, James P. Parker had been elected lieutenant colonel of the 1st Mississippi Light Artillery Regiment on May 14, 1862. Along with Companies B, F, and K, 1st Mississippi Light Artillery Regiment, he was stationed at Port Hudson. Captured on July 9, 1863, he remained in prison until July 21, 1865. Service record of James P. Parker, First Light Artillery, Roll 88, CSR MS.
85. Dr. R. B. Scott was born in Virginia about 1818. A resident of Warren County in 1860, he owned $5,000 real and $20,000 personal property, including eighteen slaves. R. B. Scott, p. 72, 1860 Free Schedule, Mississippi, Warren, Not Stated, Roll 592, M653; R. B. Scott, p. 96, 1860 Slave Schedule, Mississippi, Warren, Not Stated, Roll 603, M653.
86. All six were transports; the *Tigress* was sunk, and the *Empire City* and *Anglo-Saxon* were seriously damaged. Additionally, six of twelve barges that accompanied the transports were sunk. Bearss, *The Vicksburg Campaign,* 2:78–79.
87. This comment refers to the most successful of Grant's efforts to keep Pemberton off balance. Colonel Benjamin Grierson led the 6th and 7th

Illinois Cavalry regiments over 600 miles, from La Grange, Tennessee, to Baton Rouge, Louisiana, destroying supplies, railroad equipment, and track. See Dee Alexander Brown, *Grierson's Raid: A Cavalry Adventure of the Civil War* (Dayton, OH: Morningside Bookshop, 1981).

88. Probably Minerva B. Scott Reid, wife of **Luther R. Reid**.

89. The Confederate batteries fired at an army tugboat that was running the gauntlet with a number of barges in tow. *ORN*, 24:705.

90. The tug and accompanying barges were damaged, and one barge loaded with hay was sunk. Ibid.

91. The shelling was from Union gunboats attempting to knock out the Confederate heavy cannon at Grand Gulf. Bearss, *The Vicksburg Campaign*, 2:259.

92. Grierson's raiders continuing on their way to Baton Rouge, Louisiana. Also see p. 139n87.

93. This show of force in the lower Yazoo prevented Pemberton and Stevenson from determining if the main threat would come from above or below Vicksburg. Bearss, *The Vicksburg Campaign*, 2:259.

94. The ironclads *Choctaw* and *De Kalb* shelled the heavy gun emplacements on Drumgould's Bluff, while other Federal vessels engaged the lower defenses, all in an effort to keep the Confederates from transferring troops from the Yazoo River south to oppose Grant's crossing of the Mississippi below Vicksburg. Ibid., 259, 261.

95. This must have been written before 3 p.m., as the gunboats opened fire shortly thereafter. Ibid., 265–66.

96. The deserter was an orderly of brigade commander Colonel T. Kilby Smith. Ibid., 266.

97. This bombardment lasted from 3 to 7:30 p.m., and included firing by both gunboats and mortars. *OR*, 24, pt. 1:578.

98. Along with Company G, Company A, 1st Mississippi Light Artillery Regiment, had been assigned to Hébert's Brigade. Eggleston is correct regarding the number of casualties, but 2nd Lieutenant James R. Cottingham, Company I, 3rd Louisiana Infantry Regiment, was severely wounded and captured while commanding a party skirmishing with some Federals when they landed on the east bank of the Yazoo. He remained a prisoner of war until June 12, 1865. The other two casualties did occur in the heavy batteries: Corporal Frank Haggerty (who lost a leg from amputation) and Private D. Houston, Companies D and C, respectively, 21st Louisiana Infantry Regiment. Ibid., pt. 3:624 and pt. 1:578; Service record of James R. Cottingham, Third Infantry, Roll 117, CSR LA.

99. Aunt Mary Wilkinson (see p. 132n42) was accompanied by her daughter Molly. Ross is probably a typographical error and should be Rose, another of her daughters. "Robert Andrews Wilkinson," Smolenski Family Tree.

100. Their departure marked the end of the Federal diversion north of Vicksburg.

101. No fighting occurred at Grand Gulf on April 30 or May 1. Union vessels did periodically fire on Port Hudson, Louisiana, but nothing noteworthy occurred on these days. The Battle of Port Gibson, however, was fought on May 1. Though the rumor regarding Grand Gulf was incorrect, it is possible that the original transcriber of the diary misread "Hudson" for "Gibson".

102. Brigadier General John S. Bowen.

103. Born in North Carolina on December 4, 1818, William W. Loring grew up in Florida, where he fought against Seminole Indians at the age of fourteen. A lawyer and politician at the outbreak of the Mexican War, Loring was commissioned a captain in 1846 when the U.S. Army organized its Regiment of Mounted Rifles. After distinguishing himself during that conflict and losing an arm from a wound received at the Battle of Chapultepec, Loring remained in the army and eventually became colonel of the regiment. Entering Confederate service as colonel on March 16, 1861, he was promoted to brigadier general on May 20. After serving in northwestern Virginia and having charges filed against him by "Stonewall" Jackson, Loring was promoted to major general on February 15, 1862. Transferred to Mississippi in November, he would spend the remainder of the conflict commanding a division, and briefly a corps, in the Western Theater. After the war, he spent four years in banking in New York before entering a decade of service in the Egyptian army. Returning to the United States in 1879, he had a varied career before dying in New York on December 30, 1886. Davis and Hoffman, eds., *The Confederate General*, 4:97–98.

104. Born on January 26, 1816, in Maryland, Lloyd Tilghman graduated near the bottom of the West Point class of 1836. After a few months with the 1st U.S. Dragoons, he resigned and worked as an engineer on various railroads and canals. After serving in the Mexican War, Tilghman returned to civilian life. Though he had married a native of Maine in 1843, Tilghman moved his family to Paducah, Kentucky, in 1852. He entered Confederate service as colonel of the 3rd Kentucky Infantry Regiment on July 5, 1861. Promoted to brigadier general on October 18, the following month he was placed in command of Forts Henry and Donelson in Tennessee. Captured at the former when he surrendered the post on February 6, 1862, he remained a prisoner of war until August. After returning to the Confederacy, Tilghman was ordered to northern Mississippi, where he commanded a division. Spring 1863 found him commanding a brigade outside of Vicksburg, when Eggleston's unit was assigned to his command. Bruce S. Allardice and Lawrence Lee Hewitt, eds., *Kentuckians in Gray: Confederate*

Generals and Field Officers of the Bluegrass State (Lexington: Univ. of Kentucky Press, 2008), 264–69.

105. Thomas A. Roach was the son of Eggleston's sister, Mahala P. H. Eggleston Roach. In 1860, 14-year-old Thomas was a student living with his parents in Vicksburg. His father, James Roach, was a 47-year-old Irishman. A banker, James claimed a net worth of $5,300 in real property and $50,000 in personal property, including ten slaves. On February 1, 1863, Thomas enlisted as a private in Company A, 2nd Mississippi State Cavalry Regiment. He was wounded in the left arm and captured May 21, 1863, and treated at Branch 2, U.S. Army General Hospital, at La Grange, Tennessee, on May 24. Forwarded to Memphis, Tennessee, he was treated for chronic diarrhea at the Jefferson Military Hospital on July 6. On July 18 he was transferred to the General Hospital in Memphis and the following day was sent north. No further records of his military service was found. Thomas Roach, p. 78, 1860 Free Schedule, Mississippi, Warren, Not Stated, Roll 592, M653; James Roach, p. 16, 1860 Slave Schedule, Mississippi, Warren, Not Stated, Roll 603, M653; Service record of Thomas A. Roach, Second State Cavalry, Roll 15, CSR MS.

106. By the afternoon of May 6, the Confederates were fortifying a line from the Big Black Bridge to Warrenton to prevent Grant's advance on Vicksburg from the southeast. Bearss, *The Vicksburg Campaign*, 2:454.

107. Rather than moving directly on Vicksburg, Grant moved northeast to strike the railroad running between Vicksburg and Jackson, eliminating the possibility of a major engagement involving Company G for several days. Ibid., 459–555.

Notes to Interlude

1. Ibid., 454.
2. Grabau, *Ninety-eight Days,* 204; *OR,* 24, pt. 2:74.
3. Born in Tennessee about 1817, Mrs. Sarah A. Ellison and her two grown children resided with J. H. Thompson's family in 1860, but she possessed greater wealth, owning $8,000 real and $6,000 personal property, including six slaves. S. A. Ellison, p. 54, 1860 Free Schedule, Mississippi, Hinds, Not Stated, Roll 582, M653; S. A. Ellison, p. 95, 1860 Slave Schedule, Mississippi, Hinds, Not Stated, Roll 597, M653; *OR,* 24, pt. 2:74–75.
4. Timothy B. Smith, *Champion Hill: Decisive Battle for Vicksburg* (New York: Savas Beatie, 2004), 136, 145; *OR,* 24, pt. 2:75.
5. Smith, *Champion Hill,* 143, 195, 235.
6. Ibid., 343.
7. Born in Virginia about 1813, H. B. Coker had married Mrs. S. E. Cotton in the late 1850s. In 1860, he owned $3,000 personal prop-

erty, including four slaves. His wife, however, owned $20,000 real and $50,000 personal property, including forty slaves. H. B. Coker, p. 53, 1860 Free Schedule, Mississippi, Hinds, Not Stated, Roll 582, M653; S. E. Coker, pp. 93–94, 1860 Slave Schedule, Mississippi, Hinds, Not Stated, Roll 597, M653.

8. Smith, *Champion Hill*, 349; Bearss, *The Vicksburg Campaign*, 2:618.

9. *OR*, 24, pt. 3:883 and pt. 2:81.

10. Quoted in Smith, *Champion Hill*, 343–44; Bearss, *The Vicksburg Campaign*, 2:625; National Park Service, "Chicago Mercantile Battery," *Vicksburg: National Military Park, Mississippi*, http://www.nps.gov/vick/historyculture/chicago-mercantile-battery.htm (accessed July 4, 2013).

11. *OR*, 24, pt. 2:8, 82.

12. Unsigned and undated account of the engagement, in 1st Mississippi Light Artillery Regiment Collection, Mississippi State Library and Archives, Jackson.

13. E. T. Eggleston, "Scenes Where General Tilghman was Killed," *Confederate Veteran* 1, no. 10 (Oct. 1893): 296.

14. F. W. M., "Career and Fate of Gen. Lloyd Tilghman," *Confederate Veteran* 1, no. 9 (Sept. 1893): 274.

15. Smith, *Champion Hill*, 456n33; Service record of F. W. Merrin, Capt. Merrin's Battery, Roll 97, CSR MS.

16. *OR*, 24, pt. 2:81.

17. Another account states, "Tilghman killed near Lt. Tompkins guns, & taken off the field by Markhar." Unsigned and undated account of the engagement, and Geo. H. Tompkins to J. S. Power, Nov. 6, 1900, both in 1st Mississippi Light Artillery Regiment Collection.

18. J. G. Spencer, "The Death of Brigadier General Lloyd Tilghman," http://www.battleofchampionhill.org/tilghman.htm (accessed July 6, 2013).

19. *OR*, 24, pt. 2:80–81.

20. Ibid., 74, 77–78, 81.

21. Bearss, *The Vicksburg Campaign*, 2:642; *OR*, 24, pt. 2:81, 82, 86, 93.

22. Clement A. Evans, ed., *Confederate Military History, Extended Edition*, 17 vols. (Wilmington, NC: Broadfoot Publishing Company, 1988), 9:446.

23. Bearss, *The Vicksburg Campaign*, 3:782; *OR*, 24, pt. 2:381; Janet B. Hewett, Jocelyn Pinson, and Julia H. Nichols, eds., *Supplement to the Official Records of the Union and Confederate Armies* 100 vols. (Wilmington, NC: Broadfoot Publishing Company, 1996), pt. 2, 32:556 (hereafter cited as *ORS*).

24. L. S. Flatan, "Tribute to Gen. Lloyd Tilghman," *Confederate Veteran* 18, no. 9 (Sept. 1910): 423. **Spencer** went by the name of **Lewis Spense Flatau** after the war. "Flatan" was undoubtedly a typographical error. L. S. Flatau, "Only Regiment of Confederate Artillery," *Confederate Veteran* 15, no. 9 (Sept. 1907): 410.

25. Geo. H. Tompkins to J. S. Power, Nov. 6, 1900, in 1st Mississippi Light Artillery Regiment Collection.

26. From the outset of their escape, some of the men had to ride double. On May 27, the seventy-nine artillerymen obtained fodder for fifty-four horses on the Big Black River. Geo. H. Tompkins to J. S. Power, Nov. 6, 1900, in 1st Mississippi Light Artillery Regiment Collection; Isaac E. Herring to My Darling Wife, June 15, 1863, in Isaac E. Herring Letters; Requisition for forage, May 27, 1863, in service record of George H. Tompkins, First Light Artillery, Roll 90, CSR MS.

27. Isaac E. Herring to My Darling Wife, June 15, 1863, in Isaac E. Herring Letters.

28. Requisition for forage, June 13, 1863, in service record of George H. Tompkins, First Light Artillery, Roll 90, CSR MA.

29. Geo. H. Tompkins to J. S. Power, Nov. 6, 1900, in 1st Mississippi Light Artillery Regiment Collection; Isaac E. Herring to My Darling Wife, June 15, 1863, in Isaac E. Herring Letters; Service record of F. P. Derbeshire, Twenty-third Infantry, Roll 309, CSR MS.

30. Edwin C. Bearss and Warren Grabau, *The Battle Of Jackson, May 14, 1863; The Siege Of Jackson, July 10–17, 1863; Three Other Post-Vicksburg Actions* (Baltimore, MD: Gateway Press, Inc., 1981), 127.

31. Special Requisition, Aug. 10, 1863, in service record of Jacob Culbertson, Culbertson's Battery, Roll 94, CSR MS.

32. Special Requisition, Aug. 18, 1863, in service record of George H. Tompkins, First Light Artillery, CSR MS.

33. *ORS*, pt. 2, 32: 556.

34. Report of the conduct of the officers of Culbertson's Battery since its formation in June, 1863, Oct. 9, 1863, in service record of George H. Tompkins, First Light Artillery, CSR MS.

35. Isaac E. Herring to My Darling Wife, Feb. 23, 1864, in Isaac E. Herring Letters; Geo. H. Tompkins to J. S. Power, Nov. 6, 1900, in 1st Mississippi Light Artillery Regiment Collection; Rowland, *Official and Statistical Register of the State of Mississippi*, 858–59.

36. Muster Rolls for July & Aug. and Sept. & Oct., 1863, in service record of Edmond T. Eggleston, First Light Artillery, Roll 84, CSR MS.

37. A native of South Carolina, Randell was a fifty-year-old "farmer" with $10,000 in real property and $30,000 in personal property, including thirty slaves, in 1860. In August 1862, he enlisted as a private in Company C, 5th Regiment Mississippi State Troops and was elected major on September 6. After being captured at Vicksburg, the unit was disbanded on or about July 17, 1863. S. J. Randal, p. 21, 1860 Free Schedule, Mississippi, Lauderdale, Beat 5, Roll 585, M653; S. J. Randal, p. 13, 1860 Slave Schedule, Mississippi, Lauderdale, Center Beat, Roll 599, M653; Service record of Saml. J. Randall, Fifth Infantry (State Troops), Roll 154, CSR MS.

38. Sarah Antoinette McClellan was born in Maine about 1840. In 1860, she was living with her parents in New Orleans, where her father, William Henry Paine McClellan, was a contractor and owned $10,000 real and $4,000 personal property. Sarah married Callender Irvine Fayssoux, whose sister was married to Samuel Randell. Sarah, her husband, and their two children were living with her parents in New Orleans in 1870. Her husband, twenty years her senior, was born in Missouri. Sarah died in New Orleans on April 25, 1910. William H. McClellan, pp. 44, 1860 Free Schedule, Louisiana, Orleans, New Orleans Ward 1, Roll 415, M653; William McLellan, p. 123, 1870 Population Schedule, Louisiana, Orleans, New Orleans Ward 11, Roll 524, 1870 Federal Population Census, M593, National Archives and Records Service, Washington, DC; "Sarah Antoinette McLellan," *Bonney to McLellan Tree*, http://trees.ancestry.com/tree/15426776/person/1066710989 (accessed July 7, 2013; password protected site); "Family View," *Fabor-Lee-Tappan-Tanner-Boyer-Family Tree, http://trees.ancestry.com/tree/575993/family?cfpid=-1086918200* (accessed July 7, 2013; password protected site).

Notes to Volume 2

1. Born May 8, 1829, Templar Shubrick Fayssoux was a slave owner and resident of Chester, South Carolina, in 1860. For much of the war he served as chief of ordnance for Brigadier General Nathan G. Evans's Brigade of South Carolinians. Immediately before and after the period Fayssoux was in Mississippi, he was stationed at Mount Pleasant, South Carolina. Service record of T. S. Fayssoux, Roll 91, Compiled Service Records of Confederate General and Staff Officers, and Non-regimental Enlisted Men, M-331, War Department Collection of Confederate Records. RG 109, National Archives and Records Service, Washington, DC (hereafter cited as CSR CGSO); "Templar Shubrick Fayssoux," *Fabor-Lee-Tapan-Boyer-Family Tree,* http://trees.ancestry.com/tree/575993/person/-1086918194 (accessed July 7, 2013; password protected site); T. S. Fayssoux, p. 89, 1860 Slave Schedule, South Carolina, Chester, Not Stated, Roll 1233, M653.

2. In 1860, 36-year-old Maryland native Daniel O. Merwin practiced law in Vicksburg and owned $4,000 in real and $8,000 in personal property, including ten slaves. He entered Confederate service as a lieutenant in the Madison (LA) Light Artillery and was disabled when his right arm was shot off during the Battle of Garnett's and Golding's Farm, Virginia, on June 28, 1862. Resigning his commission on November 3, he returned to his home in Vicksburg, where he was captured on July 4, 1863. Apparently forced from his home, he secured a staff appointment on September 25. During the time of his association

with Eggleston, he was serving as a major and assistant adjutant general and was commandant of conscripts for the State of Mississippi with headquarters at Enterprise. D. O. Merwin, p. 16, 1860 Free Schedule, Mississippi, Warren, Vicksburg, Roll 592, M653; D. O. Merwin, p. 4–5, 1860 Slave Schedule, Mississippi, Warren, Vicksburg, Roll 603, M653; Service record of Daniel O. Merwin, Roll 176, CSR CGSO; *OR*, 11, pt. 2:747; "Family View," *Fabor-Lee-Tappan-Tanner-Boyer-Family Tree.*

3. A. M. Paxton was born in Virginia about 1813. By 1850 he was practicing law in Vicksburg and continued to do so until 1860, at which time he owned $15,000 real and $65,000 personal property, including forty-seven slaves. The election of Abraham Lincoln in November changed Paxton's life immediately; within days he became a machinist and was operating A. M. Paxton & Co., a foundry and machine shop located at the corner of Pearl and South streets in Vicksburg. Paxton & Co. cast 6-pounder brass cannon, including some for the 1st Mississippi Light Artillery Regiment; made artillery ammunition of various types and calibers; provided the necessary metal parts and tools for constructing the raft at Snyder's Mill and traverse rails for barbette carriages; and probably was instrumental in providing items necessary for the completion of the CSS *Arkansas.* The foundry continued to operate during the siege of Vicksburg. Following the garrison's surrender on July 4, 1863, Paxton was appointed major on October 2, and on October 10 was assigned to duty as Chief Inspector of Field Transportation in District No. 3, which included Alabama, West Tennessee, Mississippi, and East Louisiana. Foremost among his many duties was procuring horses for the artillery. He was paroled at Jackson on May 15, 1865. After the war, he managed to retain ownership of his foundry and was operating it in 1870 with the help of his son R. E. Paxton. A. M. Paxton was also the father of William G. Paxton. A. M. Paxton, p. 60, 1850 Free Schedule, Mississippi, Warren, Vicksburg, Roll 382, M432; A. M. Paxton, p. 11, 1860 Free Schedule, Mississippi, Warren, Vicksburg, Roll 592, M653; A. Paxton, pp. 90–91, 1860 Slave Schedule, Mississippi, Warren, Not Stated, Roll 603, M653; Papers of Paxton and Co., MS, Roll 780, Confederate Papers Relating to Citizens of Business Firms, 1861–65, M-346, War Department Collection of Confederate Records, RG 109, National Archives and Records Service, Washington, DC (hereafter cited as CPRCBF); A. M. Paxton to Lt. Col. A. H. Cole, Aug. 26, 1864, in service record of A. M. Paxton, Roll 194, CSR CGSO); S. M. Paxton, p. 14, 1870 Population Schedule, Mississippi, Warren, Vicksburg Ward 3, Roll 751, M593.

4. In 1860, the 46-year-old Maryland native Nathan G. Bryson lived in Vicksburg and owned $10,000 in real property and $5,000 in personal

property, including eight slaves. Then secretary of the Southern Railroad of Mississippi, he had previously served as Vicksburg's mayor. N. G. Bryson, p. 10, 1860 Free Schedule, Mississippi, Warren, Vicksburg, Roll 592, M653; N. G. Bryson, p. 3, 1860 Slave Schedule, Mississippi, Warren, Vicksburg, Roll 603, M653; N. G. Bryson, p. 52, 1850 Free Schedule, Mississippi, Warren, Vicksburg, Roll 382, M432.

5. Probably Philip Gill, mentioned in Jan. 18, 1864, entry.

6. Born in Alabama about 1839, Thomas J. Davenport was a student in 1860 and living in Kemper County, Mississippi. He was appointed assistant surgeon on December 4, 1862, to rank from August 6, and surgeon on June 1, 1864, to rank from February 17, 1863. He was assigned to the General Hospital in Marion when he treated Eggleston. Thos. J. Davenport, p. 101, 1860 Free Schedule, Mississippi, Kemper, Not Stated, Roll 584, M653; Service record of Matthew Davenport, Roll 71, CSR CGSO.

7. Joseph Lewis Harris married Elizabeth "Belle" Pitcher in New Orleans prior to the Civil War. Elizabeth was the daughter of Lemuel Pitcher and Mary Jane Gildart. Eggleston's mother and Mary Jane were sisters. "Family Group Sheet," *Pitcher 02–29–12,* http://trees.ancestry.com/tree/37581823/family/familygroup?fpid=19111004612&sid=19111001926 and http://trees.ancestry.com/tree/37581823/family/familygroup?fpid=19111011517 (both accessed July 7, 2013; password protected site).

8. Born in Henderson, Kentucky, about 1838, William H. Weller served as a lieutenant of artillery in the Missouri State Guard before resigning from that organization and entering Confederate service on December 8, 1861, in St. Clair County, Missouri, as 1st lieutenant in Captain John C. Landis's Company Missouri Light Artillery. Upon being exchanged following his capture at Vicksburg on July 4, 1863, he was detailed from the battery and assigned as ordnance officer for Brigadier General John C. Moore's Brigade on September 26. On October 11, he was stationed at Demopolis, Alabama, and he was granted leave March 10, 1864, for twenty-four days. Upon his return, he was assigned as ordnance officer for Baker's Brigade, Clayton's Division, Lee's Corps. Paroled at Gainesville, Alabama, on May 10, 1865. Service record of William H. Weller, Capt. John C. Landis' Co. Light Artillery, Roll 89, CSR MS.

9. A single mother of three in 1860, 37-year-old Mississippi native Sarah A. Jenkins operated a boarding house in Raymond and had personal property valued at $12,000, including twelve slaves. S. A. Jenkins, p. 8, 1860 Free Schedule, Mississippi, Hinds, Raymond, Roll 582, M653; S. A. Jenkins, p. 133, 1860 Slave Schedule, Mississippi, Hinds, Not Stated, Roll 597, M653.

10. Charles P. Ball entered U.S. service on July 1, 1857, and was cadet 3rd class on June 6, 1860. He entered Confederate service on March 16, 1861, as 2nd lieutenant of artillery and was assigned to Fort Morgan, Alabama, where he served as adjutant for Brigadier General William J. Hardee. He was stationed at New Orleans that summer and with Watson Louisiana Battery that fall. During the spring of 1862, Ball served as chief of artillery and later as acting assistant adjutant general for Major General Hardee at Corinth. He was serving as assistant adjutant general for Brigadier General S. A. M. Wood when he was relieved on December 17, having been promoted to major on November 13 and assigned as chief of artillery for Major General Patrick Cleburne's Division. On February 14, 1863, he was ordered to report to the Department of Mississippi and East Louisiana, where he served as chief of ordnance for Major General John H. Forney until captured at Vicksburg July 4, 1863. Later that summer he was stationed at the parole and exchange camp at Enterprise in charge of light artillery prisoners. On January 19, 1864, he endorsed a proposal made by **Captain Cowan** that Companies G and K, 1st Mississippi LightArtillery, be consolidated. At that time, seventy men were serving in Captain James T. Smith's (Culbertson's) battery, and twelve men of Company G and twenty-seven men of Company K were in camp at Enterprise. For officers, Ball recommended **Captain Cowan**, promotions for **T. J. Hanes**, **B. C. Edwards**, and **L. B. Cowan** to senior 1st, junior 1st, and senior 2nd lieutenant, respectfully, and two junior 2nd lieutenants from Company K, John R. Davis and William H. Buck. Apparently Ball intended Sr. 1st Lieutenant **Tompkins** of Company G to be promoted captain of another battery made up of other consolidated companies of the 1st Mississippi Light Artillery. Appointed colonel by Lieutenant General Leonidas Polk on April 20, 1864, Ball was assigned to command the 8th (also called 9th) Alabama Cavalry Regiment, which he did for the duration. Service record of Charles P. Ball, Roll 14, CSR CGSO; *OR*, 32, pt. 2:854.

11. In 1860, the 19-year-old Mississippi native George D. Lawrence was working as a clerk in Vicksburg, and resided with his mother, Martha, who operated a boarding house and owned $4,000 real and $2,000 in personal property. No record of military service was discovered. Geo. Lawrence, p. 42, 1860 Free Schedule, Mississippi, Warren, Vicksburg, Roll 592, M653; George D. Lawrence, p. 55, 1850 Free Schedule, Mississippi, Warren, Vicksburg, Roll 382, M432.

12. Probably Mrs. M. A. Cook who lived in Hinds County in 1860 with her five children. M. A. Cook, p. 82, 1860 Free Schedule, Mississippi, Hinds, Not Stated, Roll 582, M653.

13. Martha Fayssoux Randell was the wife of Major Samuel J. Randell. "Family View," *Fabor-Lee-Tappan-Tanner-Boyer-Family Tree.*

14. Joseph Lewis Harris married Elizabeth "Belle" Pitcher in New Orleans prior to the Civil War. Elizabeth was the daughter of Lemuel Pitcher and Mary Jane Gildart. Eggleston's mother and Mary Jane were sisters, making Eggleston and "Belle" first cousins. "Family Group Sheet," *Pitcher 02–29–12.*

15. Rebecca A. D. Irvine Fayssoux was also the mother of Martha Fayssoux Randell. The captain undoubtedly obtained leave to accompany his mother to his home in Chester, South Carolina. "Family View," *Fabor-Lee-Tappan-Tanner-Boyer-Family Tree.*

16. Sophia A. Gildart was born in Vermont in 1800. On January 16, 1826, in Wilkinson County she married John B. Fox, who was born in Connecticut in 1797. In 1850, the couple was living in Vicksburg, and John was a planter with $8,000 in real estate. Widowed and childless in 1860 and claiming to have been born in Virginia, Sophia owned a plantation in Warren County and had assets of $15,000 in real and $100,000 in personal property, including eighty-two slaves. Eggleston managed her plantation, and he and his family lived in her house. Sophia and his mother were sisters. Sophia A. Fox, p. 54, 1850 Free Schedule, Mississippi, Warren, Vicksburg, Roll 382, M432; John B. Fox, "Mississippi, Marriages, 1800–1911," https://familysearch.org/pal:/MM9.1.1/V28R-RBH (accessed July 7, 2013); S. Fox, p. 89, 1860 Free Schedule, Mississippi, Warren, Not Stated, Roll 592, M653; S. Fox, pp. 128–29, 1860 Slave Schedule, Mississippi, Warren, Not Stated, Roll 603, M653.

17. Benjamin Swett Tappan was born on February 25, 1799, Newburyport, Massachusetts. As a boy he worked for George Peabody in Baltimore, who gave him his start in business. Moving to Franklin, Tennessee, he married Margaret Bell Camp on May 1, 1823. They had four children, including future Confederate Brigadier General James Camp Tappan. On March 22, 1832, he married Margaret B. Wood. The family moved to Vicksburg about 1840, where he was a merchant until forced to relocate because of the war. In 1860, he had $8,000 in real property and $5,000 in personal property, including eight slaves. He died on March 1, 1866, and is buried in Vicksburg. "General" did not refer to any official military rank. Daniel Langdon Tappan, comp., *Tappan-Toppan Genealogy: Ancestors and Descendants of Abraham Toppan of Newbury, Massachusetts, 1606–1672* (Arlington, MA: privately printed by the compiler, 1915), 16–17; B. S. Tappan, p. 20, 1860 Free Schedule, Mississippi, Warren, Vicksburg, Roll 592, M653; Benj. S. Tappan, p. 49, 1850 Free Schedule, Mississippi, Warren, Vicksburg, Roll 382, M432; B. S. Tappan, p. 9, 1860 Slave Schedule, Mississippi, Warren, Vicksburg, Roll 603, M653; The Preacher's Kid, "Benjamin S. Tappan," *Find a Grave*, http://www.findagrave.com/cgi-bin/fg.cgi?page=gr&GRid=67710215 (accessed July 4, 2013).

18. The Eggleston and Davis families were well acquainted because of the long time residence of both in Warren County. Additionally, Private Dick H. Eggleston (Edmund's older brother) was killed at the Battle of Buena Vista, Mexico, (Feb. 23, 1847) while serving in Colonel Jefferson Davis's 1st Mississippi Infantry Regiment. Moreover, the first time Davis returned to Vicksburg as president, he immediately sent Mahala "a kind message." Also see Appendix C. "Buena Vista, PART TWO," *Descendants of Mexican War Veterans*, http://www.dmwv.org/honoring/bvista2.htm (accessed July 4, 2013); Jefferson Davis, *The Papers of Jefferson Davis*, vol. 4, *1849–1852*, edited by Lynda L. Crist, Mary S. Dix, and Richard E. Beringer (Baton Rouge: Louisiana State Univ. Press, 1983), 313; Jefferson Davis, *The Papers of Jefferson Davis*, vol. 8, *1862*, edited by Lynda L. Crist, Mary S. Dix, and Kenneth H. Williams (Baton Rouge: Louisiana State Univ. Press, 1995), xlviii; Mahala Roach, 1862 Diary, Dec. 20, Roach and Eggleston Family Papers; E. T. Eggleston to Jefferson Davis, Dec. 21, 1863, in service record of Edmond T. Eggleston, Roll 84, CSR MS. For more on the Confederate president, see William J. Cooper Jr., *Jefferson Davis, American* (New York: Knopf, 2000).

19. Born in Mississippi in 1827, David S. Snodgrass and his two younger brothers jointly owned a plantation in Rodney, Jefferson County, Mississippi, in 1850, having real estate valued at $38,500. In 1860, he was the minister of the Baptist Church in Vicksburg and owned $5,000 in real and $3,500 in personal property, including three slaves. After the war, he moved to Texas and was preaching in Marshall County in 1880. From July 19 to September 30, 1861, he served as chaplain of the 6th Mississippi Infantry Regiment. On the latter date he transferred to the 21st Mississippi Infantry Regiment. On November 7, 1862, he was transferred to be post chaplain at Vicksburg, where he continued to serve until August 4, 1863. In September he became post chaplain at Demopolis, Alabama, where he continued to serve in May 1864. He was paroled May 16, 1865, at Marion, Alabama. David Snodgrass, p. 7, 1850 Free Schedule, Mississippi, Jefferson, Rodney, Roll 374, M432; H. C. Clarke, "General Directory for the City of Vicksburg: Containing the Name and Address of Every Professional and Business Man and Resident of the City"; D. S. Snodgrass, p. 40, 1860 Free Schedule, Mississippi, Warren, Vicksburg, Roll 592, M653; D. S. Snodgrass, p. 11, 1860 Slave Schedule, Mississippi, Warren, Vicksburg, Roll 603, M653; D. S. Snodgrass, p. 63, Texas, Montgomery, Precinct 4, Roll 1320, T9; Service record of D. S. Snodgrass, Twenty-first Infantry, Roll 300, CSR MS; Service record of D. S. Snodgrass, Roll 235, CSR CGSO.

20. **Horatio N. King**.

21. Born about 1805 in Ireland, James H. King Sr. operated a shoe store in Vicksburg in 1860 and owned $25,000 in personal property. His

three grown sons still lived at home: James Jr., 23, and **Horatio**, 21, were clerks, and George, 19, a saddle maker. James H. King Jr. enlisted at Vicksburg on May 15, 1861, in Captain D. N. Moody's company, the Vicksburg Southrons, which eventually became Company A, 21st Mississippi Infantry Regiment. Immediately appointed 4th corporal, he was demoted to private between April and December 1862. Wounded during the Battle of Spotsylvania Court House, Virginia, on May 12, 1864, he was transported to Richmond, Virginia, and admitted to the hospital. Returning to duty on June 27, he was severely wounded in the arm and thigh at the Battle of Cedar Creek, Virginia, October 19, 1864. He was paroled at Jackson, May 19, 1865. George W. King enlisted as a private in Company H, 2nd Mississippi Infantry Battalion, on March 5, 1862, in Vicksburg. He was wounded at the Battle of Gaines' Mill, Virginia, June 27. On July 10, additional companies were added to the battalion to form the 48th Mississippi Infantry Regiment. Apparently wounded a second time and furloughed, he was admitted to Way Hospital, Meridian, February 8, 1865, suffering from his wound. Though furloughed from hospital, he was reported absent without leave from his company in Virginia on February 26, 1865. James King, p. 34, 1850 Free Schedule, Mississippi, Warren, Vicksburg, Roll 382, M432; James King, p. 73, 1860 Free Schedule, Mississippi, Warren, Vicksburg, Roll 592, M653; Service record of James H. King, Twenty-first Infantry, Roll 297, CSR MS; Service record of George W. King, Forty-eighth Infantry, Roll 418, CSR MS.

22. Born in Tennessee in 1830, Benjamin Wilkins Henry was a planter in Hinds County in 1860, owning $12,000 in real and $38,000 in personal property, including thirty-three slaves. Having previously been discharged from the military as unfit for duty, on December 24, 1863, Major A. M. Paxton requested that Henry be appointed captain and assistant quartermaster and assigned to him at Brandon. His uncle, Tennessee senator Gustavus A. Henry Sr., seconded the request on January 1, 1864, in a letter to Brigadier General and Quartermaster General Alexander R. Lawton. The senator made the same request to Secretary of War James A. Seddon on January 18, and his nephew was appointed on February 17. Initially assigned to Lexington, Captain Henry was later reassigned to Brandon. He was paroled at Jackson on May 12, 1865. B. W. Henry, p. 60, 1860 Free Schedule, Mississippi, Hinds, Not Stated, Roll 582, M653; B. W. Henry, pp. 110–11, 1860 Slave Schedule, Mississippi, Hinds, Not Stated, Roll 597, M653.

23. On June 18, 1863, F. P. Derbeshire was temporarily attached to Culbertson's Battery, where he remained until the end of 1863, when he was ordered back to his old command, Company I, 23rd Mississippi Infantry Regiment. Service record of F. P. Derbeshire, Twenty-third Infantry, Roll 309, CSR MS.

24. Mahala P. H. Eggleston Roach.

25. Mother of **Benjamin J.**, **John R.**, and **Joseph T. Hicks**.

26. Horace E. Barnes (see p. 135n51) went by "Sam." He and Mahala became quite smitten with each other in December of 1862: he visited her in Vicksburg on the first and seventh; she received a letter from him on the seventeenth; she made a shirt for him on the twenty-third; he failed to visit her as planned on the twenty-fourth; she made him a box of Christmas presents, including the shirt, on the twenty-fifth; and she received letters from him on the twenty-seventh and thirtieth. When Eggleston visited Vicksburg on March 3, he found Barnes playing cards with his wife, aunt, and Mahala; five days later he learned that Barnes is "still there and quite sick." It appears that Edmund was slow to warm to Barnes, but as the relationship between Sam and Mahala continued, he began corresponding with him as well. Mahala Roach, 1862 Diary, Dec. 1, 7, 17, 23, 24, 25, 27, and 30, Roach and Eggleston Family Papers; Eggleston entries for Mar. 3 and 5, 1863.

27. Ragsdale's was a tavern owned by Lewis A. Ragsdale, a lawyer and native of Alabama. It was located in a log plantation house build by Richard McLemore. Jack Shank, *Meridian: The Queen with a Past*, 2 vols. (Meridian, MS: Southeastern Printing, 1985–86), 1:3–6.

28. Born in Virginia about 1820, Edward H. Porter was living in Vicksburg in 1860. On January 19, 1864, Colonel Horace H. Miller requested that the War Department appoint him assistant quartermaster for his 9th Mississippi Cavalry Regiment, pointing out his prior experience as a quartermaster with the army in Virginia. The request was approved up the line and Lieutenant General Leonidas Polk, commanding the Department of Alabama, Mississippi and East Louisiana, signed off on it on January 23, 1864. The secretary of war referred the matter to the quartermaster general on December 21, 1864, who recommended another officer be transferred to the position on February 9, 1865. There is no record of Porter having served with Miller's regiment or in Virginia, but he, as a captain and assistant quartermaster, was issued provisions for four horses in Demopolis, Alabama, on April 25, 1864. E. H. Porter, p. 55, 1860 Free Schedule, Mississippi, Warren, Vicksburg, Roll 592, M653; Col. H. H. Miller to General S. Cooper, Jan. 19, 1864, in papers of Edward H. Porter, Roll 319, UPSBCCSR; Requisition for forage, Apr. 25, 1864, in papers of E. H. Porter, Roll 319, UPSBCCSR.

29. Named for an ancestor of Edmund T. Eggleston but not a blood relative, Joseph Eggleston Johnston was born in Virginia on February 3, 1807. Finishing thirteenth of forty-six graduates from West Point in 1829, his distinguished career in the U.S. Army culminated with his promotion to quartermaster general, which made him a brigadier general of staff and the highest ranking officer to resign and join the Confederate army. Rather than using his staff rank, President Davis

used Johnston's line rank of lieutenant colonel, which, to Johnston's chagrin, made him fourth instead of first among Confederate full generals. This dispute was but the first of many between the two men that would hamper the Confederacy's struggle for independence. After recovering from a wound sustained during the Battle of Seven Pines, Virginia, on May 31, 1862, Johnston was sent to the Western Theater to coordinate the efforts of General Braxton Bragg's Army of Tennessee and Lieutenant General John C. Pemberton's Department of Mississippi and East Louisiana. After Grant crossed the Mississippi River in 1863, Johnston was ordered to Jackson, where he failed to save either Vicksburg or Pemberton's army. In December he took over the Army of Tennessee, was relieved in July 1864, and reinstated in February 1865. He died March 21, 1891, and was buried in Baltimore, Maryland. Davis and Hoffman, eds., *The Confederate General*, 3:193, 197.

30. "F. W." is from Eggleston's Jan. 2, 1864, entry. Eggleston also references "the Rev. F. W. Damas" in his Dec. 21, 1863, letter to Jefferson Davis (see Appendix C). The only record found for a F. W. Damas was in the U.S. Census for 1900, which states that he was born in Alabama in 1821, was a widower, and was a professor at St. Mary's College, Oakland City, California. F. W. Damas, in "1900 Population Schedule, California, Alameda, Oakland Ward 2," http://archive. org/stream/12thcensusofpopu0082unit%23page/n211/mode/2up (accessed July 6, 2013).

31. Born in England about 1801, Frederick Elwell was an Episcopal clergyman and high school teacher living in Brandon in 1860. He owned $800 in real and $500 in personal property. In 1861, he served as the rector of both St. Luke's Church in Brandon and St. Matthew's Church in Clinton. F. Elwell, p. 9, 1860 Free Schedule, Mississippi, Rankin, Brandon, Roll 590, M653; "Journal of the Thirty-Fifth Annual Convention of the Protestant Episcopal Church, in the Diocese of Mississippi," http://docsouth.unc.edu/imls/protestant/protestant.xml%20 (accessed July 6, 2013).

32. Mary Price Perkins Tappan was born in Tennessee on June 15, 1831. Her mother died shortly after her birth, and she was afterwards called Margaret Bell for her mother, Margaret Bell Camp Tappan. In 1860, she was living with her father, Benjamin Swett Tappan, in Vicksburg. Tappan, *Tappan-Toppan Genealogy*, 16–17; Benj. S. Tappan, p. 49, 1860 Free Schedule, Mississippi, Warren, Vicksburg, Roll 592, M653; Preacher's Kid, "Benjamin S. Tappan"; B. S. Tappan, p. 20, 1860 Free Schedule, Mississippi, Warren, Vicksburg, Roll 592, M653.

33. Leonidas Polk was born in Raleigh, North Carolina, on April 10, 1806. Converting to Christianity while a cadet at West Point, he resigned from the army shortly after graduating to become ordained in the

Episcopal church. In 1841, he became the first bishop of Louisiana, but twenty years later he entered Confederate service as a major general. As commander of Department No. 2, he violated Kentucky's neutrality in September 1861. Later, while commanding a corps under General Braxton Bragg, Polk repeatedly disregarded orders and led an effort to have Bragg ousted. For the moment Bragg stayed, and in the fall of 1863 Lieutenant General Polk was transferred to Mississippi. When General Joseph E. Johnston took command of the Army of Tennessee in December, Polk became commander of the Department of Mississippi and East Louisiana, which was expanded to include Alabama in January 1864. In May, Polk exceeded his orders and took all the infantry in his department to join Johnston in northwest Georgia. On June 14, at Pine Mountain, a Union artillery shell scored a direct hit on Polk. Davis and Hoffman, eds., *The Confederate General*, 5:45, 47.

34. Samuel Williamson Tappan was born on June 19, 1841, in Tennessee. In 1860, he was a law student and boarder in Fayette, Tennessee. On May 21, 1861, at Jackson, Tennessee, Samuel enlisted in Company D, 6th Tennessee Infantry Regiment, immediately becoming 4th sergeant. On June 28, 1862, he was detached to the ordnance department and on March 1, 1864, he was transferred to field and staff. He was declared unfit for field duty on September 16, 1864, and detailed. His father, Edmund Swett Tappan, was the brother of "General" Benjamin Swett Tappan. Tappan, *Tappan-Toppan Genealogy*, 16, 19; S. W. Tappan, p. 1, 1860 Free Schedule, Tennessee, Fayette, Somerville, Roll 1248, M653; Service record of Saml. W. Tappan, Sixth Infantry, Roll 142, Compiled Service Records of Confederate Soldiers Who Served in Organizations from the State of Tennessee, M-268, War Department Collection of Confederate Records, RG 109, National Archives and Records Service, Washington, DC.

35. Undoubtedly, "General" Benjamin Swett Tappan was influential in Eggleston becoming a Mason. Tappan had served as Grand Master and Grand High Priest in Tennessee and Mississippi. Preacher's Kid, "Benjamin S. Tappan."

36. Simon B. Marye was an attorney in Vicksburg in 1860. During the war he was charged with trading with the enemy. H. C. Clarke, "General Directory for the City of Vicksburg: Containing the Name and Address of Every Professional and Business Man and Resident of the City"; Papers of Simon B. Marye, Roll 663, CPRCBF.

37. Born in Virginia on January 24, 1802, Patrick Henry was a planter in Brandon in 1860, owning $3,000 in real and $15,000 in personal property. The grandson of Revolutionary War hero Patrick Henry and brother of Confederate senator Gustavus A. Henry Sr. of Tennessee, in the fall of 1862 he applied for an appointment as colonel to serve on the Military Court in Mississippi. He died on March 14, 1864.

B. C. Henry, p. 1, 1860 Free Schedule, Mississippi, Rankin, Brandon, Roll 590, M653; G. A. Henry to Jefferson Davis, Oct. 27, 1862, and E. Barksdale to President [Jefferson Davis], Nov. 10, 1862, both in papers of Patrick Henry, Roll 435, CPRCBF; Natalie Maynor, "Patrick Henry," *Find a Grave*, http://www.findagrave.com/cgi-bin/fg.cgi?page=gr&GSln=HEN&GSpartial=1&GSbyrel=all&GSst=27&GScntry=4&GSsr=4521&GRid=11378337& (accessed July 4, 2013).

38. After Tappan moved his business from Vicksburg to Brandon, he partnered with Patrick Henry in the latter's C.S. Depositary office, which meant they operated what amounted to a branch bank of the Confederate government. E. T. Eggleston to Col. Thos. M. Jack, Jan. 1, 1864 in service record of Edmond T. Eggleston, Roll 84, CSR MS; Douglas B. Ball, *Financial Failure and Confederate Defeat* (Urbana: Univ. of Illinois Press, 1991), 138.

39. Born in Mississippi on December 30, 1813, Dr. James C. Newman was living in Warren County in 1860. He owned $25,000 real and $50,000 in personal property, including forty-four slaves. He died on September 15, 1889, and is buried in Bovina. Therese Rodgers, "Dr James C. Newman," *Find a Grave*, http://www.findagrave.com/cgi-bin/fg.cgi?page=gr&GSln=NE&GSpartial=1&GSbyrel=all&GSst=27&GScntry=4&GSsr=7121&GRid=26896043& (accessed July 6, 2013); J. C. Newman, p. 53, 1860 Free Schedule, Mississippi, Warren, Not Stated, Roll 592, M653; J. C. Newman, pp. 49–50, 1860 Slave Schedule, Mississippi, Warren, Not Stated, Roll 603, M653.

40. Captain Charles A. Jennings's Company G, Colonel H. H. Miller's 9th Mississippi Cavalry Regiment. Howell, *For Dixie Land I'll Take My Stand!*, 2:1543, 2036.

41. Born in South Carolina about 1805, Mrs. Sophia Messenger lived with her son George in 1860 in Warren County. Sophia Messenger, p. 88, 1860 Free Schedule, Mississippi, Warren, Not Stated, Roll 592, M653.

42. Eggleston was transporting this money for the C.S. Depository of Henry and Tappan. E. T. Eggleston to Col. Thos. M. Jack, Jan. 1, 1864 in service record of Edmond T. Eggleston, Roll 84, CSR MS.

43. A wagon train operated by the quartermaster department.

44. The Confederate retreat was in response to Major General William T. Sherman's advance from Vicksburg to Meridian, which began on February 3, 1864. Proclaimed by historians as the precursor to his March to the Sea later that year, Sherman's men lived off the land and destroyed supplies and the railroad as they swept through six Mississippi counties. See Buck T. Foster, *Sherman's Mississippi Campaign* (Tuscaloosa: Univ. of Alabama Press, 2006).

45. Born in North Carolina on January 3, 1827, William H. Clark attended Bethany College in Virginia before moving to Brandon to practice law.

A veteran of the Mexican War, he entered Confederate service as a lieutenant in Company D, 6th Mississippi Infantry Battalion on May 14, 1862. When his battalion was became part of the 46th Mississippi Infantry Regiment on December 1, 1862, Clark was elected major. Captured at Vicksburg on July 4, 1863, he was promoted to lieutenant colonel on November 26. Promoted to colonel on March 1, 1864, he was killed during the Battle of Allatoona, Georgia, on October 5 "while gallantly leading the third and last charge." Quoted in Allardice, *Confederate Colonels*,101.

46. Rebecca Lyon Fayssoux, wife of Thomas S. Mills, was the sister of Martha Fayssoux Randell. "Family View," *Fabor-Lee-Tappan-Tanner-Boyer-Family Tree.*

47. Born in Mississippi about 1843, Charles William Petrie was one of five siblings living with the family of Reverend John Hunter in Hinds County. Each of the siblings owned $10,000 real and $30,000 personal property, and they jointly owned seventy-four slaves. On March 22, 1862, he enlisted as a private in Company A, 1st Mississippi Light Artillery. During the summer of 1863 he was temporarily attached to Company G and served in Culbertson's Battery. He was paroled at Jackson on May 12, 1865. C. W. Petree, p. 2, 1860 Free Schedule, Mississippi, Hinds, Township 5, Roll 582, M653; Minor heirs L. W. Petre, 1860 Slave Schedule, Mississippi, Hinds, Not Stated, Roll 582, M653; Service record of Charles William Petrie, First Light Artillery, Roll 88, CSR MS.

48. A. J. Pharis of Belmont, Sumter County, Alabama. Receipt to A. J. Pharis, Sept. 5, 1863, in papers of A. J. Pharis, Roll 796, CPRCBF.

49. Born in Alabama about 1823, Louisa was married to George B. Hayden. In 1860, her husband was a school teacher in Demopolis and owned $3,000 in real and $3,500 in personal property, including four slaves. Louisa Hayden, p. 12, 1860 Free Schedule, Alabama, Marengo, Demopolis, Roll 15, M653; Geo. B. Hayden, p. 83, 1860 Slave Schedule, Alabama, Marengo, Western Division, Roll 31, M653.

50. Born on the family plantation in Camden County, Georgia, on October 12, 1815, William Joseph Hardee graduated in the middle of the West Point class of 1838. After publishing *Rifle and Light Infantry Tactics* in 1855, he served four years as commandant of the U.S. Military Academy. Promoted to lieutenant colonel in 1860, he resigned the following year and, after briefly serving with Georgia state troops, President Davis appointed him a brigadier general. Initially stationed at Fort Morgan, Alabama, Hardee was sent to Bowling Green, Kentucky, in September, following the end of that state's neutrality. Promoted to major general on October 7, he lead a division-sized corps at the Battle of Shiloh, Tennessee, in April 1862, and briefly commanded the Army of the Mississippi during the summer. Reduced to command of one

half of that army, he participated in the invasion of Kentucky that fall. Promoted to lieutenant general on October 11, he probably had the best day of his career during the Battle of Murfreesboro, Tennessee, on December 31. The following July he was transferred to Mississippi to assist General Joseph E. Johnston. He returned to command a corps in the Army of Tennessee during the Chattanooga Campaign that fall. Briefly ordered to Alabama in February in response to Major General William T. Sherman's Meridian Campaign, Hardee returned to Georgia and led his corps throughout the Atlanta Campaign. Following the fall of that city, Hardee was placed in command at Savannah, Georgia, where he remained until participating in the final campaign of the Army of Tennessee in North Carolina in 1865. He died on November 6, 1873, and is buried in Selma, Alabama. Davis and Hoffman, eds., *The Confederate General*, 58–60.

51. On February 17, President Davis ordered General Joseph E. Johnston to send Lieutenant General William J. Hardee and two divisions of his corps from the Army of Tennessee at Dalton, Georgia, to aid Polk against Sherman's advance on Meridian. *OR*, 32, pt. 1:477.

52. Usually circumspect in his comments on generals, Eggleston's praise for Hardee probably resulted from his familiarity with the general's *Rifle and Light Infantry Tactics*, which was widely used in the Confederate army.

53. The first of Hardee's troops reached Demopolis on February 21, and Polk began crossing his men over the Tombigbee two days later in preparation for an advance against Sherman. Before a full division of Hardee's had arrived, however, his entire command was ordered back to Dalton on the twenty-fourth. *OR*, 32, pt. 1:337, 340, 341, and pt. 2:793, 801.

54. Sherman's army departed Meridian on February 19, heading west to Canton. Rather than following in his wake, Polk moved Loring's Division northwest to Macon. *OR*, 32, pt. 2:786.

55. The Texan's choice of commanders and the organization of his imaginary army is interesting. Born in Iowa, Lawrence S. Ross was an infant when his family moved to Texas. Appointed a brigadier general on February 5, 1864, he commanded a brigade of Texas cavalry and was the junior officer of the group. Major General Stephen D. Lee, a West Point graduate from South Carolina, was demoted to a command equal with Ross. Having a similar background as Lee's, Brigadier General Samuel W. Ferguson commanded a cavalry brigade composed of Alabama, Mississippi, and Tennessee units. Kentuckian William Wirt Adams had lived in Mississippi since he was six. Appointed brigadier general on September 28, 1863, he commanded a brigade of Mississippi cavalry. Apparently Adams's military reputation, in the opinion of the drunken Texan, did not overcome the fact that he was neither a

Texan nor a professional soldier. Davis and Hoffman, eds., *The Confederate General*, 1:7–8; ibid., 2:122–23; ibid., 4:59, 63; ibid., 5:110–11.

56. Born in Alabama about 1832, James Huddleston was living in Harrison County in 1860. Father of five, he worked as a miller and owned $500 real and $300 personal property. He entered Confederate service on May 10, 1862, as lieutenant and adjutant for the 17th Mississippi Cavalry Battalion that on December 24, 1863, was consolidated with other units to become the 9th Mississippi Cavalry Regiment. His last record of service was at Mobile, Alabama, on January 3, 1865. J. Huddleston, p. 22, 1860 Free Schedule, Mississippi, Harrison, Police District 3, Roll 597, M653; Service record of James Huddleston, Seventeenth Battalion Cavalry, Roll 48, CSR MS.

57. William and Robert Chambers, eds., *Chambers's Information For The People*, 2 vols. (Philadelphia, PA: J. B. Lippincott & Co., 1860). First published in 1842, the work was periodically updated and several editions existed by 1864.

58. Born in Maryland about 1810, in 1860 Mississippi Supreme Court justice Alexander H. Handy was living in Canton. He owned $6,500 real and $20,000 personal property, including fourteen slaves. A. H. Handy, p. 2, 1860 Free Schedule, Mississippi, Madison, Canton, Roll 586, M653; Judge A. H. Handy, 1860 Slave Schedule, Mississippi, Madison, Not Stated, Roll 600, M653.

59. Sherman reported, "We staid at Meridian a week, and made the most complete destruction of railroads ever beheld. . . ." Yet the Confederates had the trains rolling fifteen days after his departure, and it was claimed that the rebuilt tracks were superior to what Sherman had destroyed. *OR*, 32, pt. 1:173; William M. Polk, *Leonidas Polk: Bishop and General*, 2 vols. (New York: Longman, Greens, and Co., 1893), 2:309.

60. Reaching Canton on February 26, Sherman's troops departed on February 29, withdrawing closer to Vicksburg. When Polk learned of this, he had Loring advance beyond the Pearl River north of Jackson. *OR*, 32, pt. 1:195.

61. Born in North Carolina about 1819, William J. Cowan was a farmer in Warren County in 1860 and owned $6,000 real and $15,000 personal property, including thirteen slaves. W. J. Cowan, 1860 Free Schedule, Mississippi, Warren, Not Stated, Roll 592, M653; W. J. Cowan, pp. 11–12, 1860 Slave Schedule, Mississippi, Warren, Not Stated, Roll 603, M653.

62. Either 55-year-old North Carolina native Sarah Wilkins or 49-year-old Virginian Mary Wilkins. Sarah Wilkins, p. 6, 1860 Free Schedule, Mississippi, Scott, District 1, Roll 591, M653; Mary Wilkins, p. 25, 1860 Free Schedule, Mississippi, Scott, District 5, Roll 591, M653.

63. Born about 1825 in Pennsylvania, Mrs. Harriet J. Cary and her two children lived in Clinton in 1860. She owned $10,000 real and

$10,000 personal property, including three slaves. H. J. Cary, p. 2, 1860 Free Schedule, Mississippi, Hinds, Clinton, Roll 582, M653; H. J. Cary, p. 2, 1860 Slave Schedule, Mississippi, Hinds, Clinton, Roll 597, M653.

64. Miss M. N. Gillespie was born in Ohio about 1830, and was living with her sister in Clinton in 1860. M. N. Gilispie, p. 2, 1860 Free Schedule, Mississippi, Hinds, Clinton, Roll 582, M653.

65. Isabella T. Lawrence was born in Mississippi about 1846 and resided with her family in Vicksburg in 1860. She was the sister of George D. Lawrence. Isabella T. Lawrence, p. 55, 1850 Free Schedule, Mississippi, Warren, Vicksburg, Roll 282, M432.

66. Located on the Jackson-Vicksburg road, the bridge spanned the Big Black River, which separated Warren and Hinds counties.

67. The son of A. M. Paxton, William G. Paxton was born in Mississippi about 1839. In 1860, he was a student living with his parents in Vicksburg. On March 26, 1861, in Vicksburg, he enlisted in Captain J. E. White's company (old F), 10th Mississippi Infantry Regiment, and was appointed 1st sergeant. Promoted to 1st lieutenant, he was transferred to be regimental adjutant on July 19. He resigned on October 9, returned to his company, and was discharged as a private on October 16. He was appointed adjutant of Colonel Wirt Adams's cavalry regiment on October 15 at Bowling Green, Kentucky, and was captured May 17, 1862, at Lebanon, Tennessee. Imprisoned at Camp Chase, Ohio, he was transferred to Johnson's Island, Ohio, on May 24. He was sent to Vicksburg on September 1 to be exchanged. Though Colonel Horace H. Miller requested that Paxton be assigned to his 9th Mississippi Cavalry Regiment on December 28, 1863, it appears he remained with Adams's regiment until he was paroled at Jackson May 15, 1865. Wm. Paxton, p. 11, 1860 Free Schedule, Mississippi, Warren, Vicksburg, Roll 592, M653; Service record of W. G. Paxton, Tenth Infantry, Roll 189, CSR MS; Service record of W. G. Paxton, Wood's Regiment, Roll 45, Compiled Service Records of Confederate Soldiers Who Served in Organizations Raised Directly by the Confederate Government, M-258, War Department Collection of Confederate Records, RG 109, National Archives and Records Service, Washington, DC (hereafter cited as CSRCS); Col. H. H. Miller to Lt. Col. T. B. Lamar, Dec. 28, 1863, in papers of William G. Paxton, Roll 308, UPSBCCSR.

68. Born in Kentucky about 1840, Mary E. Moody was living in Madison County in 1860 with her husband, Ed F. Moody, five years her senior and a native of Alabama, and her infant son William E., who was born in Mississippi. Mary E. Moody, p. 5, 1860 Free Schedule, Mississippi, Madison, Not Stated, Roll 586, M653.

69. First Lieutenant A. B. Coffey and 2nd Lieutenant J. M. Wilfong belonged to Captain Thomas C. Flournoy's Confederate Rangers. The

company had been organized at Memphis, Tennessee, on April 26, 1862. Comprised mostly of Tennesseans, this company was joined with two others composed of Mississippians on September 15, 1862, to form the 17th (Sanders's) Tennessee Cavalry Battalion. With Sanders's promotion to major, Coffey was elevated to 1st lieutenant and Wilfong to either junior or senior 2nd lieutenant. At this time the company was detached on scouting duty along the Big Black River, which explains their ability to deliver the mail in that region. In December 1864, it was consolidated with the 17th Mississippi Cavalry Battalion to form the 9th Mississippi Cavalry Regiment. Papers of A. B. Coffey, Roll 77, UPSBCCSR; Civil War Centennial Commission of Tennessee, *Tennesseans in the Civil War: A Military History of Confederate and Union Units with Available Rosters of Personnel*, 2 vols. (Nashville, TN: Civil War Centennial Commission, 1964), 1:36.

70. Mary Miller Bell Tappan was born in Tennessee on August 31, 1834. In 1860, she was living with her father, Benjamin Swett Tappan, in Vicksburg. Tappan, *Tappan-Toppan Genealogy*, 17; Benj. S. Tappan, p. 49, 1850 Free Schedule, Mississippi, Warren, Vicksburg, Roll 382, M432; Preacher's Kid, "Benjamin S. Tappan."

71. Born in Canada about 1840, Archibald D. McInnis was working as a telegraph operator in Evergreen, Alabama, when he enlisted at Sparta, Alabama, on April 25, 1861, as a private in Company E, 4th Alabama Infantry Regiment. Wounded at First Manassas on July 21, the following day he was appointed 1st sergeant. On December 4, he was detached on special service at the telegraph office in Richmond, Virginia, and, on January 1, 1862, he resigned as ordnance sergeant. Promoted to ordnance sergeant on April 23, 1862, he was elected later that year junior 2nd lieutenant and promoted to senior 2nd lieutenant October 9. He became a 1st lieutenant June 1, 1863, was wounded at Gettysburg July 2, and promoted to captain the following day. Admitted to C.S.A. General Hospital, Charlottesville, Virginia, on August 6, he was furloughed on September 2. Declared absent without leave on February 7, 1864, he returned to the Army of Northern Virginia in time to participate in the Battle of the Wilderness (May 5–7) and retired to the Invalid Corps on January 17, 1865. Service record of Archibald D. McInnis, Fourth Infantry, Roll 126, Compiled Service Records of Confederate Soldiers Who Served in Organizations from the State of Alabama, M-311, War Department Collection of Confederate Records, RG 109, National Archives and Records Service, Washington, DC.

72. The Confederate States of America was never recognized as an independent nation by any foreign country. Rumors circulated that a letter written by Pope Pius IX to "Your Excellency" Jefferson Davis on December 3, 1863, constituted such recognition, but Davis did not regard it as such. *OR*, ser. 4, 3:401.

73. Stephen Dill Lee was born in Charleston, South Carolina, on September 22, 1833. Finishing seventeenth out of forty-six graduates in the West Point class of 1854, he served in the artillery during the Third Seminole War, along the Kansas-Missouri border, and just before resigning in 1861, in the Dakota Territory. Appointed a captain of artillery in the South Carolina Army, he served as an aide to Brigadier General Pierre G. T. Beauregard during the firing on Fort Sumter. He commanded a battery during the Peninsula Campaign, the 4th Virginia Regiment Cavalry in mid-1862, and, as a colonel, a battalion of artillery at Second Manassas and Sharpsburg. Promoted to brigadier general on November 6, 1862, he was given command of an infantry brigade in Tennessee, which was transferred to Vicksburg in December 1862. After being captured at Vicksburg on July 4, 1863, he was promoted to major general and given command of all the cavalry in Mississippi until May 9, 1864, when he succeeded Lieutenant General Polk as commander of the Department of Alabama, Mississippi, and East Louisiana. On June 23, he became the youngest lieutenant general in the Confederate army and assumed command of a corps in the Army of Tennessee; he surrendered with that army in April 1865. After the war, he became the first president of the Agricultural and Mechanical College of Mississippi (present-day Mississippi State University), served on the board of the Vicksburg National Military Park, and helped found and was president of the United Confederate Veterans from 1904 until his death on May 28, 1908. Davis and Hoffman, eds., *The Confederate General*, 4:59, 63.

74. Born on November 22, 1835, in the Indian Territory, Frank C. Armstrong graduated from Holy Cross Academy and College in Massachusetts. In 1854, he accompanied his stepfather, Brigadier General Persifor F. Smith, on an expedition into New Mexico, where he distinguished himself fighting Indians and earned a commission as a 2nd lieutenant in the 2nd U.S. Dragoons. After participating in the Utah Expedition (1858–59), Armstrong was promoted to captain, and he led his company in the Battle of First Manassas on July 21, 1861. Immediately thereafter, he resigned and, as a volunteer aide on the staff of Brigadier General Ben McCulloch, fought for the Confederates at the Battle of Wilson's Creek, Missouri, on August 10. As a volunteer aide to Colonel James McQueen McIntosh, he fought at the Battle of Chustenahlah, Indian Territory, on December 26. Following McIntosh's death during the Battle of Pea Ridge, Arkansas, on March 7, 1862, Armstrong joined the staff of Major General Earl Van Dorn. On May 8, General Pierre G. T. Beauregard appointed Armstrong colonel of the 3rd Louisiana Infantry Regiment. On July 7, Major General Sterling Price appointed him an acting brigadier general and gave him command of all the cavalry in the Army of the West. After distinguishing

himself in several engagements, Armstrong was promoted to brigadier general on April 23, 1863, and secured command of a brigade in Brigadier General Nathan B. Forrest's division. He commanded a division at the Battle of Chickamauga, Georgia, September 19–20, and during the Knoxville, Tennessee, Campaign, November 17–December 5, 1863. On March 5, 1864, he was transferred to the Department of Alabama, Mississippi, and East Louisiana, and assigned a brigade in Brigadier General William H. Jackson's division. Soon attached to the Army of Tennessee, Armstrong lead his brigade throughout the campaigns in Georgia and Tennessee. In February 1865, his brigade was transferred to Brigadier General James R. Chalmers's division. After fighting at Selma, Alabama, on April 2, he assumed command of the division, which he led until the department was surrendered on May 4. After the war, he was involved with Indian affairs and died on September 8, 1909. Davis and Hoffman, eds., *The Confederate General*, 1:43–44.

75. Lieutenant Colonel Walter A. Rorer, 20th Mississippi Infantry Regiment, witnessed the review. In a letter written on March 31, Rorer noted that the cannoneers were well-clothed and made "a much finer [appearance] than the infantry did." He also found the horses in good condition but added that "they have been lately impressed and I am very much afraid they will soon become to look as artillery horses usually do." Walter R. Rorer to Susan Willcox, Mar. 31, 1864, James M. Willcox Papers, 1831–1871, Manuscript Department, Duke Univ. Library, Durham, NC, quoted in Daniel, *Cannoneers in Gray*, 144; Field and Staff Muster Roll for July & Aug., 1864, in service record of Walter A. Rorer, Twentieth Infantry, Roll 291, CSR MS.

76. Born in Mississippi about 1835, in 1860 Levin R. Marshall Jr. and his wife lived with his parents and siblings at Cabin Tule plantation in Adams County and worked for his father. Levin Sr., a planter, owned $35,000 real and $186,000 personal property, including 236 slaves. Levin Jr. was appointed captain on August 26, 1863. At this time, he was serving as assistant adjutant general on the staff of Major General William W. Loring. Levin R. Marshall, p. 21, 1860 Free Schedule, Mississippi, Adams, Not Stated, Roll 577, M653; Levin R. Marshall, pp. 20–23, 1860 Slave Schedule, Louisiana, Madison, Not Stated, Roll 429, M653; Service records of Levin R. Marshall, Roll 163, CSRCGSO.

77. A resident of Helena, Arkansas, Angus Grant Quaite enlisted as a private in Company F, 1st Arkansas Infantry (State Troops), on July 25, 1861. Appointed captain and assistant commissary of subsistence for Phifer's Brigade on June 10, 1862, he was assigned as major and chief quartermaster for 2nd Brigade, Maury's Division, on October 27, 1862. On April 11, 1863, Quaite was appointed major and quartermaster and ordered to report to Brigadier General John C. Moore. On January 9,

1864, he was assigned as chief quartermaster for Major General Stephen D. Lee. His duty was to travel Mississippi and purchase or impress surplus mules, artillery horses, leather, and other transportation supplies. He was paroled at Jackson on May 15, 1865. Service record of Angus G. Quaite, Roll 204, CSRCGSO.

78. Having learned of a Union buildup at Decatur, Alabama, Polk began pulling his infantry out of Mississippi to counter an enemy advance southward from Decatur. *OR*, 32, pt. 3:736.

79. Born about 1815 in Virginia, F. M. Fitzhugh lived in Madison County in 1860. A physician and planter, he owned $25,000 real and $37,800 personal property, including thirty-five slaves. F. M. Fitzhugh, p. 107, 1860 Free Schedule, Mississippi, Madison, Not Stated, Roll 586, M653; Dr. F. M. Fitzhugh, p. 205, 1860 Slave Schedule, Mississippi, Madison, Not Stated, Roll 600, M653.

80. Born in Virginia about 1812, Samuel B. Wall was a farmer in Warren County in 1860. He owned $10,000 real and $25,000 personal property. S. B. Wall, p. 7, 1860 Free Schedule, Mississippi, Warren, Not Stated, Roll 592, M653; S. B. Wall, p. 5, 1860 Slave Schedule, Mississippi, Warren, Not Stated, Roll 603, M653.

81. Born about 1836, Mississippi native Martha B. Stith resided with Samuel B. and Sarah A. Wall in 1850. In 1860, Martha Bay Wall resided with the Walls. Samuel B. Wall, p. 50, 1850 Free Schedule, Mississippi, Warren, Not Stated, Roll 382, M432; Martha Bay Wall, p. 7, 1860 Free Schedule, Mississippi, Warren, Not Stated, Roll 592, M653.

82. Mashulaville.

83. Born in Mississippi about 1822, George Messenger was a planter in Warren County in 1860, owning $100,000 in real and $130,000 personal property, including 103 slaves. Geo. Messenger, p. 80, 1860 Free Schedule, Mississippi, Warren, Not Stated, Roll 592, M653; Geo. Messenger, pp. 125–26, 1860 Slave Schedule, Mississippi, Warren, Not Stated, Roll 603, M653.

84. In 1860, 25-year-old Alabama native B. H. Craig was residing in Cahaba, Dallas County, Alabama, with his wife and two children. A lawyer, he owned $4,350 real and $20,402 personal property, including ten slaves. B. H. Craig, p. 5, 1860 Free Schedule, Alabama, Dallas, Cahaba, Roll 8, M653; B. H. Craig, p. 2, 1860 Slave Schedule, Alabama, Dallas, Cahaba Town, Roll 29, M653.

85. A civil engineer who specialized in levee construction, Joseph A. Porter was residing in Vicksburg at the outbreak of the Civil War. Major General Leonidas Polk appointed him an assistant engineer in December 1861 and assigned him to Fort Pillow, Tennessee. While serving with Major General Sterling Price in the Army of the West on October 27, 1862, Porter applied for a position as captain of engineers. Shortly thereafter, Major General William W. Loring assigned Porter to place

obstructions in the Yazoo Pass. On May 12, 1863, he served as the volunteer commander of a company in the 50th Tennessee Infantry Regiment at the Battle of Raymond. General Joseph E. Johnston nominated him for captain of engineers on May 22 and, on August 6, he was appointed captain of Company D, 2nd Regiment Engineer Troops. Eventually headquartered at Demopolis, Alabama, he remained there until May 1864, when he was transferred to Georgia. After serving on Lieutenant General Alexander P. Stewart's staff during the Atlanta Campaign and the invasion of Tennessee, he was paroled at Meridian on May 10, 1865. Service record of Joseph A. Porter, Second Confederate Engineer Troops, Roll 98, CSRCS; *OR*, 24, pt. 1:746.

86. Born about 1812 in Kentucky, Thomas A. Marshall was a lawyer in Vicksburg in 1860. He owned $33,000 real and $18,500 personal property, including nine slaves. T. A. Marshall, p. 67, 1860 Free Schedule, Mississippi, Warren, Vicksburg, Roll 592, M653; T. A. Marshall, p. 14, 1860 Slave Schedule, Mississippi, Warren, Vicksburg, Roll 603, M653.

87. Born in Kentucky on March 15, 1826, Horace H. Miller served as a sergeant major in the Mexican War. In 1860, he was practicing law in Vicksburg and owned $8,000 real and $10,000 personal property, including six slaves. A brigadier general of militia, in May 1861, Horace H. Miller entered Confederate service at Vicksburg as captain of the Vicksburg Sharp Shooters, which became Company E, 12th Mississippi Infantry Regiment. By 1863, he had been commissioned lieutenant colonel and was assigned as adjutant and inspector general for the post of Ponchatoula, Louisiana. On August 20, 1863, he was promoted to colonel of the 9th Mississippi Cavalry Regiment. Under arrest when the war ended, he returned to Vicksburg and practiced law until his death on January 26, 1877. Allardice, *Confederate Colonels*, 273–74; H. H. Miller, p. 48, 1860 Free Schedule, Mississippi, Warren, Vicksburg, Roll 592, M653; H. H. Miller, p. 12, 1860 Slave Schedule, Mississippi, Warren, Vicksburg, Roll 603, M653; Service record of H. H. Miller, Ninth Cavalry, Roll 39, CSR MS.

88. Learning on April 25 that the Federals were leaving Decatur for Chattanooga, Polk ordered his troops near Elyton to march south. *OR*, 32, pt. 3:822.

89. In 1861, Caswell C. Huckabee and Jonathan N. Smith established the Bibb County Iron Company. Initially producing cast iron, they added a blast furnace in 1862 and began producing wrought iron. The quality of their iron was so superior that Confederate officials forced the two men to sell the facility to the government for $600,000 in 1863. Renamed the Bibb Naval Furnace and connected by railroad, by 1864 the ironworks was producing twenty-five tons of iron per day for the Selma Ordnance and Naval Foundry. The Bibb Naval Furnace was destroyed

on March 31, 1865, during Brigadier General James H. Wilson's cavalry raid through Alabama and Georgia. "Brierfield Furnace," *Wikipedia: The Free Encyclopedia,* http://en.wikipedia.org/wiki/Brierfield_Furnace (accessed July 4, 2013). [Editors note: While some readers will question a reference to Wikipedia, in this case the author had access to documents generated as part of the nominating process of the property to the National Register of Historic Places. As the application was approved, we feel the information has been vetted.]

90. Private **George Marshall** left Company G to become the adjutant for the 9th Mississippi Cavalry Regiment.

91. Born in Alabama on April 15, 1828, Abner C. Steede served as a lieutenant during the Mexican War. In 1860 he was married with four children, worked as the court clerk for Jackson County, and owned $6,000 real and $3,500 personal property, including two slaves. Steede organized a two-company battalion in early spring of 1863. Commanding as major, Steede added five more companies of what became the 17th Mississippi Cavalry Battalion before it was merged with other units to form the 9th Mississippi Cavalry Regiment. He was appointed lieutenant colonel on January 13, 1865. Linda Ellis, "Col Abner Clayton Steede," *Find A Grave,* http://www.findagrave.com/cgi-bin/fg.cgi?page=gr&GSln=STE&GSpartial=1&GSbyrel=all&GSst=27&GScntry=4&GSsr=401&GRid=32474346& (accessed July 4, 2013); A. C. Steede, p. 40, 1860 Free Schedule, Mississippi, Jackson, Not Stated, Roll 582, M653; A. C. Steede, p. 8, 1860 Slave Schedule, Mississippi, Jackson, Not Stated, Roll 598, M653; Service record of A. C. Steede, Seventeenth Battalion Cavalry, Roll 48, CSR MS; National Park Service," 17th Battalion, Mississippi Cavalry," in "Regiment Details," in *The Civil War,* http://www.nps.gov/civilwar/search-regiments-detail.htm?regiment_id=CMS0017BC (accessed July 5, 2013).

92. The only possible uncle by blood was Francis Gildart [II] (1797–1871). "Family View," Jefferson College Board of Trustees Members, http://trees.ancestry.com/tree/42722266/family?cfpid=20416306342&selnode=1 (accessed Aug. 5, 2013; password protected site).

93. Eggleston was spot on. The day before Davis had sent a telegram to Demopolis ordering Polk to send Loring's Division to Rome, Georgia. *OR,* 38, pt. 4:661.

94. Major General William T. Sherman's opening move in his campaign to take Atlanta was to force General Joseph E. Johnston to abandon his fortifications along Rocky Face Ridge by threatening his line of communications. He accomplished this by having Major General James B. McPherson's Army of the Tennessee maneuver so as to threaten Johnston's left flank near Dalton, Resaca, and Rome. Richard M. McMurry, *Atlanta 1864: Last Chance for the Confederacy* (Lincoln: Univ. of Nebraska Press, 2000), 62–64. For more on the Atlanta

Campaign, see Albert Castel, *Decision in the West: The Atlanta Campaign of 1864* (Lawrence: Univ. Press of Kansas, 1992).

95. The "glorious news" concerned the Confederates' successful defense of Rocky Face Ridge and Dug Gap, Georgia, on May 8, the Battle of the Wilderness, Virginia, May 5–7, and the repulse of Major General Nathaniel P. Banks's Red River Expedition, beginning with his defeat at the Battle of Mansfield, Louisiana, on April 8, and culminating with his evacuation of Alexandria, Louisiana, on May 13.

96. Loring's Division did not arrive at Resaca simultaneously. Scott's brigade arrived on the tenth, Loring and Adams's Brigade on the eleventh, and Featherston's Brigade on the twelfth. *OR*, 38, pt. 3:874.

97. Whether due to incompetence or only confusion, Johnston's faulty troop redeployments allowed McPherson to seize Snake Creek Gap and, albeit briefly, the Western & Atlantic Railroad north of Resaca on May 9. Unable to expel McPherson, Johnston had no choice but to withdraw to Resaca. McMurry, *Atlanta 1864*, 64–68.

98. To protect Johnston's retreat from Dalton to Resaca, some of his troops had to halt to block an advance by McPherson eastward from Snake Creek Gap. Ibid., 69.

99. A Union division managed to secure a position east of the Oostanaula River at Lay's Ferry. With his left flank turned and his communications with Atlanta threatened, Johnston, once again, had to retreat. Ibid., 72.

100. On May 7, Lieutenant General Polk ordered that forty-two enlisted men of Captain J. M. McLendon's battery be temporarily detailed to strengthen the other batteries under his command. Muster Roll for Company C, Jan. 10–June 30, 1864, Fourteenth Battalion, Light Artillery, Roll 92, CSR MS.

101. Polk's infantry brought up the rear of Johnston's retreat and was fortunate enough to be well-protected by cavalry. Major General Joseph Wheeler with two divisions covered Polk to the north, northeast, and east, and Major General William T. Martin's Division covered the northwest and west. *OR*, 38, pt. 4:721.

102. At this time Featherston's Brigade consisted of the 3rd, 22nd, 31st, 33rd, and 40th Mississippi infantry regiments and the 1st Mississippi Battalion Sharpshooters. By July 31, the 1st Mississippi Infantry Regiment and Captain A. D. Brown's battalion had been attached to it, but both had been reassigned by August 31. Ibid., pt. 3:645, 664, 668.

103. Winfield Scott Featherston was born near Murfreesboro, Tennessee, on August 8, 1820. He dropped out of school at seventeen to fight in the Creek War. After being mustered out, he studied law and was admitted to the bar in Mississippi in 1840. Elected to Congress as a Democrat in 1846 and 1848, he was defeated in 1850 because of his opposition to the Compromise of 1850. When Mississippi seceded in January 1861, Featherston organized and became captain of the Mississippi Guards,

which entered Confederate service on June 7 as Company G, 17th Mississippi Infantry Regiment. Elected colonel of the regiment, Featherston led it at the battles of First Manassas and Ball's Bluff in Virginia. Promoted to brigadier general on March 6, 1862, he was given command of a brigade in Major General Daniel H. Hill's Division, which he led during the siege of Yorktown and the Battle of Williamsburg. On June 12, Featherston was placed in command of a newly created all-Mississippi brigade in Major General James Longstreet's Division. Seriously wounded at the Battle of Glendale, by the time Featherston rejoined his brigade two months later, it had been assigned to Major General Richard H. Anderson's Division. He commanded two brigades on August 30 at Second Manassas, but Longstreet criticized his performance. After leading his brigade at the Battle of Fredericksburg, he was transferred to Mississippi on January 19, 1863, where he was assigned an all-Mississippi brigade under Major General William W. Loring. As part of Lieutenant General Leonidas Polk's Army of Mississippi, Featherston's Brigade was sent to Georgia in May 1864, where it participated in the Atlanta Campaign. When Polk was killed on June 14, Loring succeeded him and Featherston took command of Loring's Division. When Lieutenant General Alexander P. Stewart took command of the Army of Mississippi on July 7, Loring and Featherston resumed their regular commands. Featherston distinguished himself during the Battle of Peachtree Creek on July 20, where his brigade suffered nearly 50 percent casualties. When Loring was wounded during the Battle of Ezra Church on July 28, Featherston took over the division until Loring returned in mid-September. After participating in General John B. Hood's invasion of Tennessee, Featherston's was one of six infantry brigades on December 20 deemed fit to fight a rear guard action. In February 1865, Featherston's Brigade was transferred from Tupelo to North Carolina, where Featherston was paroled at Greensboro on May 1, 1865. After the war, he practiced law, dabbled in politics, and became a judge. He died on May 28, 1891. Davis and Hoffman, eds., *The Confederate General*, 2:119–21.

104. Francis Asbury Shoup was born in Laurel, Indiana, on March 22, 1834. He graduated fifteenth in the West Point class of 1855 and became a 2nd lieutenant of artillery. He was stationed at various coastal forts and participated in the Third Seminole War. Resigning on January 10, 1860, he returned to Indiana, studied law, and was admitted to the bar. He also organized a company of zouaves and was elected its captain. During the winter of 1860–61, he moved to St. Augustine, Florida, and began practicing law. Though a recent transplanted Yankee, when Florida seceded, Shoup offered his services to Governor M. S. Perry. Commissioned a lieutenant of artillery in the Confederate army on March 16, 1861, he was assigned to the staff of Colonel

William J. Hardee at Fort Morgan, Alabama. He accompanied Hardee to northern Arkansas and then to Kentucky. Promoted to major on November 7, Shoup commanded an artillery battalion at Cave City, Kentucky, and served as Hardee's chief of artillery during the Battle of Shiloh, where he assisted in massing the sixty-two cannon that blasted the Hornets' Nest. Following the retreat to Corinth, General P. G. T. Beauregard appointed him chief of artillery for the Army of the Mississippi. Returning to Arkansas, he commanded a battalion of artillery until September 28, 1862, when Major General Thomas C. Hindman put him in charge of an infantry brigade. Plagued with regimental commanders who outranked him, Shoup's troubles soon doubled when he was elevated to command of a two-brigade division, which he led at the Battle of Prairie Grove on December 7. Promoted to brigadier general on April 11, 1863, to rank from September 12, 1862, he was ordered east and soon found himself besieged at Vicksburg in command of a brigade of Louisiana infantry. After being exchanged following his capture on July 4, he was assigned to command an infantry brigade at Mobile. On April 3, 1864, he became the chief of artillery for the Army of Tennessee. His excellent performance influenced General John B. Hood to make him his chief of staff on July 24. Relieved at his own request on September 14, he remained unassigned until February 21, 1865, when he was ordered to report to General Joseph E. Johnston in North Carolina. On March 13, he was placed in command of the black troops being raised to fight in the Confederate army but before he could lead them into battle, Johnston surrendered the army to Maj. Gen. William T. Sherman. Paroled at Greensboro on May 2, 1865, Shoup found employment as professor of applied mathematics at the University of Mississippi. Three years later he became an Episcopal priest and spent the remainder of his life serving the church and teaching. He died at Columbus, Tennessee, on September 4, 1896. Ibid., 5:150–51.

105. Regulations did not provide for Shoup having a chief surgeon, therefore it is probable that the individual Eggleston arrested was a Dr. Foster, who had served as Shoup's volunteer surgeon during the siege of Vicksburg. *OR*, 24, pt. 2:410.

106. Born in Georgia, Assistant Surgeon Andrew J. Foard resigned from the U.S. Army on April 1, 1861, and was assigned to duty as assistant surgeon at Pensacola, Florida, on April 10, 1861, where he was in charge of the general hospital. Promoted to surgeon on June 1, he became the medical director on Major General Braxton Bragg's staff on October 14. General Albert S. Johnston made Foard medical director for the Army of the Mississippi on March 30, 1862, and General P. G. T. Beauregard made him medical director for the Western Department on May 10. Later that year Bragg named him the medical director for both the

Department of Tennessee and the Army of Tennessee. On January 6, 1863, Foard was ordered to report to General Joseph E. Johnston, who made him medical director for the Department of the West. On November 27, he was assigned as medical director for the Army of Tennessee. On February 12, 1864, he joined J. E. Johnston's staff as medical director and continued as such under Johnston's successor, General John B. Hood. Relieved from duty with the Army of Tennessee on February 8, 1865, Foard was inspecting hospitals when he was assigned to J. E. Johnston's staff on March 13. After the war, he was a professor at the Washington Medical College in Baltimore, Maryland. Hugh T. Harrington, *Civil War Milledgeville: tales from the Confederate capital of Georgia* (Charleston, SC: The History Press, 2005), 31–32; Service record of Andrew J. Foard, Roll 95, CSRCGSO.

107. Determining the position at Adairsville untenable, Johnston resumed his retreat. McMurry, *Atlanta 1864,* 77.

108. The new line they occupied that afternoon ran along a ridge from northeast of Cassville to about a mile and a quarter south of the town, with Polk's Army of Mississippi occupying the center. Ibid., 82.

109. After Union artillery deployed opposite Johnston's new line, the Confederates discovered that a sizeable portion of the center could be enfiladed. Once again Johnston opted to retreat, even before learning that the Federals had managed to cross the Etowah River. Ibid., 82–83.

110. Possibly the Confederates were keeping their opinions to themselves, for even their commander was becoming demoralized. On May 23, Johnston wrote his wife, "I have seen so much beautiful country given up [to the enemy] as to be made unhappy by it. You can not imagine how disheartening it is & at the same time humiliating to see the apprehension of the people of a country abandoned to the enemy. I had rather have the agony of defeat as far as my own feelings are concerned." Johnston to wife, May 23, 1864, McLane-Fisher Papers, ca. 1800–1905, Maryland Historical Society, Baltimore, quoted in McMurry, *Atlanta 1864,* 84.

111. Resuming his advance, Sherman attempted to turn Johnston's left flank, but this time, instead of retreating, Johnston shifted two of his three corps, including Cowan's Battery, southwest from Allatoona. McMurry, *Atlanta 1864,* 86.

112. The heavy firing was Major General Joseph Hooker's 20th Corps advancing toward New Hope Church. Though 2,000 casualties (1,500 Federal, 500 Confederate) were nominal at best by this stage of the war, Eggleston had seen little combat in his twenty-five months of service. Ibid., 88–89.

113. Loring's Division moved two miles to the right and occupied the position previously held by Hindman's Division of Hood's Corps. *OR,* 38, pt. 3:875.

114. The assault against Cleburne occurred on May 27 and was known as the Battle of Pickett's Mill. The Confederates lost 448; the Federals had approximately 1,600 killed, wounded, and missing. Though not as one-sided as Lieutenant General William Hardee supposedly speculated, it was bad enough for one eyewitness, Union lieutenant Ambrose Bierce, to write "The Crime of Pickett's Mill" after the war. Castel, *Decision in the West*, 234, 235, 241, 639.

115. Battle of Murfreesboro, Tennessee, December 31, 1862–January 2, 1863.

116. Considerable artillery and musketry firing at various points along the line, but no Union assault took place. *OR*, 38, pt. 3:988.

117. Despite all the fighting that Cowan's artillerymen had experienced, they had the good fortune to have been deployed in locations the Federals did not attack. One reason for their luck was that after Resaca, where they were deployed on the left flank, Polk's command occupied the center, and Civil War armies usually attacked the enemy's flanks. Additionally, between May 25 and June 4, the opposing armies faced each other along a ten-mile front stretching from south of Dallas to northeast of Pickett's Mill. Often half a mile apart, with intervening woods, skirmishing dominated combat, with little need for 12-pounder howitzers. Castel, *Decision in the West*, 155, 199, 247–48, 258.

118. Sherman had extended his lines as far from Western & Atlantic Railroad as possible. Having failed to turn Johnston's left flank, he had no choice but to move northeastward toward the railroad. On June 1, Federal cavalry seized the undefended Allatoona Pass; two days later Federal infantry occupied Acworth, three miles to the south. McMurry, *Atlanta 1864*, 91–92.

119. Born in Missouri about 1819, Thomas R. Holloman was a planter in Yazoo County in 1860. He owned $35,000 real and $76,100 personal property, including sixty-seven slaves. T. R. Holloman, p. 50, 1860 Free Schedule, Mississippi, Yazoo, Not Stated, Roll 594, M653; T. R. Holloman, pp. 110–11, Mississippi, Yazoo, Not Stated, Roll 604, M653.

120. Major General Samuel G. French commanded one of three infantry divisions in Polk's Army of Mississippi. *OR*, 38, pt. 3:645.

121. The movements of Cowan's Battery were part of Johnston's grand design to counter Sherman's advance along the railroad against his right flank. McMurry, *Atlanta 1864*, 92.

122. Walter J. Morris was serving as a 1st lieutenant on ordnance duty on October 28, 1861, but by February 1862 he was an engineer on the staff of Brigadier General Lloyd Tilghman. After being released from prison following his capture at Fort Henry, Tennessee, he was appointed a 1st lieutenant of engineers from Kentucky on October 4, 1862, and assigned to the staff of Lieutenant General Leonidas Polk on December 11. On May 27, 1863, he was appointed captain from Tennessee. Relieved from duty with the Army of Tennessee in Decem-

ber, he was stationed in Richmond, Virginia, until returning to Polk's staff on May 12, 1864. On September 23, he was relieved from duty with the Army of Tennessee; assigned to the Department of Alabama, Mississippi, and East Louisiana; and stationed at Mobile, Alabama. He was paroled at Meridian on May 10, 1865. Service record of Walter J. Morris, Roll 108, CSRCS.

123. T. F. Folkes enlisted as a private in Company D, 28th Mississippi Cavalry Regiment at Camp Holly on August 19, 1862. Reported as having deserted on December 24, 1863, he died June 9, 1864, in the hospital at Marietta, Georgia, from wounds received near Dallas, Georgia. This Tom Folkes, however, is not Thomas M. Folkes of Vicksburg, who survived the war. Service record of T. F. Folkes, Twenty-eighth Cavalry, Roll 55, CSR MS.

124. Barbour was the assistant quartermaster general for the Army of Mississippi. Service record of W. A. Barbour, Roll 15, CSRCGSO.

125. The 12th Louisiana Infantry Regiment was in a brigade with five Alabama regiments so that its commander, Thomas M. Scott, would command the brigade as senior colonel. He was promoted to brigadier general on May 24, 1864, to rank from May 10. His was one of three brigades in Loring's Division. Davis and Hoffman, eds., *The Confederate General*, 5:131; *OR*, 38, pt. 3:645.

126. Abram M. Feltus Jr. enlisted April 21, 1861, at Woodville in what became Company K, 16th Mississippi Infantry Regiment. Initially a 2nd lieutenant, at twenty-six he became captain when the regiment was organized on June 6, 1861. During his service in the Army of Northern Virginia, he was promoted to major on December 20, 1862, and to lieutenant colonel on March 7, 1864. He was killed at Spotsylvania Court House, Virginia, on May 12, 1864. Service record of Abram M. Feltus, Sixteenth Infantry, Roll 241, CSR MS.

127. Born in Ireland about 1837, John Lee was working as a clerk in Vicksburg when he enlisted on May 15, 1861, at Vicksburg, and was mustered in as a private in what eventually became Company A, 21st Mississippi Infantry Regiment. Slightly wounded in the arm at Gettysburg on July 2, 1863, he was transferred to Company L on February 16, 1864, and promoted to 3rd sergeant and to 2nd sergeant before being killed during the Battle of the Wilderness, Virginia, on May 6. Service record of John Lee, Twenty-first Infantry, Roll 297, CSR MS.

128. Battle of the Wilderness, Virginia, May 5–7, and Battle of Spotsylvania Court House, Virginia, May 8–21.

129. The Vicksburg Southrons became Company A, 21st Mississippi Infantry Regiment.

130. Born in Alabama about 1831, William M. Bullock resided in Warren County in 1860 with his wife and son. A merchant, he owned $1,000 real and $12,000 personal property. He enlisted at Vicksburg on

March 7, 1862, and was immediately appointed 2nd corporal in Company H, 2nd Mississippi Infantry Battalion, which later became Company H, 48th Mississippi Infantry Regiment. Elected junior 2nd lieutenant on December 24, 1862, he was promoted to 2nd lieutenant on April 20, 1863. Originally listed as missing in action at Spotsylvania Court House, Virginia, on May 12, 1864, he in fact had been captured. Initially taken to Belle Plain, he was received at Fort Delaware (DE) on May 17. He was sent to Hilton Head, South Carolina, on August 20, and from there to Fort Pulaski, Georgia, by October 20. He returned to Hilton Head and then to Fort Delaware on March 12, 1865. After signing the Oath of Allegiance, he was released from Fort Delaware on June 16. W. Bullock, p. 78, 1860 Free Schedule, Mississippi, Warren, Not Stated, Roll 592, M653; Service record of William M. Bullock, Forty-eighth Infantry, Roll 415, CSR MS.

131. Born in Mississippi about 1838, James M. Crump was a book merchant in Vicksburg in 1860, owned $2,000 personal property, and resided with his parents. His father, R. H. Crump, was mayor and owned $2,000 real and $15,000 personal property, including four slaves. James enlisted at Vicksburg on March 6, 1862, and was immediately appointed 2nd sergeant in Company H, 2nd Mississippi Infantry Battalion, which later became Company H, 48th Mississippi Infantry Regiment. Crump was reduced to private on February 16, 1863, but before the end of spring he was again 2nd sergeant and, by the fall, was 1st sergeant. Initially reported missing in action, it was later determined that he was killed in action at Spotsylvania Court House, Virginia, on May 12, 1864. James Crump, p. 7, 1860 Free Schedule, Mississippi, Warren, Vicksburg, Roll 592, M653; R. H. Crump, p. 2, 1860 Slave Schedule, Mississippi, Warren, Vicksburg, Roll 603, M653; Service record of James M. Crump, Forty-eighth Infantry, Roll 416, CSR MS.

132. Sherman had allowed his soldiers to rest while the railroad bridge over the Etowah River was being rebuilt. He resumed his advance on June 10, which caused the increased activity noticed by Eggleston. McMurry, *Atlanta 1864*, 102.

133. The Federals completed the railroad bridge over the Etowah River on June 11, enabling trains to reach the front. Ibid., 100.

134. Major General Francis P. Blair and two divisions of the 17th Corps, about 9,000 men, reinforced Sherman on June 8. Ibid., 100.

135. Elizabeth Yoste, the only sister of **George W. Yoste** old enough (nineteen) to be traveling alone. In 1860 she lived with her parents and attended school in Vicksburg. Her father, B. Yoste, was a farmer, owning $9,000 real and $3,000 personal property. B. Yoste, p. 3, 1860 Free Schedule, Mississippi, Warren, Not Stated, Roll 592, M653.

136. Born in Bavaria in 1833, Henry S. Gwinner lived with his two brothers in Vicksburg in 1863; all three were saddle tree makers, and Henry

owned $1,000 personal property. He enrolled in Company C, 28th Mississippi Cavalry Regiment, at Vicksburg on February 12, 1862, and was mustered in as a bugler on February 25. He was appointed chief bugler for the regiment on July 1, and brigade bugler in February 1863. On February 3, 1864, Lieutenant General Polk detached him to secure the proper wood for saddle trees and inspect the finished products, and he was working as a foreman at Demopolis, Alabama, in January 1865. In addition, during part of this time, he served as bugler on the staff of Brigadier General William H. Jackson. He was paroled twice, at Gainesville, Alabama, on May 12 and at Grenada on May 19. Henry Gwinner, p. 16, 1860 Free Schedule, Mississippi, Warren, Vicksburg, Roll 592, M653; Service record of Henry S. Gwinner, Twenty-eighth Cavalry, Roll 55, CSR MS.

137. Appointed a captain and assistant commissary of subsistence from Florida on November 4, 1861, William S. Harris was assigned to the 1st Florida Cavalry Battalion. Promoted to major and assistant quartermaster on November 11, 1862, he was assigned to Brigadier General William G. M. Davis's Brigade in East Tennessee. Relieved on June 16, 1863, he was transferred to the Army of Mississippi on June 24, 1863. Reporting to General Johnston on July 8, he was made inspector of field transportation. That fall, his duty was to purchase or impress mules, artillery horses, leather, "& other materials of Field Transportation," first in Alabama beginning October 21 and in northeastern Mississippi and northwestern Alabama on November 16. Ordered to the Trans-Mississippi Department on December 2, he was working at Shreveport, Louisiana, as inspector general of field transportation on January 11, 1865. Service record of William S. Harris, Roll 119, CSRCGSO.

138. A Parrott shell passed through Polk's left arm, body, and right arm before striking a chestnut tree and exploding. Jack D. Welsh, M.D., *Medical Histories of Confederate Generals* (Kent, OH: Kent State Univ. Press, 1995), 174.

139. Born in Maine about 1813, C. K. Marshall was a Methodist preacher in Vicksburg in 1860. He owned $100,000 real and $7,000 personal property, including seven slaves. C. K. Marshall, p. 24, 1860 Free Schedule, Mississippi, Warren, Vicksburg, Roll 592, M653; C. K. Marshall, p. 7, 1860 Slave Schedule, Mississippi, Warren, Vicksburg, Roll 603, M653.

140. **Augustus A. Folkes.**

141. Johnston's left flank had been compromised on June 16, forcing Hardee to withdraw to a position that could be enfiladed by Federal artillery. They had to endure the fire for two days while engineers constructed a new line of defenses, which the army moved into on the night of the 18–19. McMurry, *Atlanta 1864*, 103.

142. Shortly before 6 p.m., the Federals began advancing along the Bell's Ferry Road and, shortly after 6 p.m., deployed a battery and opened fire. *OR*, 38, pt. 4:787.

143. During the Battle of Kennesaw Mountain, Cowan's and Bouanchaud's batteries were deployed near the center of Scott's Brigade, which was stretched thin on the extreme right of the Confederate line of infantry. Brigadier General Featherston wrote after the war that these guns were:

> pretty well fortified. These batteries commanded a large public road, running north from Marietta, and running parallel with the public road at the base of Kennesaw, and about 1,000 yards east of it, where our lines crossed the two roads. These two batteries, with others still further to the right and left of this road where the principal attack was made, were directed to give a converging and concentrated fire upon the enemy at this point. The order was obeyed with apparent pleasure, and artillery has been rarely served so effectively, within my knowledge, during the late war. The firing was rapid, well directed, and very destructive to the compact lines of the advancing foe. As usual, they advanced in three lines of battle.
>
> Here we had in our front, with the exception of a narrow space on each side of the road, woodlands with tolerably large growth. The fire of our artillery began when our skirmish line was driven in, and was continued until the enemy had passed beyond the reach of our guns. Our skirmish line held their position until confronted by an overwhelming force, when they fell back in good order to the main line of defense. The enemy advanced until they came within full view of our works, and received then a well-directed fire from our entire line of infantry behind their breastworks.
>
> This joint fire of the infantry and artillery was well calculated to arrest the onward march of experienced veterans. The enemy halted, wheeled, and retreated in confusion under its shock and deadly effect. Some hour or two after they retired, our skirmish line was reestablished on the same spot.

In his official report, written three days after the battle, Featherston noted that "the artillery was ably and skillfully served, and so terrible was the fire and severe its results that the enemy retired before it, leaving some of their dead upon the field unburied and hastily burying others." He concluded: "The action of the artillery was not only highly beneficial to us in its results, but very creditable to the batteries—both officers and men." Eggleston was conservative, if anything, in his estimate of enemy casualties in his front. *ORS*, pt. 1, 7:147–48; *OR*, 38, pt. 3:879–81.

144. The Battle of Kennesaw Mountain cost the Federals 3,000 casualties and the Confederates about 1,000. McMurry, *Atlanta 1864*, 109.

145. Born in Vicksburg on June 5, 1847, Honora "Nora" Elizabeth Roach was a student living with her parents, James Roach and Mahala Perkins Harding Eggleston, in Vicksburg in 1860. Her father was a banker and owned $5,300 real and $50,000 personal property, including ten slaves. Nora married Dr. Robert J. Turnbull on June 17, 1865, and died on September 28, 1881. She was the niece of Edmund T. Eggleston. "Honora 'Nora' Elizabeth Roach," *Vicksburg Connections*, http://trees.ancestry.com/tree/28580183/person/13191968059?pgNum=1 (accessed July 7, 2013; password protected site); James Roach, p. 78, 1860 Free Schedule, Mississippi, Warren, Vicksburg, Roll 592, M653; James Roach, p. 16, 1860 Slave Schedule, Mississippi, Warren, Vicksburg, Roll 603, M653.

146. On June 26, a Union brigade successfully crossed Olley's Creek beyond Johnston's left flank. By the time the Federal attacks got underway at Kennesaw Mountain the following day, more Yankees had crossed Olley's Creek. The equivalent of a Union division now stood closer to the Chattahoochee River than the Confederates on Johnston's left. Rain prevented Sherman from exploiting this advantage until July 1, but when he did, Johnston retreated once again. McMurry, *Atlanta 1864*, 109–10.

147. Upset that the Confederates had slipped away, Sherman's pushed his pursuit in hopes of either bringing Johnston to battle before his men could entrench or catching them crossing the Chattahoochee River. Loring's Division deployed west of the Pace's Ferry Road. Ibid., 110, 113; *OR*, 38, pt. 5:863.

148. Describing the Confederate fortifications along the Chattahoochee "the best line of field intrenchments I have ever seen," Sherman decided to turn Johnston's right flank instead. Quoted in McMurry, *Atlanta 1864*, 115.

149. Major Generals Sherman, George Thomas, and Oliver Howard were out in front reconnoitering on the morning of the sixth. Sherman later wrote, there "was a space concealed by dense woods, in crossing which I came near riding into a detachment of the enemy's cavalry; and later in the same day Colonel Frank Sherman, of Chicago, then on General Howard's staff, did actually ride straight into the enemy's camp, supposing that our lines were continuous." Howard reported that Colonel Francis T. Sherman, his chief of staff, was captured while reconnoitering on July 7. *OR*, 38, pt. 1:894; William T. Sherman, *Memoirs of Gen. W. T. Sherman, written by himself, with an appendix bringing his life*

down to its closing scenes, also a personal tribute and critique of the memoirs, by Hon. James G. Blaine, 2 vols. (4th rev. ed., New York: Charles L. Webster & Co., 1891-1892), 1:67.

150. Earlier that day, Sherman had secured several bridgeheads across the Chattahoochee, forcing Johnston, once again, to retreat. McMurry, *Atlanta 1864,* 116.

151. Johnston did not issue the order because it was demoralizing. It concluded: "Yesterday the enemy had a great interest in finding the fords in the Chattahoochee, and easily attained their object, the pickets by mutual agreement bathing in the river together. The engineers of the enemy most probably mingle with the bathers." *OR,* 38, pt. 5:876.

152. In a letter to his girlfriend, Dr. P. F. Whitehead wrote: "The Enemy's Artillery annoyed Bouanchauds Battery this morning, he and **Cowan** 'let loose the dogs of war' and soon silenced their batteries." W. to Miss Irene [Cowan], July 17, 1864, in Whitehead (Dr. P.F.) Letters, McCain Library and Archives, Univ. of Southern Mississippi, Hattiesburg.

153. Actually, Johnston was relieved on July 17 and relinquished command that night between 10:30 and midnight. *OR,* 38, pt. 5:885, 887.

154. Though he mentions the change of army commanders, Eggleston follows his pattern of not commenting on general officers. Similarly, he failed to even mention that, on July 7, Lieutenant General A. P. Stewart was assigned to command Polk's Army of Mississippi, which resulted in Loring resuming command of his division and Featherston command of his brigade. Ibid., 868.

155. Considering it was written the day of the engagement, Eggleston's succinct appraisal of the Battle of Peachtree Creek was insightful. Casualties amounted to about 10 percent of the number engaged on both sides, approximately 1,900 Federals and 2,500 Confederates. Castel, *Decision in the West,* 381.

156. In Featherston's Brigade alone, of the ten field officers on the field, Colonel Jabez L. Drake (33rd) and Major F. M. Gillespie (31st) were killed; Major W. McD. Gibbens (40th) was mortally wounded; and Colonel T. A. Mellon (3rd), Major Martin A. Oatis (22nd), Lieutenant Colonels J. W. Drane (31st) and George P. Wallace (40th) were severely wounded, the latter losing an arm. *OR,* 38, pt 3:883–84.

157. The Army of Mississippi deployed on the left of the Confederate line, from a redoubt on a hill to the left of Turner's Ferry Road eastward to Peach Tree Street. Ibid., 872.

158. This was the Battle of Atlanta, which cost Major General James B. McPherson, commander of the Union Army of the Tennessee, his life. Eggleston's summary, as well as Hood's telegram to Richmond that night, read as if the Confederates won a great victory. Hardee even claimed that it was "the only decided success achieved by the army at Atlanta," but that was not the case. McPherson's army had not been

destroyed, and Sherman was not forced to withdraw behind Peachtree Creek. Union casualties amounted to 3,722, including 1,733 missing; 5,500 would be a high estimate of Confederate losses. The Rebels had captured at least twenty-three cannon, but Wheeler claimed to have captured six wagons and failed to mention burning even one. Castel, *Decision in the West*, 410–12; *OR*, 38, pt. 3:29, 699, 953.

159. Born in Tennessee on October 2, 1821, Alexander P. Stewart finished twelfth of fifty-six graduates from West Point in 1842. After serving in the artillery and teaching at his alma mater, he resigned in 1845 and pursued a teaching career in Tennessee. Though opposed to secession, he promptly entered Confederate service as a major of artillery when Tennessee seceded. Appointed a brigadier general on November 8, 1861, he led an infantry brigade in the Western Theater until promoted to major general on June 5, 1863. Following Polk's death, he was promoted to lieutenant general and given command of the Army of Mississippi, which became a corps in the Army of Tennessee in July. Stewart commanded that corps until it was surrendered in North Carolina in 1865. He returned to teaching after the war, dying on August 30, 1908. Davis and Hoffman, eds., *The Confederate General*, 6:10–11.

160. It is surprising that Eggleston wrote "Hardee" instead of Stewart, since he goes on to mention that the latter was wounded. Confederate divisions engaged at the Battle of Ezra Church belonged to corps led by Stewart and Lieutenant General Stephen D. Lee, the latter having succeeded Hood, who had been elevated to army command.

161. A shell fragment made a deep, extensive cut in his thigh, but the wound was not deemed dangerous. P. F. Whitehead to Miss Irene [Cowan], Aug. 1, 1864, in Whitehead (Dr. P.F.) Letters.

162. Born in Alabama about 1822, Horatio P. Powers was living in Tallahatchie County in 1860. A farmer, he owned $3,000 real and $4,512 personal property, including one slave. He enlisted as a private in Company C, 14th Mississippi Light Artillery Battalion, at Charleston in September 1863. On May 7, 1864, Lieutenant General Polk temporarily detached him to Cowan's Battery. He was killed while carrying **Warren Cowan** off the field. Horatio P. Powers, p. 20, 1860 Free Schedule, Mississippi, Tallahatchie, Not Stated, Roll 591, M653; Horatio P. Powers, p. 17, 1860 Slave Schedule, Mississippi, Tallahatchie, Not Stated, Roll 603, M653; Service record of H. P. Powers, Fourteenth Battalion, Light Artillery, Roll 92, CSR MS. P. F. Whitehead to Miss Irene [Cowan], Aug. 1, 1864, in Whitehead (Dr. P. F.) Letters.

163. **John T. Williams**.

164. The latter proved to be the case. With sixth-sevenths of his force, Sherman cut loose from his bridgehead on the Chattahoochee River to swing around Atlanta to the west before turning eastward to seize the remaining railroads that supplied the city. McMurry, *Atlanta 1864*, 171.

165. Surprisingly, there are several possibilities, all of whom were distant cousins of Edmund T. Eggleston. Most likely it was Captain John Peyton Eggleston, who was assigned to duty on August 18, 1864, as assistant commissary of subsistence for Anderson's Division, Lee's Corps. Service record of John P. Eggleston, Roll 84, CSRCGSO.

166. Colonel William H. Clark. See p. 155n45.

167. A resident of Calhoun County, Texas, Sergeant Major Raymond Burke of the "Hawkin Artillery" was paroled at Jackson on May 19, 1865. This is the only military service record for Raymond Burke, and no record was found for "Hawkin Artillery." Papers of Raymond Burke, Roll 51, UPSBCCSR.

168. This was the opening move in the two-day Battle of Jonesboro. McMurry, *Atlanta 1864*, 172.

169. Hood's religious conversion did not occur until May 18, 1864, when Bishop-General Polk received him into the Episcopal Church. One onlooker claimed it was "one of the most imposing ceremonies I ever witnessed." Quoted in Castel, *Decision in the West*, 148.

170. Major General Edward C. Walthall commanded one of the three divisions in Stewart's Corps. *OR*, 38, pt. 3:665.

171. The failure of the Confederates to drive the Federals from Jonesboro on August 31 allowed the Federals to sever the last rail line supplying the city. Consequently, the Confederates had to evacuate Atlanta on the night of September 1–2.

172. On September 3, Sherman telegraphed Washington, "Atlanta is ours, and fairly won. I shall not push much farther on this raid, but in a day or so will move to Atlanta and give my men some rest." Ibid., pt. 5:777.

173. Born in Virginia on January 25, 1816, Nathaniel Green Watts served as sergeant and quartermaster in Colonel Jefferson Davis's 1st Mississippi Rifles during the Mexican War. Before the Civil War, he worked as a clerk, was a deputy U.S. marshal, and resided in Vicksburg. Commissioned a captain in the C.S. Regular Army on March 16, 1861, he was serving as assistant quartermaster and assistant commissary of subsistence for Brigadier General Charles Clark in June. Promoted to major in the provisional army on October 4, he served as quartermaster for Brigadier General Richard Griffith's Brigade in the Army of Northern Virginia. On August 4, 1862, he was assigned to duty in the prisoner exchange bureau and was serving as a lieutenant colonel by November 19, 1863. In 1865, he was on duty as a colonel in charge of prisoner exchanges in Alabama and Mississippi. He died on January 27, 1866, and was buried in Vicksburg. No official record of his promotion above major has been found. Allardice, *Confederate Colonels*, 388.

174. Born in South Carolina about 1818, Joseph D. Hudson was a widower with five children in 1860, living in Brookhaven and working as an overseer. He entered Confederate service as a private in Captain J. A.

Hoskins's Brookhaven (MS) Artillery, and rose to the rank of 2nd lieutenant. J. D. Hudson, p. 8, 1860 Free Schedule, Mississippi, Lawrence, Brook Haven, Roll 584; National Park Service, "Hudson, Joseph D.," in "Soldier Details," in *The Civil War*, http://www.nps.gov/civilwar/search-soldiers-detail.htm?soldier_id=720372aa-dc7a-df11-bf36-b8ac6f5d926a (accessed July 7, 2013).

175. Sherman claimed the evacuation was necessary because he was not going to feed the populace and fortifying the city to enable a small garrison to defend it would require the destruction of numerous houses, while the remainder would be required "for military storage and occupation." He admitted to having removed 705 adults, 867 children, and 79 servants. *OR*, 39, pt. 2:414, 481.

176. Sister of Charles William Petrie. See p. 156n47.

177. On September 28, Davis authorized Hood to move north and strike Sherman's supply line. *OR*, 39, pt. 2:880.

178. Because these places were taken by Loring's and Walthall's divisions, Eggleston was in close proximity. Consequently, his information is quite accurate, as opposed to the rumors he recorded regarding the battles around Atlanta. Ibid., pt. 1:812.

179. Born in New Jersey on November 22, 1818, Samuel G. French graduated from West Point in 1843 and served with distinction during the Mexican War, where the wound he received during the Battle of Buena Vista changed his life forever. The person on the litter next to him at the field hospital was Jefferson Davis. They became friends, and when French resigned from the army in 1856, he became a planter in Mississippi. Appointed brigadier general on October 23, 1861, he served in North Carolina and Virginia. Promoted to major general on October 22, 1862, French was sent west to assist General Joseph E. Johnston's efforts to raise the siege of Vicksburg. He commanded a division in the Western Theater for the remainder of the war, after which he moved to Florida, where he died on April 29, 1910. Davis and Hoffman, eds., *The Confederate General*, 2:148–49.

180. Eggleston is factually correct regarding the performance of Sears's Brigade, but French did not hold Brigadier General Claudius W. Sears responsible, instead thanking him for his "bravery, skill, and unflinching firmness." *OR*, 39, pt. 1:813–20.

181. For more on the fighting at Allatoona, see Robert C. Jones, *The Battle of Allatoona Pass: The Forgotten Battle of Sherman's Atlanta Campaign* (n.p.: CreateSpace Independent Publishing Platform, 2011).

182. Battles of New Hope Church, Dallas, and Pickett's Mill.

183. While the army moved north via Resaca to Dalton, the balance of the artillery and surplus wagons moved to Jacksonville. J. B. Hood, "The Invasion of Tennessee," in *Battles and Leaders of the Civil War: Being for the most part contributions by Union and Confederate officers based*

upon "The Century War Series," edited by Robert U. Johnson and Clarence Clough Buel, 4 vols. (1884–88; repr., New York: Thomas Yoseloff, 1956), 4:426.

184. Cowan's Battery was one of the two left behind. See diary entry for October 22, 1864.

185. Eggleston was incorrect about why Beauregard had come to the army, but such a rumor is worth noting. In truth, Beauregard was only consulting with Hood seven days before he assumed command of the newly created Military Division of the West, which placed him over Hood's Department of Tennessee and Georgia and Lieutenant General Richard Taylor's Department of Alabama, Mississippi, and East Louisiana, but Hood remained in command of the Army of Tennessee, as well as his department. Anne J. Bailey, *The Chessboard of War: Sherman and Hood in the Autumn Campaigns of 1864* (Lincoln: Univ. of Nebraska Press, 2000), 34; *OR*, 39, pt. 3:824.

186. Born in Virginia about 1827, John D. Myrick had a plantation in Hertford County, North Carolina, and resided in Norfolk in 1860. He owned $150,000 real and $160,000 personal property, including sixty-five slaves. Myrick apparently entered Confederate service on June 14, 1862, when Brigadier General William W. Loring added him to his staff as captain and aide de camp. Though commissioned 1st lieutenant on October 4, he continued to serve as a captain and, in early 1863, took on the additional duties of chief of artillery and inspector general. By May 1, 1864, his battalion had been reduced to the three companies that would compose it until it was disbanded: Cowan's; Captain Robert L. Barry's Lookout (TN) Artillery; and Captain Alcide Bouanchaud's Company C, Pointe Coupée (LA) Artillery. Unfortunately, each was armed with four 12-pounder Napoleons; there was not a single long-range rifled gun. His commission as major of artillery on August 19 legitimized his command of the battalion of artillery attached to Loring's Division, a position he held until January 1865. He was paroled at Meridian on May 10, 1865. John D. Myrick, p. 19, 1860 Free Schedule, Virginia, Norfolk, Norfolk, Roll 1366, M653; John D. Myrick, pp. 11–12, 1860 Slave Schedule, North Carolina, Hertford, Not Stated, Roll 923, M653; Service record of John D. Myrick, Roll 185, CSRCGSO; *OR*, 38, pt. 3:652; ibid., pt. 4:656.

187. Decatur was too well fortified and garrisoned to assault. Hood used his artillery to make a "slight demonstration," while his army marched westward south of the town. Hood, "Invasion of Tennessee," 427.

188. Either **Albert F. Auter** or **Solomon B. Auter**.

189. Actually, it was seventeen barges. *OR*, 39, pt. 3:900.

190. In 1850, 1-year-old Mississippi native John R. **Wilkins** lived with his parents in Warren County. In 1860, 9-year-old John attended school

and lived with his mother and three siblings in Warren County; his mother, Caroline, was a farmer with $5,000 real and $18,000 personal property, including twenty-seven slaves. In 1870, 21-year-old John B. Wilkins lived with his mother in Warren County. Not only was Bob an example of the Confederacy robbing the cradle, there is no record that he ever served in the army. Caroline V. Wilkins, p. 5, 1850 Free Schedule, Mississippi, Warren, Not Stated, Roll 382, M432; C. E. Wilkins, p. 71, 1860 Free Schedule, Mississippi, Warren, Not Stated, Roll 592, M653; C. Wilkens, p. 94, 1860 Slave Schedule, Mississippi, Warren, Not Stated, Roll 603, M653; John B. Wilkins, p. 35, 1870 Population Schedule, Mississippi, Warren, Bovina Precinct, Roll 751, M593.

191. Born in Tennessee on June 8, 1806, Gideon J. Pillow was a politically connected lawyer in Columbia, Tennessee. Before the Civil War, his partners included future president James K. Polk, and thanks to Polk, Pillow served as a brigadier and major general during the Mexican War. In 1861, Governor Isham G. Harris appointed Pillow senior major general in the Provisional Army of Tennessee. Upset at having to enter Confederate service as a brigadier general, he ruined his career by fleeing from Fort Donelson before the garrison was surrendered in February 1862. He served with the volunteer and conscript bureau in Tennessee until February 1865, when he became commissary general of prisoners. In 1861, he reportedly had $2 million in assets, including the home Eggleston found so impressive. Davis and Hoffman, eds., *The Confederate General*, 5:38–39.

192. Born in Maury County, Tennessee, on May 24, 1815, William H. Polk served as a major in the Mexican War and in Congress (1851–1853). In 1860, he was a lawyer who owned $30,000 real and $60,000 personal property, including fifteen slaves, residing in Maury County, Tennessee. He died in Nashville, Tennessee, on December 16, 1862. "Polk, William Hawkins, (1815–1862)," in *Biographical Directory of the United States Congress, 1774–Present*, http://bioguide.congress.gov/scripts/biodisplay.pl?index=P000412 (accessed July 4, 2013); W. H. Polk, p. 71, 1860 Free Schedule, Tennessee, Maury, District 9, Roll 1264, M653; W. H. Polk, p. 15, 1860 Slave Schedule, Tennessee, Maury, District 9, Roll 1284, M653.

193. William H. Polk was the brother of former president James K. Polk and a second cousin to Leonidas Polk. Frank M. Angellotti, *The Polks of North Carolina and Tennessee* (Greenville, SC: Southern Historical Press, 1923), 22.

194. Lee's Corps had arrived in front of Columbia on November 26 and relieved Major General Nathan B. Forrest's cavalry. On November 27, Lee's men drove the enemy's skirmishers into their main fortifications surrounding the city. *OR*, 45, pt. 1:687.

195. Darden's Mississippi Battery had replaced Captain Barry's Lookout (TN) Artillery in Myrick's Battalion. Ibid., 668.

196. Lee, with Stevenson's and Clayton's infantry divisions and almost all the army's artillery, was ordered "to engage and occupy the enemy near Columbia," while the other two corps and Johnson's Division along with one battery from each corps went on an expedition. The artillery was limited because the horses were exhausted, and the infantrymen had been having to assist getting the guns up hills for several days. It was an honor for **Cowan** to be selected to command the ad hoc battery for Stewart's Corps, which was no doubt supplied with the best horses available in Myrick's Battalion. That force crossed the Duck River above Columbia "and moved to the rear of the enemy in the direction of Spring Hill." Hood's brilliant plan to block the Federals' escape route from Columbia came to naught, because though both could have, neither Stewart nor Cheatham blocked the road at Spring Hill. Ibid., 652–53, 687, 719.

197. Initial reports indicated that twelve generals and forty-five field officers were casualties, but those figures have been revised upward to fifteen and sixty-five, respectively. Major General Patrick R. Cleburne and Brigadier Generals John Adams, States R. Gist, Hiram B. Granbury, and Otho F. Strahl were killed; Brigadier General John C. Carter was mortally wounded; Major General John C. Brown and Brigadier Generals Francis M. Cockrell, Zachariah C. Deas, Arthur M. Manigault, W. A. Quarles, Daniel H. Reynolds, Thomas M. Scott, and Jacob H. Sharp were wounded; and Brigadier General G. W. Gordon was captured. It should be noted that Reynolds made no mention of his wound in his wartime diary. Ibid., 684–86; Eric A. Jacobson and Richard A. Rupp, *For Cause & For Country: A Study of the Affair at Spring Hill and the Battle of Franklin* (Franklin, TN: O'More Publishing, 2008), 418–20; Bruce Allardice to Lawrence Hewitt, e-mail, June 6, 2013.

198. None of the troops left behind under Lee south of the Duck River on the twenty-ninth arrived in time to participate in the Battle of Franklin. *OR*, 45, pt. 1:687.

199. On December 2, Stewart's Corps formed the left of Hood's line, with Lee's in the center, and Cheatham's on the right. Each day the corps commanders tweaked their lines, so Cowan's artillerymen had more time behind the line than most of Hood's troops. Ibid., 671.

200. Both Stewart's and Lee's corps moved their lines a short distance to their rear so their troops could gather wood more conveniently. Ibid., 672.

201. Weather finally cooperating, Major General George H. Thomas advanced to turn Hood's left flank, which consisted of four detached redoubts along the Hillsborough Turnpike running off to the southwest. Walthall's and French's divisions were deployed along the road, while

Loring's Division faced north along the main line where it turned eastward. Hood immediately began shifting troops from his right; the brigades of Johnson's Division, Lee's Corps, being the first to arrive. Because the Federals were not pressing Loring's Division, Stewart ordered Loring to send one of the three batteries on his front to the left, and Cowan's was soon on the move. They arrived, dropped trail, and managed to get off one or two rounds before the Confederate infantry in their front, Deas's and Manigault's brigades of Johnson's Division, broke and fled to the rear. The Federals on their heels seized all four of Cowan's guns. Lieutenant **Tompkins** recalled, "in the first days fight at Nashville our Battery was ordered to report to Genl Ed Johnson on our extreme left, where we arrived at a gallop and went into position just in time to be run over and loose our guns." Union Brigadier General Joseph A. Cooper reported, "As soon as the rebel battery opened the men, without waiting for orders, commenced cheering and rushed forward, charging up the hill at double-quick. The lines were necessarily much broken owing to the extreme difficulty of climbing the hill, but the men rushed forward as best they could and soon gained the top off the hill, and captured three pieces of artillery and a number of prisoners." Ibid., 371, 709; Geo. H. Tompkins to J. S. Power, Nov. 6, 1900, in 1st Mississippi Light Artillery Regiment Collection.

202. Captain James A. Hoskins's Brookhaven (MS) Battery was part of the battalion attached to French's Division. About May 1, 1864, Hoskins's Battery contained two 3-inch rifles, one 10-pouder Parrott (rifled), and one 6-pounder smoothbore. If the section (normally two guns) assigned to **Cowan** on December 15 contained even one rifled gun, it is surprising that it was not fired on December 16. *OR*, 38, pt. 3:653 and pt. 4:656.

203. Stewart's Corps occupied the center and was not pressed as were the corps on either side of him. It is more likely that Cowan's section was on the line and lacked a suitable target than that they had been left in the rear. *OR*, 45, pt. 1:710–11.

204. Because Stewart's Corps was in the van of the retreat, Eggleston could travel without worrying about the enemy, while the rearguard, Lee's Corps, was hard-pressed and pushed just south of Franklin by dark. Ibid., 673, 690.

205. Stewart's Corps led the retreat on the eighteenth as well, but upon reaching the Duck River it deployed in line of battle, where it remained on the nineteenth while the rest of the army crossed the river ahead of it. Ibid., 673.

206. Lieutenant General Stewart detached Lieutenant **Tompkins** with the two guns Cowan's Battery had successfully withdrawn from Nashville and Sergeant T. G. Dabney with the only remaining gun of Hoskins's Mississippi Battery to engage a gunboat that threatened to destroy the

pontoon bridge the army was using to cross the Tennessee River. They delayed the gunboat from daylight until 2 p.m. on December 27, when a shell exploded, dismounting one gun, killing Private **John B. Ferrell**, and wounding Lieutenant **Tompkins** and Private **Walton Whatley**. T. G. Dabney, "Gen. A. P. Stewart on Strong Topics," *Confederate Veteran* 17 (Jan. 1909): 31; Rowland, *Official and Statistical Register of the State of Mississippi*, 859; diary entry for December 30, 1864.

207. The balance of Cowan's Battery crossed with Lee's and Cheatham's corps; Stewart's Corps and the cavalry crossed on the twenty-seventh. *OR*, 45, pt. 1:674.

208. John Lucius Eggleston was born in Virginia about 1808. In 1860, he was a farmer in Lawrence County, Alabama, and owned $2,560 real and $14,630 personal property, including fifteen slaves. John and Edmund were distant cousins. William Eggleston (1720–1780) was the great-grandfather of the former and great-great-grandfather of the latter. John Eggleston, p. 38, 1860 Free Schedule, Alabama, Lawrence, Northern Division, Roll 12, M653; John Eggleston, p. 23, 1860 Slave Schedule, Alabama, Lawrence, Northern Division, Roll 31, M653; "Family View," *Powell/Eggleston/Watts/Pruitt/Key*, http://trees. ancestry.com/tree/398579/family?cfpid=-2086854451 (accessed July 7. 2013; password protected site).

209. Samuel Overton Eggleston was born in Hanover County, Virginia, on April 24, 1797. A resident of Lawrence County, Alabama, since before 1849, in 1860 he was a small planter owning $2,820 real and $31,520 personal property, including twenty-eight slaves. "Samuel Overton Eggleston," *Powell/Eggleston/Watts/Pruitt/Key*, http://trees.ancestry. com/tree/398579/person/-2086854451?ssrc= (accessed July 7, 2013; password protected site); S. O. Eggleston, p. 39, 1860 Free Schedule, Alabama, Lawrence, Northern Division, Roll 12, M653; S. O. Eggleston, p. 24, 1860 Slave Schedule, Alabama, Lawrence, Northern Division, Roll 31, M653.

210. Either H. P. or William J. Carloss. H. P. Carloss and Wm. Carloss, p. 10, 1860 Free Schedule, Alabama, Franklin, Western Division, Roll 10, M653.

211. Eggleston was fortunate to have someone to visit on the twenty-seventh while the balance of the army was crossing the Tennessee River. He pushed his French leave by visiting another relative on the twenty-eighth, because Stewart's Corps began marching for Burnsville that afternoon. Undoubtedly, he was enjoying this break from the army, because he opted to spend a third night under a roof instead of with his comrades in the field. *OR*, 45, pt. 1:674.

212. **John B. Ferrell**.

Notes to Epilogue

1. Quoted in Daniel, *Cannoneers in Gray*, 182–85; *OR*, 45, pt. 1:668–69, 674, 682, and pt. 2:1323.
2. I. E. Herring to My Darling Wife, Feb. 10, 1865, in Isaac E. Herring Letters; *OR*, 49, pt. 1: 1047.
3. Ibid., 1047, 1048; Dabney H. Maury, "The Defence of Mobile in 1865," 3, no. 1 *Southern Historical Society Papers* (Jan. 1877), 8; James G. Spencer, Application for Pension, Series 1201: Confederate Pension Applications, 1889–1932, Mississippi Office of the State Auditor, Mississippi Department of Archives and History, Jackson; *ORS*, pt.1, 7:944, 952.
4. *ORS*, pt. 1, 7:945, 959–62, 964.
5. Application S12982, Tennessee Confederate Pension Applications: Soldiers & Widows, Tennessee State Library and Archives, Nashville.
6. In 1860, 33-year-old Edwin F. Stafford, a native of England, was living in Indian Point, Knox County, Illinois, with his wife and three children. He was working as a farm laborer and owned $200 personal property. He had become a minister before being commissioned a 1st lieutenant in Company B, 124th Illinois Infantry Regiment. Promoted to captain on July 9, 1863, he was mustered out on August 15, 1865. Edwin Stafford, p. 30, 1860 Free Schedule, Illinois, Knox, Indiana Point, Roll 195, M653; Edwin Stafford, p. 333, vol. 3, Consolidated Lists of Civil War Draft Registration Records (Provost Marshal General's Bureau; Consolidated Enrollment Lists, 1863–1865), RG110, Records of the Provost Marshal General's Bureau (Civil War), National Archives and Records Administration, Washington, DC; National Park Service, "Stafford, Edwin F.", in "Soldier Details," in *The Civil War*, http://www.nps.gov/civilwar/search-soldiers-detail.htm?soldier_id=b48771d4-dc7a-df11-bf36-b8ac6f5d926a (accessed July 7, 2013); "Edwin F. Stafford," *U.S., Civil War Soldier Records and Profiles, 1861–1865*, http://search.ancestry.com/ . . . (accessed July 7, 2013; password protected site). Complete citation available from UTP.
7. Original documents in possession of Andrew Stevens, Dallas, TX.
8. Howard A. M. Henderson was appointed captain of Company E, 28th Alabama Infantry Regiment, on February 18, 1862. After resigning for medical reasons on October 2, 1862, he served as acting provost marshal of Demopolis, Alabama. Appointed captain on August 14, 1863, he was assigned as the assistant commissioner for the exchange of prisoners and stationed at Cahaba, Alabama. Promoted to major in 1864 and lieutenant colonel by February 1865, Henderson ended the war working with Union Brigadier General Morgan L. Smith at Vicksburg. Service record of Howard A. M. Henderson, Twenty-eighth Infantry, Roll 322, M-311; *OR*, ser. 2, 6:203 and 8:284.

9. New York native Morgan Lewis Smith left home at the age of twenty-one. After teaching school, five years in the army, and a decade as a riverboat man, Smith recruited the 8th Missouri Infantry Regiment and became its colonel. He commanded a brigade at Fort Donelson and Shiloh. Promoted to brigadier general on July 16, 1862, he was seriously wounded at Chickasaw Bluffs in December. Returning the following October, he commanded a division at Chattanooga and temporarily commanded the 15th Corps during the siege of Atlanta. Incapacitated by the aggravation of his wound, he finished the war in command of the District of Vicksburg. Resigning on July 12, 1865, he served as consul general in Honolulu under presidents Andrew Johnson and Ulysses S. Grant. He died suddenly while on a trip to New Jersey and was buried in Arlington National Cemetery. Ezra J. Warner, *Generals in Blue: Lives of the Union Commanders* (Baton Rouge: Louisiana State Univ. Press, 1964), 460.

10. Born in New York, Archie C. Fisk entered the army on June 1, 1861, as 2nd lieutenant, 23rd Ohio Infantry Regiment. Promoted to 1st lieutenant on October 15, 1862, he served with distinction as aide-de-camp to Brigadier General Hugh Ewing during the Vicksburg campaign. Promoted to captain on June 23, 1863, Fisk became the assistant adjutant general for the 2nd Brigade, 2nd Division, 15th Corps. In 1865, he held the same position for the District of Vicksburg until mustered out on July 20. Francis B. Heitman, *Historical Register and Dictionary of the United States Army, from its organization, September 29, 1789, to March 2, 1903,* 2 vols. (Washington, DC: U.S. Congress, 1903), 1:421; *OR*, 24, pt. 2:257, 38, pt. 3:237, and 48. pt. 1:711.

11. Original documents in possession of Andrew Stevens, Dallas, TX.

12. Original document in possession of Andrew Stevens, Dallas, TX.

13. "City Directory Listing for F. T. Eggleston," *Database=City Directories,* http://userdb.rootsweb.ancestry.com/citydir/cgi-bin/citydir. cgi?main_id=9453&database=City%20Directories&return_to=http:// userdb.rootsweb.com/citydir/&submitter_id= (accessed July 7, 2013).

14. A native of Georgia, David Washington Lamkin was working as a clerk in Yazoo County in 1850 and gave his age as 21. In 1860, the 29-year-old was living in Yazoo City with his 22-year-old Tennessee-born wife J. A. He gave no occupation and owned $5,000 in personal property, including four slaves. On April 27, 1862, at Yazoo City, he enlisted as quartermaster sergeant in Company I, 1st Mississippi Light Artillery Regiment. Elected junior 2nd lieutenant on March 2, 1863, he was captured at Vicksburg on July 4 and again at Fort Blakely, Alabama, on April 9, 1865. Exchanged in New Orleans on May 1, he was paroled at Jackson on May 15. In 1870, David W. Lamkin worked as a grocer in Vicksburg and owned $3,000 in personal property. Claiming to be 30, he was living with 25-year-old Martha from Georgia and five children,

ages 3 to 15. As with Eggleston, Lamkin fell on economic hard times. In 1880, his wife and children were living with her sister and brother-in-law in Vicksburg, while D. W. died of pneumonia that December at the age of 50, while working in a factory in Warren County. D. W. Lamkin, p. 521A, 1850 Population Schedule, Mississippi, Yazoo, not stated, Roll 382, M432; D. W. Lamkin, p. 136, 1860 Population Schedule, Mississippi, Yazoo, Yazoo City, Roll 594, M653; D. W. Lamkin, p. 209, 1860 Slave Schedule, Mississippi, Yazoo, Yazoo City, Roll 604, M653; Service record of D. Wash Lamkin, First Light Artillery, Roll 87, CSR MS; David W. Lamkin, p. 15, 1870 Population Schedule, Mississippi, Warren, Vicksburg, Roll 751, M593; Martha Lamkin, p. 36, 1880 Population Schedule, Mississippi, Warren, Vicksburg, Roll 667, T9; "Washington Lamkin," *U.S. Federal Census Mortality Schedules Index, 1850–1880,* http://search.ancestry.com/cgi-bin/sse.dll?db=mortality cen&h=453836&indiv=try&o_vc=Record:OtherRecord&rhSource =7163 (accessed Aug. 13, 2013; password protected site).

15. *Daily Commercial* (Vicksburg, MS), May 8, 1877, May 9, 1877, Jan. 16, 1878, May 5, 1879, and Nov. 25, 1879.

16. Trent Eggleston, p. 58, 1880 Population Schedule, Mississippi, Warren, Vicksburg, Roll 667, T9; Roach-Eggleston Family Pedigree, Roach-Eggleston Family Papers; *Daily Commercial* (Vicksburg, MS), Nov. 23, 1878, p. 3.

17. *Daily Commercial* (Vicksburg, MS), July 5, 7, 1879.

18. *Daily Commercial* (Vicksburg, MS), Sept. 24, 1881, May 26, 1882, Oct. 26, 1882.

19. Roach-Eggleston Family Pedigree, Roach-Eggleston Family Papers.

Notes to Appendix A

1. Samuel Williamson Tappan.

2. "General" Benjamin Swett Tappan.

3. Captain Edward H. Porter.

4. Though out of sequence, Eggleston spent the night of March 8 at Dr. Lee's. See diary entry for March 8, 1864.

5. A. M. Paxton.

6. **Pryor Lawson**.

7. In 1860, North Carolina native Thomas W. Allen worked as a clerk in Carroll County, Mississippi. He was one of three siblings living with their father, Thomas Allen, who was a farmer and purportedly owned $600 real and $2,500 personal property. On April 20, 1861, 22-year-old Thomas entered the army as 3rd lieutenant of what became Company E, 15th Mississippi Infantry Regiment. Captured at the Battle of Fishing Creek, Kentucky, on January 19, 1862, he was exchanged that fall. In June 1863, he was detached to serve in Culbertson's Battery

when it was organized. Near the end of the year he was detached by Major General Loring to be acting assistant quartermaster of Myrick's artillery battalion in late 1863. He returned to his company by September of 1864. Thomas W. Allen, p. 17, 1860 Free Schedule, Mississippi, Carroll, Police District 1, Roll 578, M653; Service record of Thomas W. Allen, Fifteenth Infantry, Roll 229, CSR MS.

8. **ETE**'s wife.

9. In 1860, 25-year-old Alabama native Greek P. Rice was a farmer living in Tallahatchie County with his wife and three children, and he owned $4,479 personal property, including five slaves. On December 20, 1862, G. P. Rice enlisted as a private in Company C, 14th Mississippi Light Artillery Battalion. By order of Lieutenant General Polk on May 7, 1864, he was temporarily detailed to Cowan's Battery. By November, he had returned to his former command, but the 14th Battalion was broken up about July, and on August 19, 1864, Company C was designated as Captain Merrin's Battery. He was paroled at Grenada on May 19, 1865. Greek P. Rice, p. 61, 1860 Free Schedule, Mississippi, Tallahatchie, Not Stated, Roll 591, M653; Greek P. Rice, p. 52, 1860 Slave Schedule, Mississippi, Tallahatchie, Not Stated, Roll 603, M653; Service record of G. P. Rice, Capt. Merrin's Battery, Roll 97, CSR MS.

10. **Eggleston, Tompkins,** and **Greene**.

11. **Reid, Eggleston, Tompkins, Levy, Bentley, DeMoss**.

12. **George H. Tompkins**.

13. **Ludwell B. Cowan, Warren Cowan, Benjamin J. Hicks, Luther R. Reid**, and **Eggleston**.

Notes to Appendix B

1. On March 9, 1862, at Greenville, 29-year-old William Lewis Nugent enlisted in what eventually became Company D, 28th Mississippi Cavalry Regiment, and was elected junior 2nd lieutenant. By May, he was on special duty as acting adjutant for the regiment. Relieved on August 10, 1863, five days later he began serving on the staff of Brigadier General Samuel W. Ferguson. On September 7, he was appointed captain in the adjutant general's department and assigned as the assistant adjutant general for Ferguson's Brigade, a position he held for the remainder of the war. Service record of William L. Nugent, Twenty-eighth Cavalry, Roll 58, CSR MS; Service record of William Lewis Nugent, Roll 188, CSRCGSO.

2. Kelley in May 3, 1864, diary entry.

3. This is undoubtedly Benjamin Swett Tappan.

4. The 15th Mississippi Infantry Regiment was in Brigadier General John Adams's Brigade, Loring's Division, Stewart's Corps. *OR*, 39, pt. 2:854.

5. Captain Charles E. Fenner's Louisiana Battery was in Major J. Wesley Eldridge's Battalion of Lee's Corps. Ibid., 858.

6. A jeweler's apprentice in 1860, Ohio native George B. Hunter was twenty-one and residing in Oskaloosa, Iowa, when he enlisted on October 1, 1861. Mustered into service on October 21 as a corporal in Company B, 13th Iowa Infantry Regiment, he was promoted to 2nd lieutenant on April 20, 1862. Wounded in the right leg during the Battle of Atlanta on July 22, 1864, Hunter resigned his commission on November 8. George Hunter, p. 17, 1860 Free Schedule, Iowa, Mahaska, Oskaloosa, Roll 334, M653; Adjutant General's Office, *Roster and Record of Iowa Soldiers in the War of the Rebellion: together with Historical Sketches of Volunteer Organizations, 1861–1866,* vol. 2, *9th—16th Regiments—Infantry* (Des Moines, IA: Emory H. English, 1908), 621.

7. The 13th Iowa Infantry Regiment was in the 4th Division, 17th Corps, from April 1864 until July 1865. Frederick H. Dyer, *A Compendium of the War of the Rebellion,* 3 vols. (repr., New York: Thomas Yoseloff, 1959), 1:520.

8. A 31-year-old native of Connecticut and resident of Delhi, Iowa, in 1860, John H. Peters was an attorney and owned $3,400 real and $598 personal property. Appointed captain of Company B, 4th Iowa Cavalry Regiment, he was mustered in on November 23, 1861. He was slightly wounded on November 8, 1862, at Marianna, Arkansas. Promoted to major on June 20, 1863, and to lieutenant colonel on September 2, Peters was mustered out on August 8, 1865, at Atlanta, Georgia. John H. Peters, p. 21, 1860 Free Schedule, Iowa, Delaware, Delhi, Roll 318, M653; Adjutant General's Office, *Roster and Record of Iowa Soldiers in the War of the Rebellion: together with Historical Sketches of Volunteer Organizations, 1861–1866,* vol. 4, *1st–9th Regiments—Cavalry and Two Independent Companies—Cavalry* (Des Moines, IA: Emory H. English, 1910), 782.

9. No information was found to explain why Eggleston mentioned these two Union officers, and his references are partially incorrect. The 4th Iowa Cavalry Regiment was never part of Brigadier General Marcellus M. Crocker's brigade. The 13th Iowa Infantry Regiment had served in Crocker's brigade, but that was before the regiment was in the 4th Division, 17th Corps. As the 4th Iowa Cavalry Regiment was never part of Crocker's brigade, Eggleston must have confused Peters with Hunter as to which served in Crocker's brigade. Dyer, *A Compendium of the War of the Rebellion,* 1:479, 482, 502, 520, 521.

10. Born about 1809 in South Carolina, James Pagan was living in Chester County, South Carolina, with his wife Ann C. Fayssoux. He was a merchant and owned $700 personal property. He entered military service on January 7, 1861, as acting brigade commissary for Brigadier General

James Dunovant at Charleston, South Carolina. When the South Carolina Army was organized, he was appointed major and chief commissary. On June 25, he resigned to accept an appointment as captain and assistant commissary of subsistence for the 6th South Carolina Infantry Regiment. He was appointed major in the Commissary Department on March 13, 1862, and assigned to Brigadier General Nathan G. Evans, then commanding the 3rd Military District of South Carolina. On October 23, he became commissary general for Evans's Brigade, and remained in that position under Evans's successors, Brigadier Generals Stephen Elliott and William H. Wallace. Pagan was paroled at Appomattox Court House, Virginia, April 9, 1865. Jas. Pagan, p. 141, 1860 Free Schedule, South Carolina, Chester, Not Stated, Roll 1217, M653; Service record of James Pagan, Roll 192, CSRCGSO.

Notes to Appendix C

1. Born in Wilmington, North Carolina, in 1798, William Mercer Green graduated from the University of North Carolina and, in 1837, he became the Episcopal chaplain and professor of belles-lettres at his alma mater. He became the first Episcopal bishop of Mississippi in 1847 and was residing in Jackson in 1860, where he owned $13,300 in personal property, including fifteen slaves. Green was instrumental in the founding of the University of the South at Sewanee, Tennessee, and became chancellor of that institution in 1867. He died in 1887. Collection Overview, William Mercer Green Papers, 1843–1887, Southern Historical Collection, Louis Round Wilson Special Collections Library, Univ. of North Carolina, Chapel Hill; W. M. Green, p. 3, 1860 Free Schedule, Mississippi, Hinds, Township 5, Roll 582, M653; W. M. Green, p. 1, 1860 Slave Schedule, Mississippi, Hinds, Township 5, Roll 597, M653.

2. Born in New York in 1819, William Wilberforce Lord was an Episcopal preacher living in Vicksburg in 1860. He owned $4,000 in personal property, including one slave. He was appointed chaplain of the 1st Mississippi Light Artillery Regiment on May 14, 1862, and resigned the position on October 24. He died in 1907. W. W. Lord, *A discourse, by the Rev. W.W. Lord, D.D. in honor of Capt. Paul Hamilton, Adjutant General, Third Brigade, Army of Miss., killed in the battle of Chickasaw Bayou, Dec. 29th, 1863, buried from Christ Church, Vicksburg, December 31, commemorated in this discourse Sunday, January 4th, 1863* (Vicksburg, MS: M. Shannon, 1863); W. W. Lord, p. 14, 1860 Free Schedule, Mississippi, Warren, Vicksburg, Roll 592, M653; W. W. Lord, p. 3, 1860 Slave Schedule, Mississippi, Warren, Vicksburg, Roll 603, M653; Service record of W. W. Lord, First Light Artillery, Roll 87, CSR MS.

3. See p. 153n30.

4. Born in New York City on December 25, 1829, Joseph Christmas Ives attended Yale before graduating from West Point in 1852. While serving as an engineer in the U.S. Army, he explored the Grand Canyon and was briefly in charge of building the Washington Monument. Having married the daughter of a U.S. senator from Louisiana, he was appointed captain in the regular Confederate Army on March 16, 1861, and served as chief engineer on the staff of General Robert E. Lee in South Carolina later that year. On April 19, 1862, he was promoted to colonel and assigned as an aide to President Davis. He left the country following the war, but eventually returned to New York City, where he died of alcoholism on November 12, 1868. Allardice, *Confederate Colonels*, 210.

5. Service record of Edmond T. Eggleston, First Light Artillery, Roll 84, CSR MS.

6. Born in Maysville, Kentucky, on June 1, 1815, William Henry McCardle edited a newspaper in New Orleans and was a long-time resident of Mississippi when, in January 1861, he joined the staff of Charles Clark, commander of Mississippi's state troops. He entered Confederate service on September 7, 1861, as a 1st lieutenant and aide-de-camp for Clark. Promoted to captain on April 11, 1862, and later to major, he acted as Clark's assistant adjutant general. After Clark was disabled by wounds at the Battle of Baton Rouge, McCardle was granted a leave of absence by Brigadier General John C. Breckinridge. That leave was repeatedly extended by Major General Earl Van Dorn, but after Lieutenant General John C. Pemberton took command of the Department of Mississippi and East Louisiana in October, McCardle joined his staff as assistant adjutant general. Pemberton's fall from grace following his surrender of Vicksburg left McCardle having to hustle once more to find an assignment. Though repeatedly recommended for promotion by Clark and Pemberton, McCardle finished the war as a major, being paroled at Meridian on May 11, 1865. He died in Jackson on April 28, 1893. Robert E. L. Krick, *Staff Officers in Gray: A Biographical Register of the Staff Officers in the Army of Northern Virginia* (Chapel Hill: Univ. of North Carolina Press, 2003), 205–6; Service record of Wm. H. McCardle, Roll 168, CSRCGSO.

7. Appointed from Louisiana, William A. Broadwell entered Confederate service on July 19, 1861, as a major in the Commissary Department. Appointed lieutenant colonel on September 16, 1862, he was assigned to Jackson as commissary general. He was appointed chief of the Cotton Bureau for the Trans-Mississippi Department on August 3, 1863. When that bureau was abolished in August of 1864, General Edmund Kirby Smith retained him to settle its outstanding affairs; he was not relieved from that position until May 19, 1865. Service record of W. A. Broadwell, Roll 34, CSRCGSO.

8. Robert Witherspoon Memminger (1839–1901) was appointed captain on January 13, 1862, and assigned as assistant adjutant general on General Robert E. Lee's staff. When Lee was transferred to Virginia, Memminger remained in the Department of South Carolina, Georgia, and East Florida on Major General Pemberton's staff. Appointed major on January 9, 1863, he was assigned to the staff of Major General William W. Loring. He also served on the staffs of Robert Ransom and Daniel Harvey Hill. Krick, *Staff Officers in Gray*, 344; Service record of Robert W. Memminger, Roll 176, CSRCGSO.

9. Sheet containing the endorsements and letter in Series 1: Unbound Papers, 1844–1899 and undated, Roach and Eggleston Family Papers, 1825–1905, in Southern Historical Collection, Louis Round Wilson Special Collections Library, Univ. of North Carolina, Chapel Hill.

10. Born in Texas in 1831, Thomas M. Jack, a lawyer who claimed to own no property, was living in Galveston with his wife and two children in 1860. He claimed to be twenty-seven when he enlisted at Houston on September 7, 1861, as a private in what became Company B, 8th Texas Cavalry Regiment. By January 7, 1862, he had been promoted to lieutenant and was serving as aide de camp to General Albert S. Johnston. Following Johnston's death at Shiloh on April 6, 1862, Jack was promoted to major by August 20 and was serving as assistant adjutant general on the staff of Lieutenant General Leonidas Polk by November 26. By September 29, 1863, Jack was promoted to lieutenant colonel, and by the time of Polk's death on June 14, 1864, he was serving as his chief of staff, a position he continued to hold under Polk's successors, Major General William W. Loring and Lieutenant General Alexander P. Stewart, at least through September. In the Trans-Mississippi by February 1865, Jack served as chief of staff and assistant adjutant general for Major General John B. Magruder and, at some point, on the staff of Major General John G. Walker, as well. He died in 1880. Service record of Thomas M. Jack, Eighth Cavalry (Terry's) Regiment, Roll 51, Compiled Service Records of Confederate Soldiers Who Served in Organizations from the State of Texas, M-323, War Department Collection of Confederate Records, RG 109, National Archives and Records Service, Washington, DC; *OR*, 52, pt. 2:342; 20, pt. 2:426; 30, pt. 2:58; 38, pt. 4:777 and pt. 3:880; 53:1044; 48, pt. 2:1263; Capt. M. G. Howe to Col. Thos. M. Jack, Feb. 9, 1865, in service record of M. G. Howe, Fourth Confederate Engineer Troops, CSRCS; Krick, *Staff Officers in Gray*, 335.

11. Ord. Sgt. http://www.fold3.com/image/271/66987574/

Notes to Appendix D

1. Captain R. G. Harper, Company G (from Madison Parish), Colonel
   J. Frank Pargoud's 3rd Louisiana Cavalry Regiment. The regiment was
   organized about October 1862 by adding four independent companies
   to the 13th Louisiana Cavalry Battalion. The regiment was broken up
   in February 1863, with the restoration of the 13th Battalion and the
   four independent companies soon becoming part of the 15th Louisiana
   Cavalry Battalion. Arthur W. Bergeron Jr., *Guide to Louisiana Confederate Military Units, 1861–1865* (Baton Rouge: Louisiana State Univ.
   Press, 1989), 45.
2. J. J. Cowan to Irene, Apr.11, 1865, James J. Cowan Papers.

BIBLIOGRAPHY

Manuscripts

Compiled Service Records of Confederate General and Staff Officers, and Non-regimental Enlisted Men. M-331. War Department Collection of Confederate Records. RG 109. National Archives and Records Service, Washington, DC.

Compiled Service Records of Confederate Soldiers Who Served in Organizations from the State of Alabama, M-311, War Department Collection of Confederate Records, RG 109, National Archives and Records Service, Washington, DC.

Compiled Service Records of Confederate Soldiers Who Served in Organizations from the State of Louisiana. M-320. War Department Collection of Confederate Records. RG 109. National Archives and Records Service, Washington, DC.

Compiled Service Records of Confederate Soldiers Who Served in Organizations from the State of Mississippi. M-269. War Department Collection of Confederate Records. RG 109. National Archives and Records Service, Washington, DC.

Compiled Service Records of Confederate Soldiers Who Served in Organizations from the State of Tennessee. M-268. War Department Collection of Confederate Records. RG 109. National Archives and Records Service, Washington, DC.

Compiled Service Records of Confederate Soldiers Who Served in Organizations from the State of Texas. M-323. War Department Collection of Confederate Records. RG 109. National Archives and Records Service, Washington, DC.

Compiled Service Records of Confederate Soldiers Who Served in Organizations Raised Directly by the Confederate Government. M-258. War Department Collection of Confederate Records. RG 109. National Archives and Records Service, Washington, DC.

Confederate Papers Relating to Citizens of Business Firms, 1861–65. M-346. War Department Collection of Confederate Records. RG 109. National Archives and Records Service, Washington, DC.

Consolidated Lists of Civil War Draft Registration Records (Provost Marshal General's Bureau; Consolidated Enrollment Lists, 1863–1865). RG110.

Records of the Provost Marshal General's Bureau (Civil War). National Archives and Records Administration, Washington, DC.

Cowan, James J. Papers. Old Court House Museum, Vicksburg, MS.

Eggleston-Roach Papers. Louisiana and Lower Mississippi Valley Collections. Special Collections. Hill Memorial Library, Louisiana State University, Baton Rouge.

1850 Federal Population Census. M432. National Archives and Records Service, Washington, D.C.

1860 Federal Population Census. M653. National Archives and Records Service, Washington, D.C.

1870 Federal Population Census. M593. National Archives and Records Service, Washington, D.C.

1880 Federal Population Census. T9. National Archives and Records Service, Washington, D.C.

Fifth Census of the United States, 1830. M-19. National Archives and Records Service, Washington, D.C.

1st Mississippi Light Artillery Regiment. Collection. Mississippi State Library and Archives, Jackson.

Green, William Mercer, 1843–1887. Papers. Southern Historical Collection. Louis Round Wilson Special Collections Library, University of North Carolina, Chapel Hill.

Herring, Isaac E. Letters. Old Court House Museum, Vicksburg, MS.

Markham, Thomas R. Papers. Louisiana and Lower Mississippi Valley Collections. Special Collections. Hill Memorial Library, Louisiana State University, Baton Rouge.

McLane-Fisher. Papers. ca. 1800–1905. Maryland Historical Society, Baltimore.

Order Book, 1st Mississippi Light Artillery Regiment. Mississippi Department of Archives and History, Jackson.

Roach and Eggleston Family. Papers. 1825–1905. Southern Historical Collection. Louis Round Wilson Special Collections Library, University of North Carolina, Chapel Hill.

Roach-Eggleston Family Papers. Old Court House Museum, Vicksburg, MS.

Tennessee Confederate Pension Applications: Soldiers & Widows. Tennessee State Library and Archives, Nashville.

Series 1201: Confederate Pension Applications, 1889–1932. Mississippi Office of the State Auditor. Mississippi Department of Archives and History, Jackson.

Sixth Census of the United States, 1840. M704. National Archives and Records Service, Washington, DC.

Unfiled Papers and Slips Belonging in Confederate Compiled Service Records. M-347. War Department Collection of Confederate Records. RG 109. National Archives and Records Service, Washington, DC.

Whitehead (Dr. P. F.). Letters. McCain Library and Archives, University of Southern Mississippi, Hattiesburg.

Willcox, James M. Papers. 1831–1871. Manuscript Department. Duke University Library, Durham, NC.

Government Documents

Adjutant General's Office. *Roster and Record of Iowa Soldiers in the War of the Rebellion: Together with Historical Sketches of Volunteer Organizations, 1861–1866.* 6 vols. Des Moines, IA: Emory H. English, 1908–11.

Heitman, Francis B. *Historical Register and Dictionary of the United States Army, from Its Organization, September 29, 1789, to March 2, 1903.* 2 vols. Washington, DC: U.S. Congress, 1903.

Population of the United States in 1860: compiled from the original returns of the eighth census, under the direction of the secretary of the interior, by Joseph C. G. Kennedy, superintendent of census. Washington, DC: Government Printing Office, 1864.

U.S. Navy War Records Office. *Official Records of the Union and Confederate Navies in the War of the Rebellion.* 31 vols. Washington, DC, 1894–1927.

U.S. War Department. *The War of the Rebellion: A Compilation of the Official Records of the Union and Confederate Armies.* 128 vols. Washington, DC, 1880–1901.

Newspapers

Daily Commercial (Vicksburg, MS)

Printed Primary Sources

Dabney, T. G. "Gen. A. P. Stewart on Strong Topics." *Confederate Veteran* 17 (Jan. 1909): 31–32.

Davis, Jefferson. *The Papers of Jefferson Davis, 1808–1879.* 13 vols. Edited by Haskell L. Monroe Jr., Lynda L. Crist, et al. Baton Rouge: Louisiana State University Press, 1971–2012.

Eggleston, E. T. "Scenes Where General Tilghman was Killed." *Confederate Veteran* 1, no. 10 (Oct. 1893): 296.

F. W. M. [Merrin]. "Career and Fate of Gen. Lloyd Tilghman," *Confederate Veteran* 1, no. 9 (Sept. 1893), 274–75.

Flatan [Flatau], L. S. [Lewis M. Spencer]. "Tribute to Gen. Lloyd Tilghman." *Confederate Veteran* 18, no. 9 (Sept. 1910): 423.

Flatau, L. S. [Lewis M. Spencer]. "Only Regiment of Confederate Artillery." *Confederate Veteran* 15, no. 9 (Sept. 1907): 410.

Hewett, Janet B., Jocelyn Pinson, and Julia H. Nichols, eds. *Supplement to the Official Records of the Union and Confederate Armies*. 100 vols. Wilmington, NC: Broadfoot Publishing Company, 1996.

Hood, J. B. "The Invasion of Tennessee." In vol. 4 of *Battles and Leaders of the Civil War: Being for the most part contributions by Union and Confederate officers based upon "The Century War Series,"* edited by Robert U. Johnson and Clarence Clough Buel, 426–37. 4 vols. 1884–88; reprint, New York: Thomas Yoseloff, 1956.

Lord, W. W. *A discourse, by the Rev. W.W. Lord, D.D. in honor of Capt. Paul Hamilton, Adjutant General, Third Brigade, Army of Miss., killed in the battle of Chickasaw Bayou, Dec. 29th, 1863, buried from Christ Church, Vicksburg, December 31, commemorated in this discourse Sunday, January 4th, 1863*. Vicksburg, MS: M. Shannon, 1863.

Maury, Dabney H. "The Defence of Mobile in 1865." *Southern Historical Society Papers* 3, no. 1 (Jan. 1877): 1–13.

Noyes, Edward, ed. "Excerpts from the Civil War Diary of E. T. Eggleston." In "Notes and Documents." *Tennessee Historical Quarterly* 17, no. 4 (Dec. 1958): 336–58.

Sherman, William T. *Memoirs of Gen. W. T. Sherman, written by himself, with an appendix bringing his life down to its closing scenes, also a personal tribute and critique of the memoirs, by Hon. James G. Blaine*. 2 vols. 4th rev. ed., New York: Charles L. Webster & Co., 1891-1892.

Printed Secondary Sources

Allardice, Bruce S. *Confederate Colonels: A Biographical Register*. Columbia: University of Missouri Press, 2008.

Allardice, Bruce S., and Lawrence Lee Hewitt, eds. *Kentuckians in Gray: Confederate Generals and Field Officers of the Bluegrass State*. Lexington: University of Kentucky Press, 2008.

Angellotti, Frank M. *The Polks of North Carolina and Tennessee*. Greenville, SC: Southern Historical Press, 1923.

Bailey, Anne J. *The Chessboard of War: Sherman and Hood in the Autumn Campaigns of 1864*. Lincoln: University of Nebraska Press, 2000.

Ball, Douglas B. *Financial Failure and Confederate Defeat*. Urbana: University of Illinois Press, 1991.

Baskervill, P. Hamilton. *Andrew Meade of Ireland and Virginia; his ancestors, and some of his descendants and their connections, including sketches of the following families: Meade, Everard, Hardaway, [Eggleston,] Segar, Pettus, and Overton*. Richmond, VA: Old Dominion Press, Inc., 1921.

Bearss, Edwin C. *Rebel Victory at Vicksburg*. Little Rock, AR: Vicksburg Centennial Commemoration Commission, 1963.

———. *The Vicksburg Campaign*. 3 vols. Dayton, Ohio: Morningside House, Inc., 1985–86.

Bearss, Edwin C., and Warren Grabau. *The Battle Of Jackson, May 14, 1863; The Siege Of Jackson, July 10–17, 1863; Three Other Post-Vicksburg Actions*. Baltimore, MD: Gateway Press, Inc., 1981.

Bergeron, Arthur W., Jr. *Guide to Louisiana Confederate Military Units, 1861–1865*. Baton Rouge: Louisiana State University Press, 1989.

Brown, Dee Alexander. *Grierson's Raid: A Cavalry Adventure of the Civil War*. Dayton, OH: Morningside Bookshop, 1981.

Castel, Albert. *Decision in the West: The Atlanta Campaign of 1864*. Lawrence: University Press of Kansas, 1992.

Chambers, William, and Robert Chambers, eds. *Chambers's Information For The People*. 2 vols. Philadelphia, PA: J. B. Lippincott & Co., 1860.

Civil War Centennial Commission of Tennessee. *Tennesseans in the Civil War: A Military History of Confederate and Union Units with Available Rosters of Personnel*. 2 vols. Nashville, TN: Civil War Centennial Commission, 1964.

Cooper, William J., Jr. *Jefferson Davis, American*. New York: Knopf, 2000.

Daniel, Larry J. *Cannoneers in Gray: The Field Artillery of the Army of Tennessee, 1861–1865*. University: University of Alabama Press, 1984.

Davis, William C., and Julie Hoffman, eds. *The Confederate General*. 6 vols. Harrisburg, PA: National Historical Society, 1991.

Dyer, Frederick H. *A Compendium of the War of the Rebellion*. 3 vols. Reprint, New York: Thomas Yoseloff, 1959.

Evans, Clement A., ed. *Confederate Military History, Extended Edition*. 17 vols. Wilmington, NC: Broadfoot Publishing Company, 1988.

Foster, Buck T. *Sherman's Mississippi Campaign*. Tuscaloosa: University of Alabama Press, 2006.

Glatthaar, Joseph T. *Soldiering in the Army of Northern Virginia: A Statistical Portrait of the Troops Who Served under Robert E. Lee*. Chapel Hill: University of North Carolina Press, 2011.

Grabau, Warren E. *Ninety-eight Days: A Geographer's View of the Vicksburg Campaign.* Knoxville: University of Tennessee Press, 2000.

Harrington, Hugh T. *Civil War Milledgeville: Tales from the Confederate Capital of Georgia.* Charleston, SC: The History Press, 2005.

Hewitt, Lawrence Lee. *Port Hudson: Confederate Bastion on the Mississippi.* Baton Rouge: Louisiana State University Press, 1987.

Howell, H. Grady, Jr. *For Dixie Land I'll Take My Stand! A Muster Listing of All Known Mississippi Confederate Soldiers, Sailors and Marines.* 3 vols. [Madison, MS]: Chickasaw Bayou Press, 1998.

Jacobson, Eric A., and Richard A. Rupp. *For Cause & For Country: A Study of the Affair at Spring Hill and the Battle of Franklin.* Franklin, TN: O'More Publishing, 2008.

Jones, Robert C. *The Battle of Allatoona Pass: The Forgotten Battle of Sherman's Atlanta Campaign.* N.p.: CreateSpace Independent Publishing Platform, 2011.

Krick, Robert E. L. *Staff Officers in Gray: A Biographical Register of the Staff Officers in the Army of Northern Virginia.* Chapel Hill: University of North Carolina Press, 2003.

Lewis, Charles Lee. *David Glasgow Farragut: Our First Admiral.* Annapolis, MD: U.S. Naval Institute, 1943.

Lowry, Robert, and William H. McCardle. *A History of Mississippi, from the Discovery of the Great River by Hernando De Soto, including the Earliest Settlement made by the French, Under Iberville, to The Death of Jefferson Davis.* Jackson, MS: R. H. Henry & Co., 1891.

McMurry, Richard M. *Atlanta 1864: Last Chance for the Confederacy.* Lincoln: University of Nebraska Press, 2000.

Moore, Albert Burton. *Conscription and Conflict in the Confederacy.* 1924; reprint, New York: Hillary House Publishers Ltd., 1963.

Polk, William M. *Leonidas Polk: Bishop and General.* 2 vols. New York: Longman, Greens, and Co., 1893.

Rowland, Dunbar. *The Official and Statistical Register of the State of Mississippi, 1908.* Nashville, TN: Brandon Print. Co., 1908.

Shank, Jack. *Meridian: The Queen with a Past.* 2 vols. Meridian, MS: Southeastern Printing, 1985–86.

Smith, Timothy B. *Champion Hill: Decisive Battle for Vicksburg.* New York: Savas Beatie, 2004.

Tappan, Daniel Langdon, comp. *Tappan-Toppan Genealogy: Ancestors and Descendants of Abraham Toppan of Newbury, Massachusetts, 1606–1672.* Arlington, MA: privately printed by the compiler, 1915.

Warner, Ezra J. *Generals in Blue: Lives of the Union Commanders.* Baton Rouge: Louisiana State University, 1964.

Welsh, Jack D., M.D. *Medical Histories of Confederate Generals.* Kent, Ohio: Kent State University Press, 1995.

Internet Resources

Some of the information documented here was obtained from subscription websites protected by password and inaccessible to non-subscribers. In those cases, only part of the web address has been cited. The complete URL is on file with the publisher.

Achee, Ben. *1865 Orleans Parish Death Index—O through Z.* http://files. usgwarchives.net/la/orleans/vitals/deaths/index/1865dioz.txt. Accessed July 7, 2013.

"Appendix A." "Appendices A through E." Mersey Heritage Society. http:// www.mersey.ca/RaddallAppendices.html#APPENDIX A. Accessed July 4, 2013.

Application for Membership of Lemuel Eggleston Montgomery, descendant of Richard Eggleston of Virginia, to The Mississippi Society of the National Society Sons of the American Revolution, National Number 58272, State Number 98, filed April 24, 1944, and certified May 15, 1944. http://search.ancestry.com/Browse/BookView.aspx?dbid=2204& iid=32596_242517–00151&sid=&gskw=Dick+Hardaway+Eggleston—. Accessed July 7, 2013; password protected site.

Blake Girl. "Benson Blake." Find A Grave, http://www.findagrave.com/cgi-bin/fg.cgi?page=gr&GSln=BL&GSpartial=1&GSbyrel=all&GSst=27& GScntry=4&GSsr=4241&GRid=13610756&. Accessed July 5, 2013.

"Brierfield Furnace." Wikipedia: The Free Encyclopedia. http://en. wikipedia.org/wiki/Brierfield_Furnace. Accessed July 4, 2013.

"British Legion, Gildart's Troop." *The On-Line Institute for Advanced Loyalist Studies.* http://www.royalprovincial.com/military/musters/ britlegn/blgild1.htm. Accessed July 4, 2013.

"Buena Vista, PART TWO." *Descendants of Mexican War Veterans.* http:// www.dmwv.org/honoring/bvista2.htm. Accessed July 4, 2013.

"City Directory Listing for F. T. Eggleston." *Database=City Directories.* http://userdb.rootsweb.ancestry.com/citydir/cgi-bin/citydir.cgi?main_ id=9453&database=City%20Directories&return_to=http://userdb. rootsweb.com/citydir/&submitter_id=. Accessed July 7, 2013.

Clarke, H. C. "General Directory for the City of Vicksburg: Containing the Name and Address of Every Professional and Business Man and

Resident of the City." http://homepages.rootsweb.ancestry.com/ ~holler/dir1860.htm. Accessed July 5, 2013.

"Confederate Park, Memphis, TN. getting new cannons." Steen Cannons, Ashland, KY http://steencannons.com/confederate-park-memphis-tn-getting-new-cannons/. Accessed July 4, 2013.

"Edwards to Feltus." *Mississippi, Wilkinson County Newspaper Slave Ads, 1823–1849.* http://search.ancestry.com/Browse/BookView.aspx?dbid =1943&iid=32010_219165–00060&sid=&gskw=Doctor+Dick+H+ Eggleston-. Accessed July7, 2013; password protected site.

"Edwin F. Stafford." *U.S., Civil War Soldier Records and Profiles, 1861–1865.* http://search.ancestry.com/cgi-bin/sse.dll?new=1&MSAV=1&msT= 1&gss=angs-c&gsfn=Edwin+F&gsln=Stafford&msrpn__ftp=Illinois &_83004002=white&cpxt=0&uidh=l06&_83004003-n_xcl=f&cp= 0&rank=1&pcat=39&h=361131&db=civilwar_histdatasys&indiv=1. Accessed July 7, 2013; password protected site.

Eggleston, Robert. "The Egglestons of Virginia." http://www.pennlaird. com/eggleston/Rframe.html. Accessed July 4, 2013.

Ellis, Linda. "Col Abner Clayton Steede." *Find A Grave.* http://www.find agrave.com/cgi-bin/fg.cgi?page=gr&GSln=STE&GSpartial=1&GSby rel=all&GSst=27&GScntry=4&GSsr=401&GRid=32474346&. Accessed July 4, 2013.

"Family Group Sheet." *Pitcher 02–29–12.* http://trees.ancestry.com/ tree/37581823/family/familygroup?fpid=19111004612&sid= 19111001926. Accessed July 7, 2013; password protected site.

———. http://trees.ancestry.com/tree/37581823/family/familygroup? fpid=19111011517. Accessed July 7, 2013; password protected site.

"Family View." *Fabor-Lee-Tappan-Tanner-Boyer-Family Tree.* http://trees. ancestry.com/tree/575993/family?cfpid=-1086918200. Accessed July 7, 2013; password protected site.

"Family View." Jefferson College Board of Trustees Members. http://trees. ancestry.com/tree/42722266/family?cfpid=20416306342&selnode=1. Accessed Aug. 5, 2013; password protected site.

"Family View." *Powell/Eggleston/Watts/Pruitt/Key.* http://trees.ancestry. com/tree/398579/family?cfpid=-2086854451. Accessed July 7, 2013; password protected site.

Gara, Don. "Gildart, Francis." *Biographical Sketches of the Cavalry Officers of the British Legion.* http://home.golden.net/~marg/bansite/odds/ bl_cavalry.html. Accessed July 4, 2013.

"Honora 'Nora' Elizabeth Roach." *Vicksburg Connections.* http://trees. ancestry.com/tree/28580183/person/13191968059?pgNum=1. Accessed July 7, 2013; password protected site.

"Isaac Newton Brown of Navarro County, Texas." *Navarro County Texas: Genealogical and Historical Web Site.* http://www.rootsweb.ancestry.com/~txnavarr/biographies/b/brown_isaac_newton.htm. Accessed July 7, 2013.

"Journal of the Thirty-Fifth Annual Convention of the Protestant Episcopal Church, in the Diocese of Mississippi." http://docsouth.unc.edu/imls/protestant/protestant.xml. Accessed July 6, 2013.

"Mary Farrar Stark Gildart (Wilkinson)." *Jefferson College Board of Trustees Members.* http://trees.ancestry.com/pt/RequestTreeAccess.aspx?tid=42722266&pid=19918035062. Accessed July 7, 2013; password protected site.

Maynor, Natalie. "Patrick Henry." *Find A Grave.* http://www.findagrave.com/cgi-bin/fg.cgi?page=gr&GSln=HEN&GSpartial=1&GSbyrel=all&GSst=27&GScntry=4&GSsr=4521&GRid=11378337&. Accessed July 4, 2013.

"Mississippi, Marriages, 1800–1911." https://familysearch.org/pal:/MM9.1.1/V28R-RBH. Accessed July 7, 2013.

National Park Service. "Battle of Fredericksburg." *Fredericksburg & Spotsylvania: National Military Park, Virginia.* http://www.nps.gov/frsp/fredhist.htm. Accessed July 4, 2013.

———. "Chicago Mercantile Battery." *Vicksburg: National Military Park, Mississippi.* http://www.nps.gov/vick/historyculture/chicago-mercantile-battery.htm. Accessed July 4, 2013.

———. "1862 Battle of Harpers Ferry." *Harpers Ferry: National Historical Park, WV, VA, MD.* http://www.nps.gov/hafe/historyculture/1862-battle-of-harpers-ferry.htm. Accessed July 4, 2013.

———. "Hudson, Joseph D." In "Soldier Details." In *The Civil War.* http://www.nps.gov/civilwar/search-soldiers-detail.htm?soldier_id=720372aa-dc7a-df11-bf36-b8ac6f5d926a. Accessed July 7, 2013.

———. "John Jones Pettus." http://www.nps.gov/resources/person.htm?id=25. Accessed July 4, 2013.

———. "17th Battalion, Mississippi Cavalry." In "Regiment Details." In *The Civil War.* http://www.nps.gov/civilwar/search-regiments-detail.htm?regiment_id=CMS0017BC. Accessed July 5, 2013.

———. "Stafford, Edwin F." In "Soldier Details." In *The Civil War.* http://www.nps.gov/civilwar/search-soldiers-detail.htm?soldier_id=b48771d4-dc7a-df11-bf36-b8ac6f5d926a. Accessed July 7, 2013.

Niles, Jason. *Diary of Jason Niles, June 22, 1861–December 31, 1864: Electronic Edition.* Academic Affairs Library, University of North Carolina at Chapel Hill, http://docsouth.unc.edu/imls/niles/niles.html. Accessed July 31, 2013.

"1900 Population Schedule, California, Alameda, Oakland Ward 2." http://archive.org/stream/12thcensusofpopu0082unit#page/n211/mode/2up. Accessed July 6, 2013.

"Polk, William Hawkins, (1815–1862)." *Biographical Directory of the United States Congress, 1774–Present.* http://bioguide.congress.gov/scripts/biodisplay.pl?index=P000412. Accessed July 4, 2013.

The Preacher's Kid. "Benjamin S. Tappan." *Find A Grave.* http://www.findagrave.com/cgi-bin/fg.cgi?page=gr&GRid=67710215. Accessed July 4, 2013.

"Robert Stark." *lewiscomplete.* http://trees.ancestry.com/tree/45292422/person/6340077700/photo/d50eb1cd-972a-48e5-9189-bae1c4f25d62?src=search. Accessed July 7, 2013; password protected site.

Rodgers, Therese. "Dr James C. Newman." *Find a Grave.* http://www.findagrave.com/cgi-bin/fg.cgi?page=gr&GSln=NE&GSpartial=1&GSbyrel=all&GSst=27&GScntry=4&GSsr=7121&GRid=26896043&. Accessed July 6, 2013.

"Samuel Overton Eggleston." *Powell/Eggleston/Watts/Pruitt/Key.* http://trees.ancestry.com/tree/398579/person/-2086854451?ssrc=. Accessed July 7, 2013; password protected site.

"Sarah Antoinette McLellan." *Bonney to McLellan Tree.* http://trees.ancestry.com/tree/15426776/person/1066710989. Accessed July 7, 2013; password protected site.

"Robert Andrews Wilkinson." Smolenski Family Tree. http://trees.ancestry.com/tree/22740791/person/1445777568. Accessed July 23, 2014. password protected site.

Spencer, J. G. "The Death of Brigadier General Lloyd Tilghman." http://www.battleofchampionhill.org/tilghman.htm. Accessed July 6, 2013.

"Templar Shubrick Fayssoux." *Fabor-Lee-Tapan-Boyer-Family Tree.* http://trees.ancestry.com/tree/575993/person/-1086918194. Accessed July 7, 2013; password protected site.

"Washington Lamkin." *U.S. Federal Census Mortality Schedules Index, 1850–1880.* http://search.ancestry.com/cgi-bin/sse.dll?db=mortalitycen&h=453836&indiv=try&o_vc=Record:OtherRecord&rhSource=7163. Accessed Aug. 13, 2013; password protected site.

"Wilkinson 1825." *Mississippi State and Territorial Censuses, 1792–1866.* http://interactive.ancestry.com/. . . . Accessed July 7, 2013; password protected site.

Miscellaneous Sources

Allardice, Bruce, to Lawrence Hewitt, e-mail, June 6, 2013.

Coyle, Tiffany, to Lawrence Hewitt, e-mail, Aug. 6, 2013.

Faller, Phillip, to Lawrence Hewitt, e-mail, Mar. 2, 2013.

Stevens, Andrew. Original Eggleston documents.

Winschel, Terrence, to Lawrence Hewitt, e-mails, Apr. 7, June 11, 2013.

Index

All military personnel, armies, departments, units, and subunits are Confederate unless otherwise indicated. All numbered and named military units, from armies to companies, are listed directly below. References to named units can also be found listed under its commander's name. Names of men in Eggleston's unit, page number locations of maps and illustrations are in **bold**. Blood relatives of Edmund Trent Eggleston are indicated by [brackets]. Vicksburg and Warren County, MS, present throughout this book, have not been indexed.